Contemporary Developments and Issues in China's Economic Transition

Also by Charles Harvie

CAUSES AND IMPACT OF THE ASIAN FINANCIAL CRISIS (*co-editor with Tran Van Hoa*)

VIETNAM'S REFORMS AND ECONOMIC GROWTH (*with Tran Van Hoa*)

Contemporary Developments and Issues in China's Economic Transition

Edited by

Charles Harvie
Associate Professor
Department of Economics
University of Wollongong
New South Wales
Australia

First published in Great Britain 2000 by
MACMILLAN PRESS LTD
Houndmills, Basingstoke, Hampshire RG21 6XS and London
Companies and representatives throughout the world

A catalogue record for this book is available from the British Library.

ISBN 0–333–74617–1

First published in the United States of America 2000 by
ST. MARTIN'S PRESS, INC.,
Scholarly and Reference Division,
175 Fifth Avenue, New York, N.Y. 10010

ISBN 0–312–23026–5

Library of Congress Cataloging-in-Publication Data
Contemporary developments and issues in China's economic transition / edited
by Charles Harvie.
    p.   cm.
A collection of 11 research papers written for this volume by specialists.
Includes index.
ISBN 0–312–23026–5 (cloth)
1. China—Economic conditions—1976–   2. China—Economic policy—1976–
3. Mixed economy—China.   I. Harvie, Charles, 1954–

HC427.92 .C664   1999
338.951—dc21
                                                                99–048151

This book is printed on paper suitable for recycling and made from fully managed and sustained
forest sources.

10   9   8   7   6   5   4   3   2   1
09   08   07   06   05   04   03   02   01   00

Printed and bound in Great Britain by
Antony Rowe Ltd, Chippenham, Wiltshire

To Colin and Wendy

Contents

Part 1   Recent developments

Part 2   Key issues

List of Figures

List of Tables

Notes on Contributors

Khorshed Chowdhury is a Senior Lecturer in the Department of Economics at the University of Wollongong. He received his BA (Honours) and MA from the University of Chittagong (Bangladesh), MEc from the University of New England (Australia), and Ph.D from the University of Manitoba (Canada). He has held positions at the University of Chittagong, University of Manitoba and the Australian National University. His research interests include development economics, international monetary economics and macroeconomics. He has published several journal articles in these areas.

Charles Harvie is an Associate Professor in the Department of Economics at the University of Wollongong. He received his PhD from the University of Warwick (UK) in 1986. He has taught in the United Kingdom, Australia, Thailand and Vietnam in the areas of macroeconomics, international economics, monetary economics and comparative economic systems. His recent research has focused upon economies in transition from plan to market, with a particular interest in related issues for the Chinese economy. He has numerous publications in the form of journal articles, books and book chapters in this area.

Martin Hovey is a Lecturer in finance in the School of Accounting and Finance at Griffith University. He has extensive experience in the banking industry in Papua New Guinea and as a consultant in Australia. His current research interests are in alternative corporate governance models as they prevail in Australia, China, Japan, Korea, and the Czech Republic and are applicable to China, and in identifying suitable corporate governance systems for China.

Robyn Iredale is an Associate Professor in the Department of Geo-Sciences and Centre for Research Policy at the University of Wollongong. She is a human geographer with a particular interest in population studies. Her research interests include international and internal migration, human resources development and issues of skills transfer. She has conducted research on a wide range of topics to do with migration, women migrants, education and training and skills transfer and accreditation. She is currently carrying out research in China on the internal mobility of Minority Nationalities. This is part of a wider project—part of the Asia Pacific Migration Research Network,

Management of Social Transformations (MOST) project—funded by UNESCO.

Amnon Levy is an Associate Professor in the Department of Economics at the University of Wollongong. He obtained his BA and MA from Tel Aviv University and Ph.D from the University of California at Berkeley. He has held academic positions at Ben Gurion, Tel Aviv and the Hebrew Universities in Israel. He has taught and published in the areas of development economics, macroeconomics, financial economics, agricultural economics, natural resource economics and comparative economics. His recent research has focused upon intercountry income inequality, external debt and growth problems of developing countries.

Xielin Liu is an Associate Professor working for the National Research Centre for Science and Technology for Development and Tsinghua University in Beijing. He is also Deputy Director of the Research Center for Innovation Strategy and Management in Beijing. He has a PhD in Business Administration from Tsinghua University and has held research fellowship positions at the Sloan School of management, MIT and the Centre for Research Policy, University of Wollongong. His current research and teaching interests include: Chinese enterprise development; S&T policy; and management of technology and innovation. He has published widely on Chinese technology management and business and innovation policy.

Darren McKay is an Associate Lecturer in the Department of Economics at the University of Newcastle. He has extensive teaching experience in the area of urban and regional economics. His research includes examining the regional employment impact of overseas student expenditures, and analyzing the comparative advantage of Australian tertiary institutions in exporting education. Currently he is completing a doctoral dissertation on the role of urban land markets on the competitiveness of Australian cities. In particular, this research involves analyzing the influence of infrastructure charges, urban planning and property taxes on urban form and economic growth.

Tony Naughton is Professor of International Finance in the School of Accounting and Finance at Griffith University. His research interests are in the financial markets of Asia and he has published widely in this field as well as working as an academic and consultant in many countries of the region. His current work includes a study of firm performance and ownership change in China.

Greg O'Leary is a Senior Lecturer in Politics at the University of Adelaide where he teaches International Politics. Having initaially specialized in

Chinese foreign policy – publishing *The Shaping of Chinese Foreign Policy* (ANU Press, Canberra; Croom Helm, London, 1980) – he subsequently worked on Chinese rural reform and in recent years on the reforms in industry, particularly those affecting labour. His most recent work in this area is in *Adjusting to Capitalism: Chinese Workers and the State* (ME Sharpe, New York, 1998), which he also edited.

Jung-Soo Seo is a Lecturer in Economics at the Australian Defence Force Academy in Canberra, Australia. He obtained his PhD in 1997 from the University of New South Wales, Australia. He has written a number of book chapters and seminar papers in the field of foreign direct investment and international trade. His current research interests are multinational enterprises' strategy, foreign direct investment and dynamics of comparative advantage, especially in the Asia-Pacific region.

Chung-Sok Suh is a Senior Lecturer at the School of International Business, University of New South Wales, Australia. He has studied at Seoul National University and obtained his PhD from the University of New South Wales. He has published in the areas of Resource Economics, International Trade, Foreign Direct Investment, with a strong emphasis on the Asia-Pacific Economies, and the economic relationship between Australia and Korea. Currently, his research focus is in the areas of Foreign Direct Investment, MNE strategies and Management in the Asia-Pacific region.

Tran Van Hoa is an Associate Professor in the Department of Economics at the University of Wollongong. He holds higher degrees from the University of Western Australia and Monash University, Australia. He has taught widely at universities in Australia, Asia and the US and spent many of his sabbaticals and visits at major international research institutes and universities in the US, UK, France, Belgium, Thailand, China and Vietnam. He has published widely in the major applied and theoretical areas of economics, business, finance, energy and econometrics in Australia and overseas, and been a consultant to a number of organizations and authorities in Australia and various ministries in Thailand and Vietnam.

Tim Turpin is an Associate Professor and Director of the International Business Research Institute and the Centre for Research Policy at the University of Wollongong. He has a PhD in Sociology from La Trobe University and has worked in government, private sector and university environments. He has researched and published widely on issues concerning research policy, cultural adaptation and the dissemination of knowledge. Through the past eight years he has carried out a range of research and consulting projects in China concerning the role of the

State in developing national innovation systems. Professor Turpin also teaches graduate programs on international relations, cross-cultural management and organizational behaviour.

Introduction

The People's Republic of China has, for some twenty years, been engaged in major reform of its economy, that has resulted in substantial implications not only for the growth of the economy, its integration into the global economy, its operation and management, but also for the cohesion of its society. The latter has traditionally been given a high priority by the Communist authorities, in order to maintain its legitimacy with the population. The reform process is currently in a very fluid state, with much having been accomplished but much still remaining to be done. Over the period 1978–96 the country achieved: an annual average real GDP growth rate of just under 10 per cent; its total current GDP ranked its economy as the seventh largest in the world by the mid-1990s, while on a purchasing power-parity basis it ranked second; it had become the eleventh most important trading nation; and was second only to the US as a recipient of foreign direct investment. Despite these impressive outcomes many problems remain. Lack of progress over the reform of state-owned enterprises has held back progress in other areas, such as that of the financial sector. The recent shedding of labour from the state-owned enterprises has contributed to rising urban unemployment, and the prospect of increasing social unrest. In addition, the process of reform has contributed to rising labour migration and movement of workers from the countryside to the cities, increasing income disparity between the coastal provinces and the hinterland, and pressure upon the country's cities and environment in general.

More recently the economy has experienced a growth slowdown, which is partly a reflection of earlier economic policies pursued but has also been compounded by the economic and financial crisis afflicting a number of countries in the East Asian region since mid-1997. Since the crisis began China has become a key player in terms of its contribution to regional stability. This has primarily occurred through its approach to its currency, the exchange rate of which the authorities have steadfastly maintained against the US dollar in the face of dramatic declines in the exchange rates of its regional neighbours, with whom it competes in global markets. This has not only added to the economic significance of China within the region, but has also enhanced its overall standing with its regional neighbours. It has also considerably enhanced its prospects for membership of the World Trade Organization within the foreseeable future.

While considerable literature on the Chinese economy exists, the continual state of flux of the economic, political and social situation inevitably results in this becoming rapidly out of date; hence the justification for the present volume. While the coverage of the book is comprehensive, it must inevitably, due to space limitations, be selective. However, the potential topics for coverage is, needless to say, vast. Focus is placed upon a number of contemporary and inter-linked Chinese economic and social issues, the outcomes from which will have a major bearing upon the future economic and social progress of the country. These in turn will exert a major bearing upon regional economic and political developments, as well as globally.

The coverage will be of interest to a wide audience. For the academic and business community, investor and trader, governmental and international policy decision-making agencies, and China observers in general, it is essential to be aware of recent developments as well as key emerging issues during the current crucial stage in the country's process of transition to a market economy. This is the primary objective of the book. However, it will also provide, where applicable, a historical context to such contemporary developments and issues, as well as an analysis of prospective difficulties and policy options.

The contributors to this book have extensive knowledge of the key issues involved in their particular areas, and have published widely in reputable international journals. Their objective throughout is to present the relevant material in an informative, accessible, but yet rigorous fashion, emphasizing the key issues and policy implications. In this regard the book will make an important contribution to the existing literature, while remaining accessible to as wide an audience as possible.

Completion of the book benefited substantially from a workshop held at the University of Wollongong in October 1998, which consisted of presentations by the respective contributors of their draft chapters. This greatly assisted in: providing information on the contents of each chapter with the objective of minimizing overlapping material as much as possible; providing feedback to contributors; ensuring the completion of the project on time; and finally making the editing of this book, and the maintenance of an appropriate standard throughout, considerably easier.

The book consists of eleven chapters and is divided into two parts. Part 1 consists of Chapters 1–7 and focuses upon contemporary developments in key sectors of the Chinese economy – overall macroeconomic performance, major factors contributing to the country's inflation and growth, reform options and performance of the state-owned enterprises, the development and growth of the non-state sector and in particular the township and village enterprises, reform of the financial sector, labour market, and the trade and investment regime. In Chapter 1 Charles Harvie reviews China's economic reform process, emphasizing its key characteristics and major phases. Recent macroeconomic developments are then analyzed, emphasizing those factors contributing to the economy's economic slowdown since 1997. The impact of the Asian financial crisis on the Chinese economy is also highlighted, as well as the likelihood of a devaluation of the country's exchange rate. The authorities' policy response to the economic slowdown, in terms of maintaining growth and expanding employment opportunities while maintaining low inflation, are outlined and evaluated.

In Chapter 2 Tran Van Hoa focuses upon the causal structure of growth and inflation in China, and in doing so provides substantive empirical evidence to enable a better understanding of the engines of growth and inflation. This will in itself enable better formulation and implementation of macroeconomic and restructuring policy, and minimize the consequences of the Asian financial meltdown on China.

In Chapter 3 Charles Harvie and Tony Naughton conduct a review and analysis of reform of China's of large state owned enterprises (SOEs), which is generally regarded as one of the most pressing problems facing the country. Many SOEs are recognized as being inefficient, loss-making and a major drain upon the country's resources. This chapter reviews the recent performance of China's SOEs, identifies the reforms which have already been implemented in this area, outlines the experiences of other transition economies in regard to the restructuring of their SOEs, and places emphasis upon those options which are likely to be most applicable to the Chinese situation.

In Chapter 4 Charles Harvie focuses upon the contribution which the Township and Village Enterprises (TVEs) have made to the industrial sector, and to the economy as a whole, during the period of economic reform. While the economic literature suggests that the success of the TVEs has arisen due to special circumstances, this chapter argues, to the contrary, that they are likely to remain a significant feature of the Chinese economy, albeit in new organizational and ownership forms, for some time. Their demonstrated flexibility in terms of organizational structure, delegation and incentive design, in conjunction with their evolving strategic business alliances in the form of joint ventures with foreign companies and, increasingly, alliances with science based research institutions, it is argued, will make this possible.

In Chapter 5 Martin Hovey and Tony Naughton focus upon China's gradual and cautious process of financial reform. While major changes have taken place, it is generally recognized that China still has a long way to go. The financial system remains dominated by banks, particularly state-owned institutions that retain many of the features of a repressed financial system. Experiments in developing other financial sectors have not been overly successful. Attempts are being made to free the major banks from the cycle of directed lending to inefficient state enterprises which has resulted in the accumulation of non-performing loans. The quality of the loan portfolios, supervision and regulation of the banking sector is a hindrance to progress. On the positive side the growing influence of Hong Kong and the greater freedom permitted to foreign institutions is likely to provide a much-needed stimulus to the domestic market.

In Chapter 6 Greg O'Leary focuses upon labour-market developments during China's transition to a market economy. It is suggested that the rationalization of state enterprises and the continued transfer of labour from rural to urban areas will be the major features shaping China's labour market development. The former will result in increased urban unemployment and the loss of traditional benefits to urban workers, while the latter will add to job pressure in urban labour markets. These suggest the prospect of major social unrest. Severe barriers remain to the operation of a flexible labour market, and changes to basic labour institutions will be required. In particular, the transition to a market economy will require industrial relations and trade union institutions appropriate to a market economy. However, reform in these areas has not been successful to date due to the retention by the central government of tight political control.

In Chapter 7 Chung-Sok Suh and Jung-Soo Seo focus upon international trade and foreign direct investment (FDI), which have been the engines of growth of China since its adoption of the 'open door' policy. The rapid growth of the country's foreign trade resulted by the 1990s in major surpluses in its trade balance. China also emerged as a major host country for world FDI flows. China's trade surplus in the 1990s, it is argued, is structural, for which the coastal provinces are primarily responsible. It is also argued that such surpluses should be considered in the context of the business strategy of foreign multinationals, and its impact on trade operating in China. An analytical framework is provided to show the interdependence between trade and FDI.

Part 2 focuses upon key issues that will have a major bearing upon the future performance of the economy, and the prospective policy decision-making options available to the authorities – the maintenance of international competitiveness and the contribution of science and technology policy, labour migration, regional income inequality, and urban development and efficient land usage. The issues involved, and the policy measures adopted, will have a major bearing upon the economic, social and political progress of the country in the future. This part consists of Chapters 8-11.

In Chapter 8 Tim Turpin and Xielin Liu focus upon the contribution of science and technology issues for China. They find that while production in China is predominantly concentrated along the eastern seaboard, innovation appears unevenly spread within this region. An analysis of indicators of innovation by region shows a pattern of development toward two different types of innovation system: a strong science-based system predominantly linked to public institutions and state enterprises; and a commercial system, more responsive to market forces, less science-intensive but more closely linked to the business sector and non-state enterprises. An implication is that unless the two systems become better aligned, market-driven firms will have little choice but to forge alternative innovation alliances with foreign firms.

In Chapter 9 Robyn Iredale focuses upon labour migration. The scale of internal migration in China has escalated rapidly since the introduction of economic reform. Much of this movement is labour migration, as millions of people move permanently or temporarily to find work or a better standard of living elsewhere. As the regulations controlling movement have gradually weakened, more people have decided to look for work elsewhere. This chapter discusses the trends in labour migration, including the size, spatial pattern and time frame of movements, and provides possible explanations for these trends. All population movements are now seen as part of a total system not just a response to push and pull factors. The chapter also focuses on research findings on the characteristics of labour migrants, and the impact on sending and receiving areas.

In Chapter 10 Khorshed Chowdhury, Charles Harvie and Amnon Levy focus upon analyzing developments in income inequality in China during the period of its economic reform. An overview of regional income disparity is conducted focusing upon that between the coastal, central and western provinces and regions, and the key factors behind this. A conceptual framework for measuring income disparity both between and within provinces is presented, and utilizing appropriate data the Theil index is calculated. It is found that income disparities within provinces have declined. However income disparities between regions and provinces have increased significantly during the period of the 1990s. The government's policy response to such a widening disparity, and its prospects of success, is discussed.

Finally, in Chapter 11 Darren McKay focuses upon an examination of urban development issues and land market efficiency in Chinese cities, pre- and post-economic reforms in the 1980s. It notes that urban competitiveness is fundamental to continued economic development in China. For much of the post-war era, Chinese cities were hindered by poor planning, lack of infrastructure and housing investment, and the absence of a real estate market. This chapter outlines how reforms in these areas in the 1980s for selected cities has improved their competitiveness, and changed their physical structure. However it is also noted that problems still persist that threaten sustainable urban economic development. Such problems need to be addressed if Chinese cities are to successfully absorb the extensive in migration of rural workers, and consequently various urban policy options from the literature is reviewed.

Charles Harvie
January 1999

Acknowledgments

I wish to express my sincere thanks to the various contributors to this book. Without their individual expertise, commitment and ability to meet manuscript and other deadlines, the completion of this book would not have been possible.

Special thanks are also due to the International Economic and Business Integration Research Program, the International Business Research Institute, and the Department of Economics in the Faculty of Commerce at the University of Wollongong for financial and other assistance provided.

To Robert Hood and Julie Chin I also extend my gratitude for assistance in the production of a camera-ready copy of this manuscript.

Map 1:   The Regions and Provinces of China

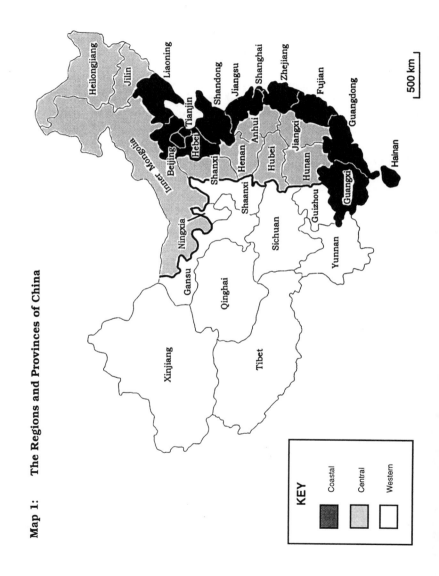

500 km

KEY

Coastal

Central

Western

Part 1

Recent Developments

1

Economic Reforms and Recent Macroeconomic Performance

Charles Harvie

This chapter briefly reviews China's economic reform process, emphasizing its key characteristics and major phases. Recent macroeconomic developments are then analyzed, focusing upon those factors contributing to the economy's recent economic slowdown. The impact of the Asian financial crisis on the Chinese economy is also highlighted as well as the likelihood of a devaluation of the country's exchange rate. The authorities' policy response to the economic slowdown, in terms of maintaining growth and expanding employment opportunities while maintaining low inflation, is outlined and evaluated.

1.1   Introduction

Since the late 1970s China has achieved impressive economic growth, rapid employment growth, and significant structural transformation, as a consequence of the economic reforms implemented during this period. China's reform process has been quite unique amongst the economies in transition from plan to market, and by any economic criteria, including the ones just identified, has been very successful. During 1978–97, real GDP grew on average by 9.7 per cent a year, contributing to a near quadrupling of per capita income and the lifting of millions out of poverty.[1] In addition the so-called township and village enterprises have generated an additional 100 million new jobs, and this is being supplemented by the significant contribution of the rapidly expanding private sector. Over the same period, many of the distortions and rigidities of the former central planning system have been eliminated, and market forces have come to play an increasingly important role in economic decision making. The state's role in the economy has been gradually reduced and a dynamic non-state sector has emerged that accounts, by the mid-1990s, for almost two-thirds of GDP.[2] In addition, as part of the normal process of economic development, employment in agriculture has declined substantially while a thriving manufacturing sector has emerged. However, despite the rapid growth of the past two decades, China has some way to go to achieve income levels comparable with those in the newly industrializing economies of East Asia such as Indonesia, Malaysia, and Thailand,[3] although the recent financial crisis afflicting these countries has significantly narrowed the gap.

Despite these impressive developments, there were worrying signs from the latter part of 1997 that the growth of the economy was faltering, primarily from a weakening of consumer and investment demand after four years of monetary austerity measures. Although net export growth remained buoyant during 1997, this became increasingly threatened by the intensification of the financial crisis afflicting other East Asian economies during 1998. Such a growth slow-down is of particular concern to the Chinese authorities since the maintenance of employment growth, for its rapidly expanding workforce, and social cohesion is seen as being paramount. It is widely perceived that the country must grow above 7–8 per cent[4] if enough new jobs are to be created to absorb the rising unemployed as well as new entrants into the labour force, and that without appropriate action by the authorities the economy will be dangerously close to this in the foreseeable future. The current economic slowdown will also threaten the government's attempts to implement badly needed restructuring of the country's state-owned enterprises (SOEs) as well as the debt-laden state banks. Both are seen as being essential for the country's future sustained economic development and growth. It will also have broader adverse implications for other Asian nations attempting to export their way out of their financial difficulties, arising from the financial and economic crisis in the region.

China's policymakers, therefore, currently face a severe problem of deflation rather than inflation. Of particular concern to China's neighbours, and indeed to the global economy, is the prospect that this deflation could be sufficiently strong that the authorities feel obliged to devalue the renminbi (RMB) as a means of regaining international competitiveness and stimulating export growth. This would have major adverse consequences for stability of both the regional and indeed global economies. The policy response will need to be innovative and unlike that used in the past, as China has become a quite different economy during its period of reform. In addition the country has become a significant regional economic player, and this too will have an important bearing upon its policy response. An analysis of these issues forms the core of this chapter.

The chapter proceeds as follows. In section 2, China's economic reform background is briefly reviewed focusing upon its key characteristics and phases. Section 3 briefly reviews recent macroeconomic developments in China, emphasizing developments which are indicative of a slowdown in the economy, and focusing upon the factors behind this. In section 4, two key issues relating to China and its regional neighbours are analyzed: the impact of the Asian financial crisis on China; and the likelihood that China will devalue its currency as a result of its economic downturn. Section 5 critically analyzes and evaluates the government's policy response to increase growth and expand employment opportunities, while maintaining low inflation. Finally, section 6 provides a summary of the major conclusions.

1.2   Economic reform since 1978: key features and phases

China has attained a remarkable performance in terms of GDP growth during its reform period, as indicated by Table 1.1. During the 1980s this arose primarily from the major structural developments in the economy which saw the transfer of labour from agriculture to rural industry,[5] resulting in a substantial improvement in labour productivity, income and domestic output growth. The period of the 1990s has seen a rapid expansion of trade and investment involving the open coastal zones, which has contributed to a further boost in output growth. However China faces two transitions, one from a developing to a developed economy, and the second from a planned to market-oriented economy. In regard to the former, the country has experienced a restructuring of its economy from agriculture to industry. Now it must move on to the next stage of economic development which will require the reform of key sectors such as that of the SOEs and the banking sector, and further structural reform. Its transition to a market economy has required the development of indirect mechanisms for macroeconomic control, to offset prospective macroeconomic cycles. These developments have proven to be much more difficult. The following presents a brief review of the key features and phases of this economic reform.

Table 1.1
East Asian Economies' GDP per Capita, and Real Growth Rates (%), 1970–97

	Per Capita GDP, PPP* 1996 US$	GDP Growth Rates (%)										
		1970–79	1980–89	1990–97	1990	1991	1992	1993	1994	1995	1996	1997**
Singapore	24 610	9.4	7.2	8.3	9.0	7.3	6.2	10.4	10.1	8.8	7.0	7.2
Hong Kong	24 085	9.2	7.5	5.1	3.4	5.1	6.3	6.1	5.4	4.5	4.9	5.3
Taiwan	15 370	10.2	8.1	6.4	5.4	7.6	6.8	6.3	6.5	6.0	5.7	6.7
South Korea	12 390	9.3	8.0	7.5	9.5	9.1	5.1	5.8	8.6	8.9	7.1	6.0
Malaysia	9 835	8.0	5.7	8.6	9.6	8.6	7.8	8.3	9.2	9.5	8.6	7.0
Thailand	8 165	7.3	7.2	7.6	11.6	8.1	8.2	8.5	8.9	8.7	6.4	0.6
Indonesia	4 140	7.8	5.7	7.6	9.0	8.9	7.2	7.3	7.5	8.2	8.0	5.0
China	3 240	7.5	9.3	10.3	3.8	9.2	14.2	13.5	12.6	10.5	9.7	8.8
Philippines	3 020	6.1	1.8	3.0	3.0	-0.6	0.3	2.1	4.4	4.8	5.7	4.3
Industrial Countries	19 400	3.4	2.6	2.0	2.5	0.8	1.7	0.9	2.9	2.2	2.5	2.8

Sources: IMF, *International Financial Statistics Yearbook*, 1996;
               IMF, *World Economic Outlook, Interim Assessment*, December, 1997.

* Purchasing power parity
** Estimates

Key features of China's economic reforms

China's economic reform process contains a number of key features. Firstly, it can be characterized as gradual and incremental. Economic reforms were not obtained from a comprehensive blueprint but rather were introduced on an experimental basis in some localities, often as a result of local initiatives, and if successful then introduced at the national level. Such a pragmatic and gradual approach to economic reform, in contrast with the 'big bang' reforms implemented in certain Eastern European countries and former states of the Soviet Union, had several advantages. It avoided major disruptions to the economy and enabled a gradual transformation of the economy from a predominantly centrally planned one to one in which the market mechanism played an important role. If the policies turned out to be successful they would be modified to accommodate national and local conditions. In addition, by implementing firstly those policies that were likely to be successful, the leadership was able to build up political support for further reform. This was particularly important in avoiding social unrest and political conflicts that could derail the whole process. For certain reforms to be effective it was also necessary to build new institutions, to set up new legal and regulatory frameworks, and to train personnel to become familiar with the new practices, all of which required time.

Secondly, the reform process utilized intermediate mechanisms to enable the transition from one economic system to another to be as smooth as possible,[6] thereby avoiding major disruptions that could arise from an abrupt shift. Specific examples of this process include: the dual track pricing system to improve the allocation of resources at the margin; establishing a swap market in foreign exchange retention rights to improve the use of foreign exchange; establishing open economic zones to introduce foreign capital and technology to the country; using a contract responsibility system in both the agriculture and industry sectors to encourage economic agents to behave in a market-oriented fashion; and authorizing some local governments to enact and experiment with market-oriented legislation. The use of such mechanisms was a means of encouraging economic agents to behave in a way compatible with a market system prior to the phasing out of central planning.

Thirdly, there was a gradually increasing role for the market determination of prices and resource allocation. As previously mentioned the dual track system was a distinctive element of the Chinese reform process. This referred to the coexistence of a traditional plan and a market channel for the allocation of a given good. Rather than initially dismantling the plan, reformers continued with a role for the plan to ensure stability and guarantee the attainment of some key government priorities (such as investment in energy and infrastructure). The dual track implies the existence of a two-tier pricing system for goods under that system: a single commodity will have both a (typically low) state-set planned price and a (typically high) market price. By the mid-1980s, most state-owned firms were still being assigned a compulsory plan for output, but had additional capacity for production of above-plan market goods. Hence the dual-track strategy was one that operated within the state system, indeed within each state-run factory, as well as in the industrial economy at large. This was essential because it meant that virtually all factories were introduced to the market, and began the process of adaptation to market processes. The dual-track system allowed state firms to transact and cooperate with non-state, marketized firms, allowing valuable flexibility. However the growing importance of collective, private, and foreign-invested firms should be considered apart from the dual-track system strictly defined, since most of these firms were predominantly market-oriented from the beginning.

Fourthly, the Chinese leadership has attempted to preserve the socialist character of the economy. The authorities have not pursued a strategy of mass privatization as in some of the transitional economies of Eastern Europe and the former Soviet Union. This has been limited to maintaining the dominance of public ownership and control of strategic sectors in the economy, supplemented by non-state and private ownership. This modified definition has allowed the authorities considerable leeway in implementing policies that promote the development of the market system, such as the use of material incentives. The household responsibility system in agriculture is one example. The emphasis on ownership allowed the authorities to implement changes to the operating mechanism of SOEs to sever the close links between them and the state, particularly with respect to their finances and management, with the aim of transforming them into autonomous units responsible for their own profits and losses. The new framework also enabled the development of the non-state sector. Indeed the rapid development of the non-state sector has strengthened the economy, facilitating the transformation of the traditional state sector.

Fifthly, the reforms have been characterized by a progressive decentralization of economic decision-making both in terms of depth and extensiveness. Prior to the reforms, decentralization had involved devolving the administrative apparatus of planning to the local authorities. However, since 1978 the process has been much deeper, involving a severing of ties between economic agents and the state, by allowing economic agents to base their decision-making on market signals and by giving considerable autonomy in resource allocation to the local authorities. This has encouraged local authorities to use their growing autonomy to influence resource-sharing arrangements with the centre, and to take initiatives in such areas as investment.

Sixthly, the partial approach to economic reform until 1992 contributed to the economy experiencing 'stop-go' periods of macroeconomic instability arising from the authorities having given up direct control of the economy while indirect instruments remained ineffective because of the incompleteness of the reforms. The traditional administrative system of control became less effective with the greater autonomy given to SOEs and local authorities, which had been pursuing their own objectives of growth promotion and development within the context of a weak framework of financial discipline. Macroeconomic instability increased with each cycle. Since 1992 economic reform initiatives have been taken with the objective of establishing a more effective system of macroeconomic management.

Finally, there has been a highly successful policy to promote the development of the non-state sector. The rapid growth of the non-state sector has strengthened the economy and has facilitated efforts to transform the traditional state sector. This growth of the non-state sector arose primarily because of the relaxation of the government's monopoly over industry. In China, the protected industrial sector was effectively opened to new entrants, beginning in 1979. A large number of start-up firms, especially rural industries,[7] took advantage of large potential profits in the industrial sector, and their entry sharply increased competition and changed overall market conditions in the industrial sector.

There has been substantial coherence to these different elements. Reductions of the state's monopoly led to the rapid entry of new firms. Entry of new firms, combined with adoption of market prices on the margin, led to enhanced competition, and began to get state-sector managers accustomed to responding to the marketplace. Gradual price decontrol was essential. Competition eroded initially high profit margins for state enterprises, and induced the government, as owner of the firms, to become more concerned with profitability. The government experimented with better incentive and monitoring devices, and this improved state-sector performance. Nonetheless, the state sector grew more slowly than the newly entrant sectors. The economy gradually grew out the plan itself[8] and the state sector as a whole became less dominant in the economy as a whole.

Phases of economic reform (1978–present)

The process of economic reform in China can be usefully broken down into a number of phases. The first phase covered the period 1978 to 1984, the second phase from 1984 to 1988, the third phase from 1988 to 1991, and the finally the fourth phase from 1992 until the present.

Phase 1 – Agricultural and rural reform (1978–84)

Economic reforms began in agriculture in the late 1970s.[9] Because this sector had been so heavily repressed under central planning, its liberalization had immediate payoffs. Between 1981 and 1984 agriculture grew on average by 10 per cent a year, largely because the shift to family farming substantially improved incentives. Key measures in this sector included: the leasing of land to farmers under the household responsibility system; higher procurement prices for key crops; the introduction of a dual (two-track) price system for agricultural produce; encouragement of diversification and specialization of crops; and restrictions on rural markets (trade fairs) were relaxed. The reforms led to: major gains in agricultural production and productivity; higher rural savings and investment; and the release and reallocation of labour for employment in the emerging rural industries. Reforms also began in other areas of the economy, but were not as dramatic in scope and effect. In the industrial sector the bonus system was reintroduced, the retention of depreciation allowance was permitted and the retention of profits by state-owned enterprises on an experimental basis began, and experiments initiated to link bonuses more closely to performance and to establish tighter links between wages and productivity. Open economic zones were established in coastal regions to attract foreign investment and promote exports, and to serve as laboratories for bolder market-oriented reforms.

Phase 2 – Broadening of reforms (1984–88)

The initial success of the rural reforms encouraged the authorities to broaden reforms to include the urban-industrial sectors in 1984, and gradually to dismantle the central planning system. In the industrial sector important reform measures implemented included: more autonomy to SOEs in production and employment decisions (the contract responsibility system); the extension of the dual-track system to industrial prices; and the introduction of enterprise taxation. Encouragement was also given to enterprises to borrow from the banking system for their investment requirements rather than depending upon funds through the state budget. This period also witnessed the growth in significance of other types of enterprises, most notably that of TVEs. In the financial sector the monobank system was dismantled and the

People's Bank was established as the central bank. In the fiscal area reforms in 1984 allowed enterprises to retain a larger share of profits, and an enterprise tax system was introduced to replace profit transfers to the budget. Revenue-sharing arrangements between the central and local governments were revised in favour of the latter, resulting in macroeconomic control problems. The trade and exchange system was further liberalized, arising from an increase in the number and scope of open economic zones, and the foreign trade plan was further reduced. Fourteen major cities were 'opened up' to encourage foreign trade and investment, including the accumulation of technical know-how. Many of these measures were further expanded and revised in 1986 to include: the establishment of swap centres for trading in retained foreign exchange earnings[10] and a decentralization of trade through the establishment of local foreign trade corporations.

The reforms during this period provided the basis for broader and sustained growth, and led to the emergence of an increasingly important and dynamic nonstate sector. However they also created difficulties in macroeconomic control which eventually gave rise to inflationary pressures, and necessitated a tightening of macroeconomic policies in the late 1980s.

Phase 3 – Rectification program (1988–91)

The success of the earlier reforms contributed to rising demand, primarily through increased fixed investment, and production, but also contributed to a sharp increase in inflation. Under a rectification program, plans for a new round of price reforms were postponed and there was a re-centralization of price controls, in conjunction with other strong measures designed to reduce the inflationary pressures within the economy. From mid-1988 to 1991, the country entered a period of retrenchment, in which further reform measure were delayed. While the retrenchment measures were successful in reducing the inflationary pressures, they contributed to a major reduction in the growth of the economy. This was felt particularly strongly in the industrial sector where the SOEs experienced a major increase in losses, inter-enterprise debt increased substantially and stock levels increased sharply. They were also felt by the TVEs which were deliberately starved of access to credit. A major crisis developed compelling the authorities in late 1990 to stimulate the economy using monetary and investment policies. By 1991 the economy began to recover. During this period, however, generally more stable prices encouraged the authorities to make substantial realignments in relative prices and liberalize certain other prices.

Phase 4 – Deepening of reforms (1992–present)

By early 1992 the authorities declared an end to the rectification program, announcing their intention to further accelerate the reform process and the opening up of the economy. This message became clear during Deng Xiaoping's tour of the prosperous southern coastal cities at this time, when he called upon the whole country to accelerate growth and to pursue vigorously the policy of reforming and opening up the whole economy. Deng's exhortation prepared the ideological groundwork for the adoption of a more comprehensive reform strategy aimed at transforming the Chinese economy to a fully market-based system. At the Fourteenth National Congress of the Chinese Communist Party in October 1992, his views were formally endorsed, setting the establishment of a 'socialist market economy' as the national goal. This goal was later included in the country's constitution during the first session of the Eighth National People's Congress in March 1993. It culminated in the adoption of a new reform strategy during the Third Plenum of the Fourteenth Central Committee in November 1993.

1.3   Recent macroeconomic developments and the growth slowdown

Following Deng's exhortations, China experienced a major increase in investment, funded primarily through bank loans. As a consequence, inflationary pressure built up within the system and became particularly acute during 1994 and 1995. In an attempt to restore order to the economy, the government introduced, in June 1993, a sixteen-point austerity program. This involved pursuing deflationary policies largely through controls on state investment via credit rationing and administered price controls, with the objective of lowering economic growth to a sustainable rate and to slow the rapid increase in prices. By 1996 it appeared that a soft landing of the economy had been achieved, in which GDP growth had declined to a more sustainable rate of 9.7 per cent and the rate of inflation[11] had been reduced to less than 6.1 per cent. It was widely anticipated that the economy was in a position for a soft take-off thereafter. However, this has not eventuated, and instead a further slowdown of the economy occurred. From Table 1.2 it can be seen that GDP growth continued to decline after 1996, falling to an annual growth rate of 7.2 per cent by the first quarter of 1998, the lowest quarterly figure in at least six years and less than the government's hoped-for 7.5 per cent, from 8.2 per cent during the last quarter of 1997 and from 8.8 per cent for the whole of 1997. The growth rate deteriorated further to 6.8 per cent for the second quarter of 1998, giving a growth rate of 7 per cent for the first half of 1998. For industrial production, similarly, growth has fallen steadily since 1994, as state firms became afflicted with declining profits. This declining growth of output is reflected in a steady decline in inflation, and by the second half of 1997, and into 1998, price deflation and not inflation has been occurring (see Table 1.2).

A number of factors have contributed towards this slowdown of the economy, some of which have arisen due to the excesses of the economic boom of 1992–95. Firstly, the austerity measures implemented against the 1992–95 overheating of the economy achieved major success in reducing inflationary pressure. Secondly, during 1992–95 the country experienced major property over-development arising from overly loose credit to this sector and from significant foreign investment. This resulted in vacant office premises. As an indication of this, the office vacancy rate in December 1997 was 37.4 per cent in Shanghai and 32.5 per cent in Beijing,[12] the two highest vacancy rates of all the cities in East Asia. Thirdly, there has been an over-expansion by Chinese enterprises in areas beyond their core business, resulting in an accumulation of unsold inventories and over-capacity in many industries. As a legacy of this development, the major problem facing China at present is a lack of domestic demand relative to the oversupply of many products. Fourthly, the country is experiencing a continued decline in domestic demand through declining retail sales growth, a decline in fixed-asset investment growth and a prospective decline in export growth and consequential reduced contribution of the net trade balance to overall economic growth.

Retail sales growth fell to 10.7 per cent in 1997 from 12.5 per cent in 1996, reflecting rising unemployment, increased job insecurity, and the need to save more for housing and for the payment of rent.[13] The growth of fixed-asset investment has declined significantly from the breakneck growth of the early 1990s, despite the recent easing of credit after the austerity program. Investment in real estate has been particularly adversely affected, declining in absolute terms. By the first quarter of 1998, fixed-asset investment was growing by 12.2 per cent over a year earlier, still well below the rates of the early 1990s (see Table 1.2), and bank loan quotas were going unfilled, indicative of declining demand for new loans for such a purpose. The supply of consumer durables (cars, household appliances, and electrical equipment) has significantly outstripped growth in domestic demand for such products, a legacy of the boom period of 1992–95 when fixed asset investment hit a peak of 50 per cent year on year as a consequence of excess industrial capacity. This situation continued into 1998. This excess production is contributing to high stock levels of which much is

Table 1.2
Indicators of China's Soft Landing and Growth Slowdown, 1992–98 (Q2)

	1992	1993	1994	1995	1996	1997	1998 (Q1)	1998 (Q2)
Output								
GDP (Real, % Change)	14.2	13.5	12.6	10.5	9.7	8.8	7.2	6.8
Industrial Production (Real, % Change)	21.2	—	21.4	16.1	15.1	13.2	9.0	7.7
Investment								
Total Fixed Asset Investment (Real, % Change)	23.5	25.2	23.9	10.0	12.7	10.5	12.2	—
Consumer Spending								
Retail Sales (Real, % Change)	10.5	12.5	7.7	11.8	12.5	10.7	—	
Prices								
RPI (%)	5.4	13.0	21.7	14.8	6.1	0.8	-1.5	
CPI (%)	6.4	14.7	24.1	17.1	8.3	2.8	-1.0*	
External								
Exports (% Change)	18.1	7.2	33.0	23.0	1.5	20.9	13.3	7.6**
Imports (cif) (% Change)	26.3	27.9	12.2	11.6	7.6	2.4	—	
FDI (% Change)	154.5	145.5	30.2	10.4	6.6	7.9	14.1	-1.5**

* Percent change over the period May 1997–May 1998
** Jan–May 1998
Source: State Statistical Bureau, *International Monetary Fund*, J.P. Morgan.

of poor quality products, amounting to an estimated US$70 billion or some 8 per cent of GDP in 1997.

Fifthly, China has been affected by the Asian financial and economic crisis that has produced a major decline in GDP and industrial output growth across the region (see Table 1.3). The region takes approximately 60 per cent of China's exports and contributes about 85 per cent of its FDI.[14] This major decline in GDP growth in the region is likely to contribute to: a decline in China's exports; a decline in its FDI; a deterioration in the corporate sector's profitability and most noticeably that of the SOEs; declining government revenue; increasing non-performing loans held by the state banks; rising unemployment; and a further slowdown in China's GDP growth.

While China's exports and FDI held up well during the initial stage of the regional crisis, as it proceeded they became more vulnerable. Net exports, or the trade balance, remained very strong after 1993, and exports contributed about 2 percentage points of China's total GDP growth of 8.8 per cent in 1997. However, this contribution weakened during 1998. During the first four months of 1998, exports were 11.7 per cent higher than a year earlier, but in May they declined by 1.5 per

Table 1.3
Internal Economic Developments–China and Selected East Asian Economies, 1998

(% Change on a Year Earlier)

	GDP	Industrial Production	Consumer Prices
China	+6.8 Q2 1998	+7.9 May 1998	−1.3 June 1998
Hong Kong	−2.8 Q1 1998	−4.0 Q1 1998	+4.0 June 1998
Taiwan	+5.9 Q1 1998	+5.4 June 1998	+0.9 July 1998
Malaysia	−1.8 Q1 1998	−8.6 May 1998	+6.2 June 1998
South Korea	−3.8 Q1 1998	−13.3 June 1998	+7.3 July 1998
Indonesia	−6.2 Q1 1998	+10.7 Q3 1997	+59.5 June 1998
Philippines	+1.7 Q1 1998	−7.7 Feb 1998	+10.6 July 1998
Singapore	+5.6 Q1 1998	−4.5 May 1998	−0.2 June 1998
Thailand	+0.4 1997	−17.5 May 1998	+10.0 July 1998

Source: *The Economist*, 8 August 1998, p. 88.

cent year on year. This represented the first contraction in 22 months. FDI remained strong during 1997 and during the first quarter of 1998. But over the five months period from January to May 1998 it amounted to US$14.9 billion, some 1.5 per cent less than for the equivalent period in 1997. Such adverse external developments suggested it was unlikely that China could export its way out of its current slowdown predicament, and that more emphasis needed to be placed upon stimulating domestic demand. This indeed provided the basis for the government's policy response outlined in more detail in section 5.

Finally, prices for various products have been falling in China. Retail price inflation was only 0.8 per cent for the whole of 1997 and during the last quarter prices actually declined, and this continued into 1998. In fact, by June 1998 the country had experienced eight consecutive months of falling prices. Consumer prices fell by 1.3 per cent by June 1998 over the previous twelve months (see Table 1.3). This was driven by chronic oversupply in manufacturing, resulting in declining profit margins that forced a cut back in production, and excellent agricultural production outcomes. Food prices, which constitute a sizeable proportion of the consumer basket, had fallen because of three years of excellent harvests. For example, grain prices fell by 13 per cent in December 1997 (over December 1996) which represented the largest explanatory factor behind the overall decline in prices. In addition the price deflation was partly due to an appreciation of the RMB relative to that of the yen and many other Asian currencies. This assisted China in maintaining the country's competitiveness by reducing the cost of imported capital goods in particular.

1.4   Impact of the Asian financial crisis on China, and implications for the RMB

Impact of the Asian crisis on China

The economic and financial crisis afflicting China's neighbours from mid-1997 gradually adversely impacted upon the Chinese economy for a number of reasons. The crisis put pressure on the country's exports and foreign investment, and, more importantly, eroded the corporate sector's profitability. Consequently, enterprises in China, SOEs in particular, were forced to reform in order to survive. Emphasis is being placed upon raising their efficiency and cutting costs, rationalizing operations, and improving management. Attempts to improve profitability have come at a social cost in the form of rapidly rising unemployment, the extent of which has already led to a rapidly deteriorating labour market. The deteriorating performance of the SOEs also has important implications for government revenue and the non-performing loans of the state banks. However, most emphasis of the crisis has tended to focus upon its impact on China's external developments.

About 65 per cent of total foreign capital flowing into China comes from Asia, equal to US$35 billion out of a total of US$54.8 billion in 1996. Of this figure, about US$33 billion was in the form of FDI. However the growth of FDI in China has been slowing for three major reasons. Firstly, the main sources of FDI for China, Hong Kong and overseas Chinese in Asian countries, have suffered severe setbacks arising from the financial and economic crisis in the region. Secondly, foreign investment in Asia generally has contracted due to the economic crisis afflicting the region. Finally, new FDI commitments to China had already begun to slow down before the crisis because of: disappointment over returns on earlier investments; a downward assessment of market potential in China; and bureaucratic difficulties facing investors in China. However, as indicated from Table 1.2, in the first quarter of 1998 FDI was some US$8.6 billion, up 9.7 per cent from a year earlier, although over the extended period January to May 1998 it amounted to US$14.9 billion which was 1.5 per cent down on the same period in 1997. Flows from a number of East Asian countries have declined dramatically during the period of the crisis. For example, Indonesian FDI in China fell 89.7 per cent, that by South Korea fell 55.8 per cent, that by Japan fell 42.2 per cent and that by Thailand fell by 35.5 per cent. However there have been increased inflows from Taiwan, Europe and the USA to offset this. FDI by the European Union (EU) is up by 75.4 per cent, and from the USA by 25.4 per cent. Hence the early indications in 1998 suggested that declines in FDI by the crisis-affected Asian economies in China were being offset to some extent by that from the EU and USA in particular.

China's exports to crisis-affected economies in East Asia were also anticipated to decline. As indicated by Table 1.2, during the first five months of 1998 exports increased by 7.6 per cent compared with those of a year previously, a sharp decline from the 20.9 per cent recorded for the whole of 1997. By May 1998, exports suffered their first year-on-year decline for 22 months, falling by 1.5 per cent. Some industries, such as textiles, experienced major difficulties. While China's trade has grown rapidly recently, with exports contributing about 2 percentage points of China's 8.8 per cent GDP growth in 1997, its significance to the overall economy, however, should not be overstated. Despite this, trade problems threaten to hamper the reform program. The government has been relying partly on the robust economic performance of its export-oriented coastal regions to provide employment for the millions of workers laid off due to SOE reform. With these areas less able to take the strain, the pressures for delay in the government's industrial reforms intensified.

Almost 30 per cent of China's exports in 1997 were with the economies of ASEAN, Korea and Japan, all of which have been badly affected by the financial and economic crisis. The ASEAN economies and Korea accounted for about 5 per cent each of China's total exports in 1997. Trade relations with Korea are complicated by the fact that many Korean export industries import components from China, and hence the net impact on trade is unclear. Although the growth of the Korean economy slowed considerably in 1998, any expansion by its export sector could lead to expanded demand for Chinese products. However this could be offset by the increased competitiveness of other crisis economies due to their substantial currency devaluations. For certain products, such as clothes, cheap electronics and other light industry products, China competes directly with a number of the ASEAN economies and especially Indonesia. However Indonesian exporters are having considerable difficulty in gaining access to trade credit and to maintaining their credibility as reliable suppliers, and hence may be unable to take advantage of their improved competitiveness arising from their massively weaker currency.

In 1997 Japan accounted for about 17.5 per cent of China's exports. Hence the biggest external threat would come from a further slowdown in the Japanese economy. There is also likely to be a moderate reduction in export growth to the USA and the EU, due to conservative fiscal and monetary policies in Europe because of the Euro, combined with the effects of greater competitiveness of ASEAN countries and Korea. The overall net effect is a likely export-growth slowdown from about 21 per cent in 1997 to perhaps around 10 per cent in 1998. Sources in China[15] suggest that even with an export slowdown to 10 per cent in 1998 its impact upon the growth of the national economy would still be relatively moderate, but in some areas, such as coastal provinces and cities like Tianjin, the effect is likely to be felt more intensely.

Will China devalue its currency?

Economic developments in the Chinese economy during 1998 and 1999 will have important regional and global implications. Should the downturn in the economy continue, and indeed intensify, it will contribute to a further increase in unemployment and rising social unrest. This will not only put in jeopardy the reforms in regard to the SOEs and banking system but could also result in intense pressure upon the authorities to devalue the currency. If China's economic downturn deepens, the world, but more particularly the region, will be watching China's currency policy nervously. As the world's seventh largest economy, and its eleventh largest trading nation,[16] China's currency policy has immense regional and global repercussions. While many participants in the region's financial markets have suggested that the RMB needs to be devalued for the sake of Chinese competitiveness, a RMB devaluation would not be an appropriate response to the Asian crisis and is in fact unlikely. China has not been subject to the currency contagion affecting countries like Thailand, Indonesia, the Philippines and Korea, due to: its successful macrostabilization measures since mid-1993; its strong agricultural performance over the past three years; and its strong external economic position. A number of factors lie behind the relative strength of the currency, making the prospect of a devaluation unlikely in the near future. The major reasons for this are now discussed.

Firstly, the country is in a very strong external position. China has experienced trade and current account surpluses since 1994, reaching record levels in 1997. In this year the country achieved a trade account surplus of US$40 billion and a current account surplus of US$24.6 billion. Figures for mid-1998 indicated that this situation remained strong. Table 1.4 indicates that over the 12-month period to June 1998 the country attained a trade account surplus of US$45 billion, and that this, as well as developments in the current account, compared very favourably with its regional neighbours. During the period January to June 1998 alone, the trade surplus amounted to US$18.6 billion, up by 33 per cent from a year earlier. Although export growth was slowing, import growth was declining even more.

Secondly, China's export growth may not be adversely affected by devaluations elsewhere in East Asia. Although devaluations elsewhere put Chinese exports in an unfavourable position, exchange rates are only one of many variables that affect export growth. For exchange rates to be significant in export competitiveness, at least two conditions must be in place. Firstly, products of competing nations must be so undifferentiated that they are nearly perfect substitutes for each other in world markets; and secondly, exports must embody the same proportions of capital, labour and technology as identical exports from competing economies. This is not the case in Asia, which consists of a number of diverse economies. The fall in the won, for instance, may not have much impact on China's exports because Korean products tend to be more capital- and technology-intensive. However, devaluations in Indonesia, Malaysia, the Philippines and Thailand could have a larger impact on China. But China exports a more diverse range of products than these countries. Also, its labour costs are below the average for the region. Regional devaluations should reduce the labour cost differential relative to China, but not eliminate it. In industries such as textiles and garments, where competition is intense, Southeast Asia is unlikely to take away significant market share from China, as such trade is mainly determined by non-tariff barriers imposed by leading importers such as the US. Direct competition with ASEAN countries is mainly limited to lower-end technology electronics and sports articles – which overlap about 35 per cent of China's exports. For major exports such as garments, toys, footwear, watches and clocks, China's sheer market share on global import markets offers a significant margin of protection. China's export tax (VAT export rebate below VAT import rate) has been reduced and is further reducible as an alternative to exchange-rate adjustment so as to maintain exporters' competitiveness. Some industries are moving from coastal areas to the interior where labour and land costs are much lower. They do not relocate to Thailand and Indonesia. Even without moving to the interior, many of China's export industries remain competitive because of low production costs and the country's virtually unlimited pool of labour.

A Southeast Asian export surge seems unlikely in the near future. Many companies in the region are finding it difficult to import raw materials and parts and to obtain letters of credit and trade finance. In addition the overall disruption to their economic systems, including the high rates of bankruptcy, has increased costs of production and turned many firms into perceived unreliable suppliers, discouraging sales even though devaluations have made their prices more attractive.[17] Such difficulties do not face Chinese enterprises. This may be more important than a competitive exchange rate, and puts China's exporters at an advantage over their financially stricken regional competitors. The falling value of the yen also allows China to buy Japanese equipment more cheaply than before. There is also the prospect that if China can weather the economic storm in 1998 and the first half of 1999, domestic inflation in the crises countries will have greatly reduced their current competitive advantage.

Exports are, however, not the most important issue facing the country. Foreign trade still remains a relatively small part of overall economic activity.[18] It is far more important for the coastal provinces, which account for about 60 per cent of China's GDP, than the interior provinces. Although export growth appears to be slowing, this is providing only a modest drag to the growth of the overall economy. Moreover, the RMB has become more competitive thanks to the concurrent sharp decline in inflation.

Thirdly, China's currency is not fully convertible – the currency is only fully convertible on current account, as of December 1996, but is not convertible on capital account, and is therefore not subject to speculative attacks. As long as China maintains its sizeable surplus on the trade and current accounts, a weakening of the exchange rate will not occur. In fact there is evidence to suggest that upward pressure on the RMB remains, almost a year after the start of the Asian crisis. The government in early 1998 relaxed foreign-exchange surrender requirements. Exporters have since accumulated US$6 billion in foreign accounts, money that the Peoples' Bank of China would otherwise have had to buy to prevent an appreciation of the RMB. As indicated in Table 1.4, over the twelve-month period from 5 August 1997 to 5 August 1998 the exchange rate has remained very stable against the US dollar. This stands in sharp contrast to developments in the currencies of its regional neighbours, with the exception of Hong Kong due to its currency peg, which have experienced sizeable deteriorations during the period of the Asian financial crisis. Interestingly, the difference between the black market rate and the official rate for the RMB appears to be small, suggesting that the exchange rate is not much out of line with market sentiment. Arising from the Asian financial crisis, the government has noted with concern the ability of a convertible currency to take a country's weak banking system to the point of collapse. The full convertibility of the currency is therefore likely to have been postponed indefinitely.

Fourthly, the country has substantial foreign-exchange reserves. China has very substantial foreign-exchange reserves in absolute terms as well as relative to imports and short-term debt. Buoyant export growth and record capital inflows in 1997, particularly in the form of FDI, contributed to the accumulation of foreign-exchange reserves worth US$140 billion by the end of 1997. As indicated by Table 1.4 these stood at US$140.9 billion by the end of June 1998[19] and compared very favourably with developments in other regional economies. However the growth of foreign reserves slowed down considerably during 1998. One reason for this was that, since October 1997, exporters have been allowed to retain 15 per cent of their export earnings in US dollar assets, whereas previously all export earnings had to be sold on the foreign-exchange market.

Fifthly, China has limited exposure to foreign debt. China's exposure to foreign debt is limited, amounting to only 17.3 per cent of GDP in 1997.[20] In addition, the bulk of its foreign-debt stock is in long-term development loans and private FDI rather than in short-term debt.[21] As a percentage of total foreign exchange reserves short-term debt amounted to only 27.6 per cent at end 1997, which compared very favourably with its regional neighbours.[22] In addition China, unlike its Asian neighbours, does not have a banking and financial system with substantial foreign debts denominated in overseas currencies. The

Table 1.4
External Economic Developments – China and Selected East Asian Economies, Twelve months to mid-1998

	Trade Balance (US$ Billion)		Current Account (US$ Billion)		Foreign Exchange Reserves (US$ Billion)		Exchange Rate Per US$		
							5 Aug 98	5 Aug 97	% Change
China	+45.0	June 1998	+24.6	1997*	140.9	June 1998	8.28	8.29	Neg
Hong Kong	−16.8	June 1998	−6.7	1997**	96.2	Apr 1998	7.75	7.74	Neg
Taiwan	+4.6	June 1998	+5.7	Q1 1998	84.4	May 1998	34.5	28.7	−20.2
Malaysia	+3.8	May 1998	−4.8	1997	21.3	Apr 1998	4.14	2.64	−56.8
South Korea	+24.7	July 1998	+23.4	June 1998	38.8	May 1998	1 265	894	−41.5
Indonesia	+17.7	May 1998	−5.8	Q4 1997	16.9	Apr 1998	12 900	2 585	−399.0
Philippines	−7.6	May 1998	−3.5	Q1 1998	7.8	Mar 1998	42.4	28.9	−46.7
Singapore	−0.5	June 1998	+13.6	Q1 1998	76.1	Apr 1998***	1.72	1.47	−17.0
Thailand	+4.8	May 1998	−2.9	Q1 1998	26.7	May 1998	40.9	31.0	−31.9

*   Estimate
**   Visible and Invisible Trade Balance
***   Includes Gold
Neg   Negligible
Source: The Economist, 8 August, 1998, p.88.

country's bad debts in the banking system are denominated in RMB and not US dollars. Finally, China's two stock markets (excluding Hong Kong) are still relatively small and would not be capable of exerting a major impact on the economy arising from a change in market sentiment.

Sixthly, the domestic economy is relatively strong. China has achieved a strong economic performance in comparison to that of other regional economies, and has attained much greater internal stability. As a result of austerity measures implemented since 1993, the country has experienced a significant decline in its rate of inflation. Although a decline in GDP growth is anticipated in 1998, both by official and non-official sources, it still remains by far and away the highest in the region. GDP growth is less dependent on export growth than is commonly assumed, with total exports amounting to only 20 per cent of GDP in 1997. Chinese exports are very import-intensive, with the exception of agricultural goods and processing industries such as cotton textiles and leather goods. Food exports account for about 10 per cent of China's total exports and textile exports are subject to MFA[23] quotas. Hence, to try and stimulate the economy through a devaluation of the currency would not be particularly effective.

Seventhly, there would be major implications for FDI arising from a currency devaluation. If China were to devalue its currency FDI would be hurt. Official figures suggest that contracted FDI, new commitments by foreigners, has been declining, which is a major cause of concern to China's leaders. Foreign corporations committing capital in China to serve the local market rely on a long-term strategy, which assumes, among other things, a relatively stable exchange rate that more or less reflects market conditions. If the RMB were to be abruptly devalued, the dollar return on foreign investment in China would be reduced. This would also spark fears about future devaluations, and as such would not be a prudent policy at a time when investors are already concerned about emerging markets in general.

Eighthly, a devaluation could also re-ignite the risk of inflation, which has abated on the back of tough austerity measures. Imports accounted for around 16 per cent of China's GDP in 1997. A devaluation would increase the domestic price of imports ranging from equipment to raw materials and intermediate goods, eventually leading to higher domestic prices for final consumption goods. Many of China's exports have a high import content, and hence this would offset any benefits from a devaluation. Sharply declining currencies elsewhere in Asia may not help reduce by much imported inflation for China, with the exception of a yen depreciation, as more than 85 per cent of its imports come from industrial economies and Hong Kong, whose currencies have not weakened in tandem with many of Asia's.

Ninthly, a devaluation could trigger a host of adverse developments for the Chinese authorities. An abrupt change in China's exchange rate policy would destabilize the Hong Kong dollar peg to the US dollar as well as its financial markets more generally, a consequence that China would prefer to avoid. Devaluation would cause friction with the US over an already spiralling bilateral trade imbalance in China's favour, which has allied diverse US groups, including labour unions, protectionist politicians, environmentalists and human rights activists, to lobby against China. Manipulating its exchange rate for trade advantages would also complicate China's negotiations on WTO membership. To enhance its WTO accession, China would be better to reduce its import restrictions and to protect its nominal exchange rate.

Finally, as Asia's second largest economy, China's role in the region is critical in containing the financial crisis and stabilizing the regional economies. The government has been concerned by developments in the ASEAN 4[24] and South Korea, and its potential implications for China. While China has pledged financial support for Thailand and Indonesia[25] under IMF bail-out packages, and not objected to Taiwanese contributions, the most effective assistance it can extend to its distressed neighbours is to maintain its own fast economic growth. A Chinese devaluation would likely trigger a fresh round of competitive devaluations in Asia and aggravate the current regional economic crisis.[26] This would neither be to the region's benefit nor to China's. Hence a currency devaluation would be an extremely risky strategy in which the potential benefit to China's export competitiveness is at best uncertain, but the negative impact of such a policy could be severe. Hence this strategy is one which China is unlikely to pursue as a response to the Asian financial crisis, and Premier Zhu Rongji has steadfastly refused to engage in a competitive devaluation. China's policy of developing constructive relations with ASEAN and other Asian neighbours also makes devaluation unwanted for external political reasons.[27]

From this discussion it is clear that China has a crucial role to play in what will happen in Asia over the foreseeable future. Most analysts agree that a move by China to devalue its currency would set off a round of competitive devaluations and depression for the entire region and the benefits to China from doing so are not at all clear.

1.5   Policy response to the economic slowdown

Since March 1998 the Chinese authorities have been implementing a domestic stimulus package, described as a Chinese style 'New Deal', that will increase expenditure on public works and other projects by as much as 20 per cent per year. Emphasis to be placed on infrastructure investment and on housing construction. By focusing upon internal growth, the Chinese are signalling their resolve not to out-export their neighbours, and to maintain their pledge of not devaluing the RMB. The key components of this new deal consists of a number of key components: increased infrastructure expenditure; a mass residential housing development program; supportive monetary measures; maintaining the reform momentum; providing tax rebates to exporters. Each of these is now briefly discussed in turn.

In February 1998, at the World Economic Summit in Davos Switzerland, Chinese Vice Premier Li Lanqing announced a US$750 billion infrastructure and environment plan for China, to be spread over three years. The aim, initially at least, was to keep economic growth in China above 8 per cent in 1998. This gave the clearest indication that the Chinese authorities were concerned about, and saw the need to respond to, the slowing economy. Such an increase in infrastructure expenditure and fixed-asset investment could boost GDP by an estimated extra 2 per cent. While the country certainly needs better roads, airports, railways, ports, bridges and irrigation schemes, housing, posts and telecommunications, particularly in the poorer inland provinces, the issue of how the program was to be funded, without fuelling inflation, needed to be resolved. The government is already running budget deficits, and this program, in conjunction with declining SOE revenue, would substantially increase the 1998 state budget deficit to as much as US$5.5 billion according to some estimates. However, with a budget deficit of just 0.7 per cent of GDP in 1997 and low domestic debt, China can afford to finance more new infrastructure projects through the issue of, for example, government bonds.

A number of funding options are available. Much of it is anticipated to come from the country's vast personal savings, some US$560 billion accumulated during the period of economic reform and held as deposits in the state-run commercial banks throughout the country, and by expanding directed lending by the state banks. Domestic savings could be mobilized in a variety of ways: through the sale of central government bonds; letting cities and provincial governments sell bonds both locally and internationally for local projects; expanding the sale of corporate bonds which are restricted at present to under US$2 billion a year; and increasing the number of highway and railroad bonds. The government could attempt to raise funds in the Hong Kong financial markets, but the market is currently depressed and there are few relatively good investment projects. Another option is to expand, and tap into, existing 'extra-budgetary' revenue. Attracting foreign investors on a build, operate and transfer basis (BOT) is possible but would be difficult for projects in the poorer inland provinces. Utilizing these alternative options meant that some 117 key infrastructure projects were carried out in 1998, more single projects than in any previous year.

The second major component of the program is the construction of low-cost housing with the objective of encouraging home ownership. The potential of this component of the program is substantial, but is unlikely to have an immediate impact. Many residential developments already stand vacant, and convincing Chinese people to buy rather than to rent will take time. State-subsidized rents would need to go much higher before consumers would consider buying their own homes. Under government reforms of 1 July 1998,[28] state housing was only to be made available for sale and not rent, and rent for existing tenants was to be increased to 15 per cent of family income or to the market level. Such developments, it was anticipated, would expand the nascent consumer finance industry, stimulate specifically a housing mortgage market as well as other services industries such as insurance and underwriting and other property ownership infrastructure. However this would take time for a country with an underdeveloped financial system. In addition, the development of a private housing market, including the sale of the current stock of housing to its occupants, would enhance labour mobility and enable the development of an effective labour market. As long as housing is limited and largely controlled by existing enterprises, labour mobility will be limited and new enterprise creation inhibited. This is particularly the case for smaller enterprises that do not have the capacity to provide housing for their employees. Private housing would also encourage the creation of small enterprises not only in construction but also in maintenance and home improvement, including plumbers, carpenters, painters and electricians. New housing units would in turn give rise to demand for new consumer products, such as appliances and furniture. Such a housing program, therefore, has the potential to be an important engine for growth. However as the economy, and in particular the labour market, has steadily deteriorated during 1998, the government has postponed reform of state housing until the end of 1998. This has arisen due to concern that rising rents and sale of the existing stock of housing will reduce funds available for consumption expenditure, and thereby exacerbate the economic slowdown.

As part of the new deal program, the central bank has eased the monetary austerity measures in place since 1993 in two major ways. Firstly, pressure has been brought to bear on the state banks to expand access to credit for key sectors such as that of infrastructure and exporters, and for home purchase consistent with attaining the overall objectives of the program, as well as struggling SOEs. Consistent with this, interest rates have been reduced to further stimulate infrastructure investment and house purchase. At the end of June 1998 the monetary authorities announced the fifth interest-rate cut in just over a year, with commercial bank lending rates cut by an average of 1.12 percentage points to 6.5 per cent for loans up to six months and around 6.9 per cent for loans up to one year. However monetary policy alone has major limitations in the present climate of excess capacity and depressed domestic demand, and its current role is therefore primarily to facilitate the attainment of the other major components of the program in stimulating aggregate expenditure.

While the first three components of the program can contribute to alleviating the short-term downturn in the economy, additional measures will be required to ensure that the growth momentum is maintained over the medium to long term. This will require: pushing ahead with reform of the SOEs; reforming the banking sector; restructuring the economy; and reducing the size of government. However the rapid deterioration of the economy has contributed to a rapid increase in unemployment and rising concern over social unrest. This has already led to an effective reversal of banking-sector reform, with state banks once again being required to extend easy loans to key sectors of the economy. Further reform of the SOEs also appears to be slowing down.

Finally, the government has offered exporters special tax rebates on exports of coal, textiles, rolled steel, cement and some machinery products to offset the loss of competitiveness brought about by the relatively strong RMB.

In addition to these core components of the stimulatory package, additional measures, or added dimensions, are likely to be required in order to make it successful. The first of which involves opening up the interior provinces of China. This has the potential to boost domestic demand significantly. The government must attempt to ensure that its ambitious public works program will spread the wealth to interior cities. In addition it is also important to assist the three-quarters of China's population that lives in rural areas, but which accounts for only 45 per cent of retail sales. This is clearly a longer-term strategy but with considerable potential for maintaining the growth momentum. There will need to be an important role for foreign investors in this process, with encouragement for them to invest in the interior where costs are lower rather than in coastal provinces. The establishment of appropriate infrastructure and other incentives would assist greatly in this process.[29]

There is also a need to put in place further incentives to attract more FDI to generate further employment growth. As indicated previously contracted FDI has declined significantly recently, suggesting that there is a need to accelerate the approval rate for new private and joint venture projects and establish a more investor friendly environment.

With the prospect over the short to medium term of further substantial increases in urban unemployment and rising social unrest, it will be essential to put a more substantive safety net in place for displaced workers. In addition there will be a need to retrain such workers for new employment opportunities in the rapidly expanding services sector, or for the prospective establishment of their own small businesses.

Should the government be unable to revive economic growth through the new deal program, and if rising unemployment and social unrest are creating major instability, in conjunction with pressure from business interests such as that of shipbuilding, petrochemicals and steel, the authorities may become sufficiently desperate to devalue the currency. If this policy is pursued it should be done so only gradually to avoid a major disturbance. However this would be a last-resort policy, and if utilized it would indicate that the authorities had lost control of macroeconomic developments elsewhere.

Many of these measures have the major drawback that they will only have a lagged effect upon the economy. While the speeding-up of infrastructure projects should have a relatively quick impact upon output and employment, and therefore has received most emphasis, the authorities should not neglect the other identified measures, so as to ensure the longer-term health of the economy. Otherwise the same situation may have to be faced up to again, but will be more intractable next time around.

1.6   Summary and conclusions

During China's reform era, the country experienced a remarkable period of economic growth and development. During the initial stages, emphasis was placed upon the country's transition from being relatively poor and technologically backward to the attainment of a higher level of economic development, primarily by improving its performance within the context of a planned economy. Much of the early economic growth success arose from improved labour productivity generated by the transfer of labour from agriculture to rural industry. However by the early 1990s the country faced a further transition from a planned to a market-oriented economy, as the objective of the government became the attainment of a socialist market economy with Chinese characteristics. This phase in the country's development process is proving to be more difficult, requiring further restructuring of the economy and the reform of key sectors such as that of the SOEs and the banking sector. If the economy is to sustain high rates of economic growth, such reform is essential, but is proving to be very difficult. This difficulty is compounded by the country's current economic downturn.

During the period of economic reform, downturns have not been uncommon, having generally occurred after the authorities implemented measures to curb bouts of inflationary pressure. The current downturn is different from that experienced in the past in that the economy is experiencing excess supply relative to demand, exemplified by: over-capacity in many industries; high stock levels; price deflation; declining retail sales growth; and declining growth of fixed asset investment. On top of these the Asian financial crisis is bringing about declining export growth and inflows of FDI. Lacklustre domestic demand is seen as being the primary culprit, rather than tight credit, and therefore traditional methods of kick-starting the economy, easing credit and expanding fixed-asset investment, will not work this time. A new approach will be required.

To this end the government has put in place a 'new deal' program which emphasizes: a public works program focusing upon infrastructure spending; housing reform; and a further loosening of monetary policy; but offers no devaluation of the currency to boost exports. There are tremendous risks involved if this program of measures is unsuccessful in reversing the downward growth trend of the economy. As the economic environment continues to deteriorate during 1998, expediency has required the authorities to focus policy on the need to reverse this downward trend in the short term and to place less emphasis on reforms required for the medium- to long-term health of the economy. Growth of less than 7–8 per cent will not be enough to absorb a growing army of laid-off workers and new labour market entrants. Social unrest would loom large. The recent experience of Indonesia would pale into insignificance if the equivalent occurred in China, and this would be hugely damaging for the regional and global economies.

Notes

1 Around 200 million during the initial stage of the reform process.
2 The non-state sector in China comprises urban and rural collectives (including township and village enterprises), joint stock companies, private businesses, joint ventures, and foreign-funded enterprises. While collectives represent a form of public ownership, they differ importantly from state enterprises in that they typically have faced harder budget constraints and less direct involvement from government ministries. In addition, in recent years, many collectives have been effectively privatized while retaining their original classification.
3 At market exchange rates, China's per capita income is currently estimated at about US$600. Purchasing power parity measures suggest a significantly higher per capita income of between US$2 000–US$3 000, roughly 30 per cent below comparable estimates for Indonesia, 60 per cent below Thailand, and 70 per cent below Malaysia (*World Economic Outlook*, 1997, May, Table 18, p. 81). The estimates of per capita income for China are subject to a considerable margin of uncertainty owing to incomplete information on the structure of domestic prices.
4 In April 1998 Huang Yukon, chief representative of the World Bank in Beijing, argued that growth below 5 per cent would initiate substantial unrest.
5 Primarily arising from the rapid growth of employment in the Township and Village enterprises, which saw an expansion of employment from 28 million in the early 1980s to 135 million by 1996.
6 However, from the outset such reformers as Chen Yun would not have envisaged that the process of economic reform involved the replacement of one economic system (planning) by another (market).
7 The township and village enterprises.
8 This expression was first used by Naughton (1996) to describe China's reform process.
9 See Naughton (1996) for an alternative viewpoint that they began in the industrial sector.
10 While foreign-funded enterprises were permitted to retain foreign-exchange earnings, domestic enterprises were subject to a general surrender requirement but received 'retention quotas' equivalent to a certain percentage of their foreign-exchange earnings. Retained foreign exchange could be traded in swap centres at a market-determined exchange rate.
11 Retail price inflation (RPI).
12 These figures are from Jones Lang Wootton, property consultants, for December 1997.

13 From 1 July 1998 state-owned housing was to be available only for sale and not rent. This represented a move towards abolishing the country's welfare housing system. Rents were to be increased to 15 per cent of family income or the market level. However this reform has been postponed in many parts of China, and the government has decided to wait until the end of the year before raising rents on state housing. It was felt that with people having to buy or pay more rent on state housing this would dissuade them from spending.

14 These figures are for 1995.

15 State Statistical Bureau chief economist.

16 See IMF, *International Financial Statistics*, March 1998.

17 See, for example, Stiglitz (1998).

18 The trade balance in 1997 was equivalent to about 4.4 per cent of GDP, in 1996 the figure was 1.5 per cent of GDP.

19 These reserves were second only in the world to that of Japan's, which stood at US$219.6 billion at end 1997.

20 As at December 1997. This compares with the equivalent figures for Indonesia – 62.4 per cent, Korea – 32 per cent, Malaysia – 43.3 per cent, Philippines – 62.3 per cent, Taiwan – 15.2 per cent, and Thailand – 62.9 per cent. These figures were obtained from JP Morgan.

21 Short-term debt comprised only 24.9 per cent of total foreign debt, or 4.3 per cent of GDP at end 1997. The equivalent figures for Indonesia are 27.2 per cent and 17 per cent, for Korea 37.3 per cent and 11.9 per cent, for Malaysia 29.8 per cent and 12.9 per cent, for the Philippines 24.7 per cent and 15.4 per cent, Taiwan 67.9 per cent and 10.3 per cent, and Thailand 29.2 per cent and 18.4 per cent respectively.

22 The equivalent figure, at end 1997, for Indonesia is 184 per cent, for Korea is 250 per cent, for Malaysia is 59.4 per cent, for the Philippines is 172 per cent, for Taiwan is 36 per cent, and for Thailand is 108 per cent.

23 Multi Fibre Agreement.

24 Indonesia, Malaysia, Philippines and Thailand.

25 US$1 billion in each case.

26 A point fully elaborated upon by Liu Lanqing, Vice Premier, at the World Economic Forum, Davos, Switzerland, February 1998.

27 The promise not to devalue the RMB was again reiterated in early June 1998 by central bank governor Dai Xianglong at a time when the Japanese currency came under further downward pressure.

28 Ultimately delayed to a later date due to the rapid deterioration in the labour market.

29 This issue is discussed in greater depth in Chapter 10.

References

Australian Department of Foreign Affairs and Trade (1996), *Country Economic Brief – China*, Canberra, February.

—— (1997), *Country Economic Brief – China*, Canberra, August.

—— (1997), *China Embraces the Market: Achievements, Constraints and Opportunities*, East Asia Analytical Unit, Canberra.

Bell, M.W., H.E. Khor, and K. Kochhar (1993), *China at the Threshold of a Market Economy*, IMF Occasional Paper 107, IMF, Washington, September.

Bottelier, P. (1998), China's Prospects in Light of the Asian Crisis, presentation at the SAIS China Forum, Johns Hopkins University, USA, March.

Businessweek (1998), *Can China Avert a Crisis?*, McGraw-Hill Inc., March 16.

IMF (1996), *People's Republic of China, Recent Economic Developments*, IMF Staff country Report No. 96/40, May.

—— (1997), *World Financial Outlook – Interim Assessment*, Washington, DC, December.

—— (1998), *World Economic Outlook*, Washington, DC, May.

Maddison, A. (1996), *Chinese Economic Performance in the Long Run*, Groningen Growth and Development Centre, University of Groningen, The Netherlands.

Naughton, B. (1995), 'China's Macroeconomy in Transition', *China Quarterly*, No. 144, December, pp 1085-1104.

—— (1996), *Growing Out of the Plan – Chinese Economic Reform 1978–1993*, Cambridge University Press.

Perkins, D. (1994), 'Completing China's Move to the Market', *Journal of Economic Perspectives*, Vol. 8, No. 2, pp. 223–46, Spring.

Rawski, T.G. (1994), 'Chinese Industrial Reform: Accomplishments, Prospects, and Implications', American Economics Association, *Papers and Proceedings*, Vol. 84, No. 2, May.

Sachs, J. and Wing Thye Woo (1994), 'Structural Factors in the Economic Reform of China, Eastern Europe and the former Soviet Union', *Economic Policy: A European Forum*, Vol. 9, April, pp. 101–45.

State Statistical Bureau (1996), *China Statistical Yearbook*, China Statistical Publishing House, Beijing.

Stiglitz, J. (1998), Second-generation Strategies for Reform for China, Address given at Beijing University, Beijing, China, 20 July.

Tisdell, C.A., and J.C.H. Chai (1997), *China's Economic Growth and Transition – Macroeconomic, Environmental and Social/Regional Dimensions*, Nova Science, New York.

Tseng, W., H.E. Khor, K. Kochar, D. Mihajek, and D. Burton (1994), *Economic Reform in China, a New Phase*, IMF Occasional Paper 114, IMF, Washington, November.

Ward, B. (1980), 'The Chinese Approach to Economic Development', in R. Dernberger (ed.), *China's Development Experience in Comparative Perspective*, Cambridge, Mass. Harvard University Press, pp. 91–119.

World Bank (1996), *World Development Report 1996 – From Plan to Market*, Oxford University Press.

—— (1997), *World Economic Outlook*, World Bank, Washington DC, May.

—— (1997), *World Economic Outlook*, World Bank, Washington DC, October.

Yusuf, S. (1993a), The Rise of China's Nonstate Sector, unpublished manuscript, World Bank.

Yusuf, S. (1993b), Property Rights and Nonstate Sector Development in China, unpublished manuscript, World Bank.

2

Growth, Inflation and the Asian Financial Crisis

Tran Van Hoa

This chapter focuses upon the causal structure of growth and inflation in China, and in doing so provides substantive empirical evidence leading to a better understanding of the engines of growth and inflation in China. This will also assist in the formulation and implementation of macroeconomic and restructuring policy to minimize the consequences of the Asian financial meltdown on China.

2.1 Introduction

The Asian financial crisis is one of the great economic phenomena in the world in recent times. While the conditions leading to it may have taken arguably months or years to build up, its occurrence was quite sudden starting initially with large short-term capital outflows from Thailand in July 1997. In a few short weeks the crisis had spread to other Asian countries with wide-ranging devastating effects on their economies, the governments and the peoples of many nations both developed and developing. Fortunately, for a number of major transition and developing economies in Asia which have a significant role in world affairs, such as China (with a population of 1 240 million people) and Vietnam (80 million), the crisis has so far not had as severe an impact. However it has been noted that, conceptually, in a global economy with multi-lateral trading and financial activities, these countries would find it difficult to avoid the flow-on of the turmoil in the medium and long term. At the time of writing,[1] the crisis is still unfolding and gripping the attention of world political and financial leaders in search of suitable short-term cures and long-term solutions. Social unrest and political instability with serious military and police crackdowns, and subsequent numerous fatalities, in such countries as Indonesia have started taking place.

Descriptive and analytical studies on the possible causes and impact of the crisis have been numerous in both the printed and electronic media in the past few months. However, they reflect what can be regarded as essentially different subjective viewpoints. A rigorous, objective and empirical analysis on the fundamental causes, and hence plausible cures, of the turmoil using time-tested theories, historical data and contemporary advanced econometric methodologies has not been formally carried out or reported for the Asian countries in trouble.[2]

This chapter adopts an economic-theoretic and empirical data-consistent perspective and is focused particularly on the causal structure of growth and inflation in China. It is an attempt at providing some substantive information on these activities' economic state of play, and the influence upon them arising from trading and financial interdependence and international competitiveness, and exposure in a modern economy-wide and global context. The findings provide a better understanding of the engines of growth and inflation in China, and informed discussion about them. This may lead to a better formulation and implementation of China's fiscal, monetary and trade policy and strategies to deal directly with the economic and financial fundamentals that may give rise to the meltdown in China itself, with disastrous global consequences, in the near future, and also to meet, contain or minimize the impact of the Asian financial crisis when it arrives in force.

2.2 Causal determination: modern methodologies

The concept of strong causality underlies all human endeavours. It underlies all theories or hypotheses known to mankind and has occupied the mind of philosophers, mathematicians, engineers and social scientists alike worldwide over many centuries. In spite of this, a unique definition of causality is still elusive in many fields. One can argue, however, that a fairly unique or generally acceptable definition of causality may be found perhaps in some special cases in such fields as physics or astronomy. Thus, the law of gravity may be able to explain why an object falls to the ground fast or slow or why hot air always rises. Similarly, the shape of the movement of the earth around the sun may be explained again by the law of gravity and mass. In medicine, however, and in the well-known medical cases such as breast cancer and hypertension, the study of what causes breast cancer, or hypertension, has generated a global industry for thousands of physicians, medical researchers and pharmaceutical corporations and worth billions of dollars each year. At the same time, even in these cases, no definitive statement can be made with authority about what actually causes breast cancer or hypertension. It is common understanding that when the causes of an event are not known, the cures for it cannot be properly prescribed.

In economics and finance, the problem of causality has no less importance and relevance in such activity as the determination of causal effects, diagnosis, and the formulation of remedial policy, prescriptions, for unemployment or the crash of a stock market. In the view of this author the current International Monetary Fund (IMF) bail-out packages for some Asian countries in trouble have not had the consequences intended. On the contrary they have caused directly or indirectly unnecessary serious social unrest simply because the real or fundamental causes of the crisis that are econometrically realistic or data-consistent have not been correctly detected and appropriately used.

The early concept of so-called Wiener-Granger causality and the formal statistical procedure for its detection were proposed by Granger (Granger, 1969) to investigate the direction of possible short-term causation between economic or financial time-series variables. Empirical applications of this Granger causality test have been extensive in the past three decades and involved many important areas of economics such as money and income (Sims, 1972), wage and price inflation (Fels and Tran Van Hoa, 1981), and energy and GNP (Abosedra and Baghestani, 1989), to name a few. The theory of long-term causal relationships, also known as the cointegration theory, was proposed by Granger (1986) and Engle and Granger (1987), and extended by Johansen and Juselius (1990) and Johansen (1991). Since then its applications have been wide-ranging in economics and finance.[3]

A comparative study on the merits of alternative causal testing procedures is avoided, and instead focus is placed on applying a simple ordinary least squares (OLS)-based method (see Granger, 1969; Fels and Tran Van Hoa, 1981; Engle and Granger, 1987; Pindyck and Rubinfeld, 1991; Tran Van Hoa, 1997) to empirically determine the short-term as well as long-term causes of growth and inflation in China. The reasons for using this method are (a) the simplicity but adequacy of the economic-theoretic assumptions underlying the model explaining growth and inflation, (b) the fairly small sample size of the data available, and (c) the simplicity and testing effectiveness of the method (Engle and Granger, 1987). In this study, for pragmatic reasons, there is assumed to be no structural break in the data-set which contains the annual data available for the period 1970 to 1995. As is well known, this period covers the two oil shocks of 1974 and 1981, the stock market crash of 1987 and the Gulf War in 1991. The implications of these external shocks, which seriously affected the Western economies, will remain the focus of a future investigation.

Thus, in the study below, the test for the presence of Wiener-Granger short-term causality between growth (denoted by say Y) and its possible cause (X) rests first on the assumption that these two variables are stationary or integrated of degree zero, that is they are $I(0)$, and the setting up of the hypothesis that X causes Y or symbolically $X \to Y$. The test is then carried out using a set of unrestricted dynamic equations of the form of say order two as follows:

$$Y_t = a_1 + a_2 Y_{t-1} + a_3 Y_{t-2} + b_1 X_{t-1} + b_2 X_{t-2} + u_t \qquad (1)$$

and restricted dynamic equations of the same order when the possible effects of X on Y have been deleted or assumed to be not relevant (that is when $b_1 = 0$ and $b_2 = 0$),

$$Y_t = a_1 + a_2 Y_{t-1} + a_3 Y_{t-2} + u_t \qquad (2)$$

In (1) and (2), the a's and b's are the parameters to be estimated and the u's the equation error terms with usual statistical properties.

The OLS applied to these equations will produce the residual, that is the difference between the actual and estimated variables, sums of squares that can be used to compute the F-statistic. This calculated F-value is then compared to the critical F-value at the appropriate degrees of freedom and the relevant significance level to determine whether or not X Granger-causes Y. That is whether the estimated F-value is greater than the critical F-value. The same procedure is applied to the test for the direction of causality from Y to X. That is whether Y Granger-causes X or symbolically $Y \to X$.

In the case of the tests for detecting long-term causality, two stages are involved. In Stage 1 the presence of unit roots or non-stationarity or $I(1)$ for all variables of interest, say Y and X above in the case of a bivariate model, is tested. This stage again consists of two steps. Firstly, the unrestricted regression equation, also known as the reduced form error correction model, is estimated:

$$Y_t - Y_{t-1} = c_1 + c_2 T_t + (c_3 - 1) Y_{t-1} + c_4 DY_{t-1} + e_t \qquad (3)$$

and the restricted regression equation, that is, with $c_2 = 0$ or zero trend and $c_3 = 1$ or unit root:

$$Y_t - Y_{t-1} = c_1 + c_4 DY_{t-1} + e_t \qquad (4)$$

In (3) and (4), T is a time trend, $DY_t = Y_{t-1} - Y_{t-2}$ an error-correction variable to take care of possible higher-order non-stationarity in the series, the c's the parameters to be estimated, and the e's the error terms with white noise properties.

Then, using the resulting OLS-based estimated residual sums of squares from (3) and (4), an F-statistic is computed and compared to the critical values of the new F-distribution tabulated by Dickey and Fuller (1981), or any other similar tabulated critical values subsequently reported. The hypothesis of random walk or unit roots for Y above is rejected if this estimated F-value is greater than the critical F-value tabulated for an appropriate significance level.

Step 2 in the long-term causality test between two variables, Y and X for example, in which both Y and X have been found to be non-stationary and $I(1)$, involves using the test of cointegration or long-term relationships. This test is carried out simply by estimating by OLS the cointegrating regression equation (Sargan and Bhargava, 1983; Granger, 1986; Engle and Granger, 1987):

$$Y_t = d_1 + d_2 X_t + v_t \qquad (5)$$

and by testing whether the residuals, that is the estimated v, from this equation are stationary. If Y and X are not cointegrated then any linear combination of Y and X will not be stationary. In this case the residuals will be non-stationary. However, for a series v to be a random walk we must have $E(v_t - v_{t-1}) = 0$, and, accordingly, the Durbin-Watson (DW) statistic which is based on the sum of squares of this condition must be zero. The test of cointegration between Y and X is therefore the test of whether DW = 0 (Sargan and Bhargava, 1983; Granger, 1986; Engle and Granger, 1987). The estimated d's represent the long-term effects of X on Y or symmetrically Y on X.

2.3   The data and substantive findings for China

In the empirical study below, a standard macroeconomic causality model for growth and inflation for China based on an earlier model used by Harvie and Tran Van Hoa, 1994a and 1994b, is intially formulated. This model for China formulates the links between nine macroeconomic variables of interest here: foreign direct investment or investment (denoted by FDI or I), external debts and long-term external debts (D and DLT), output (GDP), terms of trade (TT), current account (CA), government budget (GB) and inflation (P). From these variables two simple reduced-form equations used for testing for causality and based on the standard macro-economic hypotheses in open economies are:

GDP is caused by FDI or I, D or DLT, TT, CA and G; and similarly for P. To bring out a clear relationship between GDP and P and each of the other determinant variables in the model, only a bivariate equation for each pair of variables linking GDP or P to each of the other variables is used for the testing.

The raw annual data used for the causality tests are derived from the 1997 World Bank World Tables database, issued in July 1997. The maximum sampling size available is 26 from 1970 to 1995. Some series, such as government budget, are not available for the whole of this sampling size. All variables in monetary value are in real terms and expressed in their annual rates of change. Each testing equation is therefore a first-order or planar approximation to any mathematically arbitrary functional form. This modelling flexibility of the model used here, and its other properties, have been discussed earlier in the context of a new general modelling approach to economics, business and finance (see Tran Van Hoa, 1992a and 1992b). To approximate the cost of living index or inflation the GDP implicit price deflator is used.

The results of the tests of short-term Granger causality and long-term cointegration causality for growth and inflation in China are given in Table 2.1.

From the results given in this table, it can be noted that, at the conventional statistical significance level, the growth rate for China during this period of more than two decades has been fairly high and statistically stable, stationary, around its average rate. This is also visually observed from a graph of the movements of the data over this period. The findings are in contrast with those for other Asian countries in the same period (see Tran Van Hoa and Harvie, 1998) where all growth rates were in fact growing at an exponential rate or, in other words, they were statistically non-stationary. China's inflation rate is also found to be absent from the presence of unit roots and thus was fairly stable during the period 1970 to 1995.

China's mean annual inflation rate (5.74 per cent) was however much lower than its mean annual growth rate (7.36 per cent). This implies that a real improvement of 1.62 per cent per annum in the standard of living of the Chinese people was achieved in this period. However, the improvement had slowed down slightly in the early 1990s in which the annual growth rate continuously fell from 13.22 per cent in 1992 to 9.88 per cent in 1995, and the annual inflation rate rose from 14.16 per cent in 1993 to 19.16 per cent in 1994 and 13.69 per cent in 1995.

Next, a formal look at the possible short-term as well long-term causes of growth and inflation in the Chinese economy is considered. The results are based on an econometric analysis for an open economy,

Table 2.1 Empirical Causes of Growth and Inflation in China, 1970 to 1995

Activity	Unit Root for % series	Short-Term Causes Growth	Short-Term Causes Inflation	Long-Term Causes Growth	Long-Term Causes Inflation
Growth	No				
Inflation	No				
Investment	No	No	No	Yes(+)*	Yes(+)
FDI	Yes	Yes	Yes	Yes(+)	Yes(–)
External Debts	Yes	Yes	No	Yes(+)	Yes(+)
Long-Term Debts	Yes	Yes	No	Yes(+)*	Yes(+)
Terms of Trade	Yes	Yes	Yes	Yes(+)	Yes(+)
Current Account	No	Yes	Yes	Yes(–)	Yes(–)
Government Budget	**	**	**	Yes(–)*	Yes(–)*

Notes: No = no significant unit root or causal effect found;
Yes (– or +) = Cause found with negative or positive effect;
* = Statistically significant long-term cause found;
** = no sufficient data.

Source of data: 1997 World Bank World Tables via Australia's DX databases.

see above, having strong trends in growth and inflation as well as in trade, business, capital flows and official development assistance in the past two decades or so.

Firstly, it can be noted that the statistically significant short-term causes of China's growth were not domestic or general investment but foreign direct investment, external debts, long-term debts, terms of trade and the current account. All of these empirical findings show a high level of dependence of China's economy on international trade and capital inflows. Its inflation, however, had been caused in the short term simply by foreign direct investment, the terms of trade and the current account. These are again key activities in international trade and capital flows.

The statistically significant long-term causes of growth were investment, long-term external debt and the government budget deficit. While investment and long-term external debt have a positive effect on growth, the government budget deficit has a dampening impact on it. China's inflation was caused mainly by government budget deficits, which had a negative effect. The activity of the government sector seems therefore to have two opposite effects. On the one hand the deficit was seen as a break on the heating-up of the economy. On the other hand the same activity also had the effect of stunting growth.

2.4 Implications for macroeconomic policy

The above findings from the causality studies for both the short and long term seem to reveal a number of interesting results which are useful for policy strategic studies to monitor the economy. They are useful to check the trends towards the problems many Asian countries have been experiencing in the past ten months or so, and to control the contagion of the present Asian financial crisis.

Statements by political leaders in China and the West during 1989 were designed to assure the public in global economies that China, with its strong economic base, large international reserves and political stability, would not have the same problems other Asian countries have been having. The above study and a comparison of these findings with those for other Asian countries in Tran Van Hoa and Harvie (1998), for example, suggests a persistent conclusion – that all these economies depended significantly on international trade, business and capital flows: the international sector. It was the weaknesses of the external sector's activities that caused untold economic, social and political damage to the Asian tigers in trouble (Thailand, Indonesia, Malaysia and Korea).

From this perspective, China will not be able to escape a financial or economic crisis that has beset other Asian countries if some damaging development, such as a slow-down of foreign direct investment or growing and large external debts, occurs. Since the majority of China's foreign direct investment, trade and debts have come mainly from the newly industrialized economies in Asia, the Asian financial turmoil which chokes off capital flows from these economies must on this basis eventually affect China's economy.

2.5   Summary and conclusions

The empirical evidence presented suggests that China's economic performance, as in other Asian countries currently in trouble, during the period immediately before the crisis, July 1997, was dependent on its open economic and financial policy and relatively free trade. The prominent factors leading to its strong growth and, up to now, containable or sustainable inflation seem to be related to trade, foreign direct investment, external debts and the current account. According to these substantive findings, the causes for this performance would also be the factors that will bring about a meltdown when any reverse trends take place.

An important implication of these findings is that a rescue or recovery policy for a future economic crisis in China, when or if it happens, either initiated internally or externally imposed from the outside or by international organizations, would be more effective if these empirical findings and their important implications are taken on board. The empirical findings appear to be reasonable within the context of time-tested economic and financial theories. National and international policy that is designed to prudentially control the movement of international capital flows in order to achieve optimal growth and social improvement and minimal inflation, would appear to be a plausible, and empirically justifiable, option. This conclusion is based on the seriousness of the current crisis, its causal effects, its social turmoil and its formal fundamental analysis with appropriate tools.

Notes

1   Autumn 1998.
2   See, however, Tran Van Hoa and Harvie (1998) for a preliminary report.
3   See also Tran Van Hoa (1997).

References

Abosedra, S., and H. Baghestani (1989), 'New Evidence on the Causal Relationship between United States Energy Consumption and Gross National Product', *Journal of Energy and Development*, Vol. 14, pp. 285–92.

Dickey, D.A., and W.A. Fuller (1981), 'Likelihood Ratio Statistics for Autoregressive Time Series with a Unit Root', *Econometrica*, Vol. 49, pp. 1057–72.

Engle, R.F., and C.W.J. Granger (1987), 'Co-integration and Error Correction: Representation, Estimation and Testing', Econometrica, Vol. 55, pp. 251–76.

Fels, A.A., and Tran Van Hoa (1981), 'Causal Relationships in Australian Wage Inflation and Minimum Award Rates', Economic Record, Vol. 57, pp. 23–34.

Granger, C.W.J. (1969), 'Investigating Causal Relations by Econometric Models and Cross Spectral Methods', Econometrica, Vol. 37, pp. 424–438.

—— (1986), 'Developments in the Study of Cointegrated Economic Variables', Oxford Bulletin of Economics and Statistics, Vol. 48, pp. 213–28.

Harvie, C., and Tran Van Hoa (1994a), 'Long Term Relationships between Oil Production and Oil Price, and the Current Account, Real Exchange Rate, Capital Stock, Non-Oil Output, Manufacturing Output and Growth: The UK Experience', The Journal of Energy and Development, Vol. 20, No. 1, 1994, pp. 47–58.

—— (1994b), 'Terms of Trade and Macroeconomic Adjustments in a Resource Exporting Economy: The Case of Australia', Resources Policy, Vol. 20, pp. 101–15.

Johansen, S. (1991), 'An I(2) Cointegration Analysis of the Purchasing Power Parity between Australia and the United States', Australasian Economic Modelling Conference, 27–30 August 1991, Port Douglas, Australia.

——, and K. Juselius (1990), 'Maximum Likelihood Estimation and Inference on Cointegration – with Applications to the Demand for Money', Oxford Bulletin of Economics and Statistics, Vol. 52, pp. 169–210.

Pindyck, R.S., and D.L. Rubinfeld (1991), Econometric Models and Economic Forecasts, 3rd Edition, McGraw Hill, Sydney.

Sargan, D., and A. Bhargava (1983), 'Testing Residuals from Least Squares Regression for Being Generated by the Gaussian Random Walk', Econometrica, Vol. 51, pp. 153–74.

Sims, C.A. (1972), 'Money, Income and Causality', American Economic Review, Vol. 62, pp. 540–52.

Tran Van Hoa (1992a), 'Modelling Output Growth: A New Approach', Economics Letters, Vol. 38, pp. 279–84.

—— (1992b), 'A New and General Approach to Modelling Short Term Interest Rates: with Application to Australian Data 1962–1990', Journal of Economics and Finance, Vol. 16, pp. 327–35.

—— (ed.) (1997), *Economic Development and Prospects in the ASEAN: Foreign Investment and Growth in Vietnam, Thailand, Indonesia and Malaysia*, Macmillan, London.

—— and C. Harvie (1998), *Causes and Impact of the Asian Financial Crisis*, Macmillan, London (in press).

3

Corporate Governance, Ownership Change and State-Owned Enterprise Reform

Charles Harvie
Tony Naughton

Reform of China's large state-owned enterprises (SOEs) is one of the most pressing problems facing the country today. Many SOEs are recognized as being inefficient, loss-making and a major drain upon the country's resources. This chapter reviews the recent performance of China's SOEs, identifies the reforms which have already been implemented in this area, outlines the experiences of other transition economies in regard to the re-structuring of their SOEs, and places emphasis upon those options which are likely to be most applicable to the Chinese situation.

3.1 Introduction

The legacy of central planning for China is the existence of unique economic problems in comparison to that of other rapidly developing economies in East Asia. In particular, two pressing and inter-related problems have still to be overcome. Firstly, a financial system which is not yet run on market lines. Secondly, and the focus of this chapter, the existence of a large number of state-owned enterprises (SOEs), many of which are loss-making. China has approximately 118 000 state-run companies, employing approximately two-thirds of the urban workforce. It is widely believed that considerably more than half of these state-sector firms are currently making losses, and that this proportion is rising. Government concerns about creating mass unemployment in the cities and major social unrest arising from SOE reform has, until recently, resulted in large SOEs being heavily subsidized as well as being able to gain access to soft credit. As a result the state banks, despite measures taken in 1994 to encourage them to lend on commercial lines and the creation of three development banks exclusively responsible for policy lending from 1995, were, in reality, under pressure to keep extending credit to large state firms and on favourable terms (Tisdell and Chai, 1997). The result of this has been: an accumulation by the banks of unpaid debts which is undermining the financial system; a misallocation of domestic saving; and vulnerability of the economy to bouts of inflation. The four largest banks in China reported substantial reductions in profits in their 1997 annual reports (AWSJ, 11 May 1998).

The need to improve the performance of SOEs is, therefore, pressing, and in this regard a number of options are in the process of being implemented. For small and medium-sized SOEs these include closure, merger and sale. However the major problems lie with the large SOEs. The government is focusing upon the 1 000 largest SOEs with the objective of improving their governance and performance through corporatization and the formation of enterprise groups. They will remain predominantly publicly owned, and a key issue arises over the likelihood of whether the necessary improvement in performance can be achieved with such ownership or whether it will be necessary to allow a larger role for private ownership.

Economic theory from market economies suggests that the approach proposed for China is unlikely to improve the performance and status of large SOEs. The literature on incomplete contracting theory emphasizes the inability of contracts alone to resolve problems in enterprise management (Grossman and Hart, 1986). The literature on opportunistic behaviour identifies the potential of organizational structure to improve efficiency (Williamson, 1985). In the finance literature, concentrated institutional ownership of firms has been linked to superior performance and higher firm value (Shleifer and Vishny, 1986 and 1997). This argument rests on the ability of large shareholders to monitor the firm and its management, making changes whenever performance is unsatisfactory. The evidence from studies in market economies, therefore, suggests that greater attention be placed on ownership structure and concentration as a means of improving performance and creating value.

While the literature above relates to market economies, there is growing evidence from transition economies that privatization is a significant factor in SOE reform (see for example Dyck and Wruck, 1998). This evidence suggests that enterprise efficiency can only be achieved through transfer of ownership to the private sector. Organizational and incentive problems exist in the SOE sector because of the lack of residual claims (Vickers and Yarrow, 1988). SOEs therefore suffer a significant competitive disadvantage compared to privately owned enterprises that carry out a corresponding economic function. The evidence from transition economies also supports the theory that institutional shareholdings and greater concentration of ownership are also significant factors in the performance and wealth creation ability of former SOEs (see, for example, Claessens et al., 1997).

The remainder of this chapter proceeds as follows. In section 2 the changing contribution of the SOE sector to China's economy is presented. Section 3 traces the evolving approach to SOE reform in China. Section 4 reviews alternative approaches to SOE reform in other transition economies. Finally section 5 presents a summary of the major conclusions.

3.2 SOEs and their changing contribution to the Chinese economy

The recent economic progress of the Chinese economy has been truly remarkable. Since reform began in 1978 the economy had quadrupled in size by 1995, and is expected to increase by a further 50 per cent by the end of the decade. The major engine for this growth is to be found from the extensive investment in the industrial sector and the opening up of the economy to international trade and investment. Despite this stunning and sustained economic success for China as a whole, two unresolved and inter-related legacies remain to be overcome from the country's 'growing out of the plan'.[1] Firstly, there is the need to put the financial sector on a commercial footing and to develop indirect policy instruments, such as that of the interest rate, as a means of conducting macroeconomic control within the context of a market-oriented economy. Secondly, there is a pressing need to restructure the country's SOEs. Although the relative size of the SOE sector in the Chinese economy has declined sharply since the onset of reforms in the late 1980s, it still remains important in the economy. In 1978, about 78 per cent of the gross value of industrial output was accounted for by SOEs, declining significantly to around 31 per cent by 1995 (see Table 3.1). Despite this the SOE sector's contribution to total output remains large, and it employs about two-thirds of China's 170 million urban workforce. In addition, the SOE sector is closely linked to the banking system through the credit plan,[2] pre-empting over two-thirds of total domestic credit. It also remains important in budgetary operations, contributing directly to about one-fourth of total revenue and receiving

Table 3.1 **Industrial Production by Ownership of Enterprises (%)**

	1978	1989	1995
State	78.0	56.1	30.7
Collective	22.0	35.7	43.2
Private/Individual	0	4.8	12.5
Joint Venture/Foreign	0	3.4	13.6

Source: China Statistical Publishing House

operating subsidies amounting to two-thirds of the overall budget deficit (Naughton, 1996).

The overall financial performance of the SOE sector has remained weak. Although the gross profits of SOEs rebounded markedly in 1992–93 with the strong performance of the economy, the losses of some SOEs have continued at a very high level. A sectoral disaggregation of losses during the early 1990s suggests that they were about equally distributed among the industrial, foreign trade and commerce, and grain sectors. In the industrial sector, about one-half of the losses were concentrated in the coal and oil industries alone. Following the adoption of new accounting standards in early 1994, it was estimated that about one-half of all SOEs were incurring losses. Even on official figures the percentage of loss-making enterprises rose from 27 per cent in 1990 to 43 per cent in 1995. In the past, SOE losses have been covered about equally through budgetary subsidies and bank loans, with the latter having a consequentially detrimental effect upon the portfolio quality and capital structure of the state banking system.

This continuing weakness of SOE performance is attributable in particular to organizational structure. SOEs are characterized by: insufficient managerial autonomy and accountability; the lack of hard budget constraints; rigidities in wages and employment; overstaffing (many economists believe that SOEs have about a third more employees than they require); a heavy burden of social benefits for their workers (housing, education, health and pensions); and the use of obsolescent technology. In a number of these areas, however, progress has been made.

For some time China has simply tried to grow out of the SOE problem by letting overall GDP expansion, and a relatively faster growth rate of the non-state sector, reduce the size of the state sector (see Table 3.2). Playing a leading role in the non-state sector are the collective enterprises, consisting of both urban and rural enterprises. The collective sector has seen its share of industrial output increase from 22 per cent in 1978 to 43 per cent in 1995. There has been a particularly impressive growth of the rural enterprises, the so-called Township and Village enterprises (TVEs). In 1978 some 1.52 million TVEs employed 28.3 million workers, expanding dramatically to 22 million TVEs employing 128 million workers by 1995. Unlike the SOEs they are: small in size, averaging about five workers each; sufficiently flexible to respond to market changes in a way which the SOEs cannot; and are subject to hard budget constraints. Despite ambiguous property rights, they have been a remarkable, and somewhat unanticipated, successful consequence of China's economic reforms. The productivity performance of the collective sector, and most notably the TVEs, has been noticeably superior to that of the state sector. In addition many thousands of private companies, both domestic and foreign-owned, and joint ventures have been developed, and accounted for 26.1 per cent of industrial output in 1995, as shown in Table 3.1. The impressive growth of this sector is likely to be maintained, although the extent of this will be dependent upon its access to scarce financial resources. Yet despite these developments the SOEs still consume a far greater share of scarce state financial resources than those in the non-state sector, approximately three-quarters of state industrial investment. As a

Table 3.2 **Real Gross Value of Industrial Production (GVIO), Growth Rates, 1990–95**

| | % Growth Rate | | | |
	GVIO Total	GVIO SOEs	GVIO Collective	GVIO Other[a]
1990	5.2	2.7	6.2	47.4
1991	12.8	7.6	17.3	40.7
1992	21.4	13.1	32.9	50.6
1993	23.8	9.1	39.9	59.5
1994	21.6	2.1	30.5	43.5
1995	16.0	9.0	25.0	30.0

[a] GVIO of private, foreign-invested and other enterprises.
Source: State Statistical Bureau

consequence the government is increasingly investing scarce resources in declining industries, which will ultimately contribute to a decline in economic growth should this remain unchanged.

Although many reformers have recommended widespread bankruptcies, or privatization of the SOEs, this could create major social unrest, and the government has already rejected, at least for the meantime, large-scale privatization. Indeed the government still views the SOEs as the backbone of the economy. With 70 per cent of industrial employment provided by state enterprises, over 100 million workers, the potential risks from extensive bankruptcy would be immense. In many areas they are the sole employers and providers of social services, from housing to transport to health care and education. More recently a middle ground has emerged, described as to 'grasp the large and sacrifice the small'. This approach will involve leasing, selling or closing small failing companies, restructuring the robust ones, and sustaining with state funds those enterprises of national importance (the 'pillar industries' as described by former Premier Li Peng). This approach clearly has the objective of minimizing the adverse social consequences of a more radical form of SOE reform, but is likened to the 'failure' of the Korean model of government attempting to pick and nurture winners from the corporate sector (AWSJ, 5 May 1998).

3.3   China's evolving approach to SOE reform

Enterprise reforms prior to 1993

Prior to the reform process in the late 1970s, SOEs had little autonomy. Their production, pricing, and investment decisions were subject to the planning process. All surplus funds were transferred to the state budget, and they relied on the budget for subsidies to cover losses and grants for investment. Few incentives were available to workers or management. Wages were set by centrally determined scales, and management's main responsibility was to fulfil production quotas. Early reforms aimed to increase enterprise autonomy and accountability. In this regard the issuance of the 'Provisional Regulations on the Enlargement of Autonomy of State Industrial Enterprises' in 1984 represented an important step. These regulations permitted an increase in autonomy for above-target output in terms of price setting, output sales, and input purchases. In 1984–85 an enterprise income tax was imposed on SOEs replacing profit remittances as the main source of fiscal revenue from this sector. Enterprises were allowed to retain the bulk of after tax profits and depreciation funds. In 1986 the Contract Responsibility System (CRS) was introduced for medium-sized and larger

SOEs. Targets were specified for each enterprise over a three- or four-year period for performance in terms of output, profit remittances and taxes to the government. An enterprise's income tax liability was determined by the provisions of the enterprise's contract, instead of by law, leading to a strong element of bargaining in the fiscal process. The first generation of these contracts, signed by at least 90 per cent of the SOEs, was in place by 1988. To accompany these changes a bankruptcy law was enacted in 1986 becoming effective in 1988, but until recently rarely used against SOEs. In 1988 the authorities also enacted an Enterprise Law that sought to transform the SOEs into fully autonomous legal entities responsible for their own profits and losses. In July 1992 the implementing regulations of the Enterprise Law of 1988, entitled 'Regulations on Transforming the Operating Mechanisms of SOEs', were issued by the State Council. These regulations explicitly provided for non interference by the government in the operations of the enterprises, which were endowed with a set of fourteen rights including: the right to decide what to produce and how to price and market their products; how to invest their funds; the right to hire and fire workers and to decide on wage policy. Inefficient and loss-making enterprises were to be restructured or closed down in accordance with the Bankruptcy Law. The role of the state as owner of the enterprises was delegated to the State Asset Management Bureau.

These reforms produced an initial recovery in the output of SOEs. However, price controls persisted, production quotas for sale to the state remained and the SOEs had access to certain amounts of cheap raw materials. Credit remained readily available for investment or working capital, the budget continued to provide support for loss-making enterprises, and little advantage was taken of reforms to wage and employment practices. In short the SOEs continued to face a soft budget constraint.

Another key area of enterprise reform was aimed at changing the governance structure, accounting procedures and ownership rights, in addition to the previously mentioned management rights, to make them more appropriate in the context of a market economy. A number of experiments in this regard were applied primarily to large SOEs.

1. The establishment of 'enterprise groups' along the lines of the Japanese *keiretsus*, but more closely to the South Korean *chaebols*, integrated through a parent-subsidiary relationship. Some of these groups have been required to take over loss-making enterprises to help rationalize their operations.

2. Restructuring certain SOEs through joint ventures with foreign direct investors. In such an arrangement an SOE would typically

invite foreign participation in certain lines of production, and a joint venture would be formed under which the SOE would provide the land, buildings, and labour, and the foreign partner the equipment, technology and marketing expertise. The Chinese authorities have increasingly used this as a means for foreign investors to gain access to the Chinese market.

3. Introducing corporate forms of ownership and management to the governance structure. Provisions for the establishment of limited liability companies were introduced in 1990, and the shareholding experiment was formally sanctioned for SOEs. In late 1990, stock exchanges were established in Shanghai and Shenzhen, although provisional regulations on the issuance of securities were made public by the Shanghai and Shenzhen municipal governments only in 1992.

In addition, reform of the labour and employment systems were also initiated to provide for greater flexibility at the enterprise level in terms of worker selection, task definition and wages. Reform of the social benefits system, including unemployment benefits, pensions, and health care, aimed at establishing pooled benefits schemes and a separation of the provision of benefits from specific enterprises, were also begun. Reforms aimed at commercializing the housing market were also launched. Some SOEs have separated service activities from enterprise operations, creating autonomous units that are responsible for their own profits and losses. Other reforms affecting SOEs during this period have included: price liberalization; the reduction of the scope of the mandatory plans; the introduction of markets for land-use rights; the liberalization of the foreign exchange market; the opening of new sectors and regions to foreign trade and investment; and the deepening of financial markets.

Despite the numerous experiments with SOE reforms in the 1980s their performance remained weak with about one-third of SOEs estimated to be making losses, and another one-third only breaking even. Autonomy and financial accountability remained weak. SOEs still operated predominantly under the direct supervision of central or local governments. The retrenchment period of the late 1980s and early 1990s highlighted the weakness of the SOE sector. However, beginning in 1991, several large SOEs were transformed into joint stock companies and listed their shares on both domestic and international stock exchanges. This was to be given further impetus with reforms after 1993.

A new phase of SOE reform after 1993

The thrust of this phase of reform was to change enterprise governance with the objective of establishing a modern business sector consistent with the attainment of a socialist market economy, as proclaimed by the Chinese authorities in October 1992. This aim was to be achieved through the corporatization of SOEs, that is, the conversion of SOEs into shareholding companies through the implementation of a new Company Law that became effective in July 1994. The new companies were vested with a corporate governance structure that generally follows international practice. Through this the authorities aimed to achieve a separation of the ownership functions of the state from the management of the enterprises within a framework of greater autonomy and accountability. Specifically, the new framework attempted to:

1. clarify the rights of enterprises as legal entities entitled to make decisions concerning assets entrusted to them by owners and investors;

2. separate government ministries and departments from enterprise management to eliminate government interference in enterprise management;

3. relieve SOEs of the obligation to provide social services, while expanding the government's role in the provision of these services;

4. establish market-based relations between enterprises, so as to avoid the recurrent accumulation of inter-enterprise debt; and

5. reduce government control over wage and employment policies, while limiting its role in this sphere to a supervisory one.

In this new framework, a system for the management of state-owned assets by state holding companies, state-asset management companies, and enterprise groups would be introduced. To permit enterprises in the new system to function effectively, supporting measures were to be introduced including: the implementation of the Company Law; the enactment of a national securities law; the implementation of a new accounting system; and the development of factor markets. In addition, to support enterprise reform, the authorities set up in 1994 a fund of seven billion Yuan designated for debt repayment.

In early 1994 the government announced its intention to launch a pilot project, or experiment, for the establishment of a modern enterprise system. This project involved 10 000 medium-sized and large SOEs in a program that included asset valuation, the granting of financial autonomy, and the adoption of a new accounting system. Of these some 1 000 enterprises, deemed to be critical to the economy, were selected for an experiment that would delegate to asset management firms the authority to oversee the management of these enterprises' assets with the objective of increasing their value over time. Further, 100 of these enterprises were to become corporatized and thereby to participate in an expansion of the existing shareholding system. Finally, ten major cities, later increased to eighteen, were selected for a comprehensive enterprise reform program including pension pooling, staff lay-offs, and bankruptcies. The whole project was initially expected to take two-to-three years to complete. The medium-term goal of such reform was to transform most SOEs into autonomous, competitive, legal entities fully accountable for their profits and losses.

While the new phase of enterprise reform placed a heavy emphasis on the maintenance of public ownership as the cornerstone of the economy, it did represent a fundamental change in the concept of ownership of SOEs. A distinction was to be drawn between the ownership of an enterprise and its management. The rights of ownership were circumscribed by law, and enterprises were to be regarded as legal entities with their own rights and responsibilities. Such a clarification of the concept of ownership was seen as being necessary for a fundamental restructuring of the SOEs. This, in conjunction with the implementation of a standardized accounting system, would lay the foundations for possible privatization at a later date. In addition, the predominance of public ownership in this new ownership system was to be confined to certain strategic sectors of the economy. The Company Law of 1994, therefore, represented a major step in the SOE reform process, enabling for the first time a unified legal framework for the establishment and operation of companies as independent identities. To be effective it required resolute commitment and action on the part of the government.

In the remainder of this section, a number of experiments related to improving the performance of the SOEs will be discussed. These will focus upon: corporatization, the establishment of enterprise groups, approaches to improving the performance of small and medium-sized SOEs, and approaches to loss-making enterprises.

Corporatization

The major thrust of SOE reform has been to focus on their corporatization and commercialization, with the objective of separating government administration from enterprise management. In this regard the shareholding system is an important experiment that has major ramifications for the ownership structure of enterprises, and has consequently received widespread interest. Enterprises are allowed to restructure themselves into limited liability companies by issuing shares. Such enterprises can apply for listing in the country's two stock exchanges of Shanghai and Shenzhen. The authorities, however, do not regard the conversion of SOEs into shareholding companies as 'privatization'. Instead they see this as a means of raising funds for restructuring and introducing a more effective management system, while the state retains a significant ownership share and ultimate control over companies. In the restructuring of these enterprises the proportion of the shares belonging to the state, municipality, or township is determined by an appraisal company according to the net value of the assets in the enterprise accruing to the state, municipality or township.

Four levels of government ownership in shareholding companies were envisaged. In certain priority sectors, defined as those characterized by market failure or that produce goods deemed to be of national strategic significance, enterprises would remain wholly owned by the government. The second level consisted of enterprises with majority government ownership. The third level comprised enterprises with minority shareholding by the government. Finally, some small enterprises engaged primarily in commercial activities were to be entirely auctioned or leased to individuals.

After an enterprise had been turned into a shareholding company, the state's position as the sole owner would disappear in all but the first category. In the remaining three categories the state would only participate in the decision making to the extent of its representation. The authorities envisaged that, even in enterprises in which the state was the majority shareholder, the effective separation of ownership from management would be achieved by requiring that the government act according to the statutes of the new company law.

While the emergence of joint stock companies and equity markets is still of limited significance from an economic standpoint, they do represent a major change in the ideological framework of reforms in China. They are an important constituent part of a broader process of ownership change. The growth of the stock exchanges has also provided an important impetus for new financial reporting to replace the existing accounting standards that were inadequate to support public trading in shares. Joint stock companies are no longer seen as being at odds with the institutional underpinnings of a 'socialist' economy, since there remains the predominance of public ownership. At first, companies listed on the stock exchanges were permitted to issue only A shares which are restricted to domestic residents. Since 1991, however, some companies have been permitted to issue B shares, denominated in local currency but restricted to foreigners with payment in foreign exchange.

Foreign investors were guaranteed convertibility of their investment and earnings into foreign exchange at the then swap market rate. Indeed, some SOEs became listed on stock exchanges overseas. In addition, and more recently, there are the so called 'red chip' shares and H shares. The former are shares of mainland China owned enterprises listed on the Hong Kong stock exchange. The latter are the shares of subsidiaries of mainland China-owned enterprises based in Hong Kong and listed on the Hong Kong stock exchange.

These shareholding arrangements were seen by the authorities as reinforcing the separation of government ownership from management, and facilitating the provision of greater financial and decision-making autonomy, so that enterprises could become more efficient and respond dynamically to changing market opportunities. A further aim was to facilitate the mobilization and rational allocation of financial resources.

The major incentive for enterprises to list on the stock exchange is the ability to raise equity funds for restructuring and upgrading. However, a more significant longer-term benefit is likely to be the greater discipline on enterprise management that results from the scrutiny that listed companies are subject to from investors. This is particularly the case with those enterprises that are listed abroad where public disclosure requirements are more stringent, and the scrutiny from institutional investors more rigorous. Nevertheless, the transformation of enterprises into corporations cannot, alone, ensure greater operational efficiency or profitability. Complementary and supplementary changes in other areas are essential to create a competitive environment for SOEs. This will include the enforcement of a hard budget constraint through the commercialization of the banking sector and a wider application of the Bankruptcy Law to non-profitable enterprises. In addition it is essential to further liberalize prices and develop competitive markets for goods and factors of production. In this sense the supporting changes that are underway in the areas of taxation, banking, housing markets, and the provision of social security are at least as important for bringing about a lasting improvement in SOE performance as the process of corporatization itself.

Several problems still remain to be resolved with respect to such an enterprise experiment. The first concerns the establishment of a strong legal framework governing the issuance and trading of shares. Secondly, asset valuation and accounting practices need to be standardized across enterprises. Thirdly, the pace of reform of the social security system needs to be quickened to enable fundamental restructuring of the SOEs. Fourth, financial sector reforms need to be accelerated so that, unlike in 1996, banks can no longer be prevailed upon by central and local authorities to grant loans to uncreditworthy enterprises, which, in turn, has important implications for hardening enterprise budget constraints. Finally, some questions remain on whether a true separation of the state's role as an owner and as a manager can be achieved as long as the majority, or even the largest minority, of shareholders are agents of the state. In addition the corporatization reforms have been met by much resistance by SOE managers, especially over the issue of accountability.

Enterprise groups

Another experiment involves the formation of large enterprise groups, with the aim of: rationalizing industrial structure; taking advantage of economies of scale; and promoting the optimum use of resources. In China each locality was encouraged to be fully self-reliant during the pre-reform period. Furthermore, enterprises within one branch of an industry were normally not allowed to diversify into related fields. As a result, from a national perspective, there is: much duplication; a lack of specialization; and strong local barriers to inter-regional trade. The aim of the authorities is to break down the departmental, regional, and ownership barriers in the economy and create large conglomerates that are efficient and internationally competitive.

To this end, in the past two-to-three years, the government has selected 55 large enterprise groups for restructuring to strengthen the role of the parent or core enterprise within each group, particularly its management of the subsidiary enterprises. Preferential treatment such as trading rights or the right to diversify into other fields of activity are being provided to these enterprise groups to encourage their development into competitive conglomerates. Since there is much duplication in Chinese industry, with hundreds of inefficient small factories often making the same things, this makes economic sense. In this regard lessons can be learned from the Japanese keiretsu system in which individual Japanese companies, often with their own stock-market listings, are linked together through cross shareholdings. At the core is a bank which, in conjunction with other firms in the family, supports other group members in their business dealings. However, in the context of China the real model for the development of enterprise groups is that provided by the South Korean chaebols, which are far less structured in their range of business than the big Japanese companies and, to some extent, more closely linked to the state. In South Korea the ten leading chaebols control around two-thirds of the economy, and they have underpinned the country's rapid rate of economic development since the 1960s. The Chinese appear to be impressed by the fact that the chaebol helped to transform South Korea from a poor hungry nation into a rich one within a generation, and that the chaebol are now transforming themselves into multinationals. It is, however, ironic that just as South Korea's government is trying to reduce the influence that the chaebol exert on the domestic economy, arising from the economic and financial crisis of 1997–98, China's policy makers are contemplating the development of their own chaebol.

Small/medium-sized SOEs

The Chinese government appears, as previously indicated, to be concentrating its reform efforts on some 1 000 of the biggest SOEs. The remaining 117 000 consist primarily of smaller and medium-sized SOEs, where the plan is to turn the majority of these firms into:

1. mixed ownership through the creation of joint ventures;

2. private enterprises through sales to private domestic individuals/ firms;

3. private foreign enterprises through sales to foreign private individuals/firms as wholly foreign-funded enterprises; and

4. allowed to go bankrupt.

Both central and local governments in China have been attempting to reinvigorate small and medium-sized SOEs through ad hoc experiments with management control. The objective being to enable the development of sufficient managerial skills to enable these enterprise to operate profitably before they are released from state control. A number of 'models' for the development of these state enterprises can be found particularly at the local government level when they were given renewed authority to experiment with their own firms after 1991. With the renewed pressure of enterprise losses, it was felt that local governments were in a better position to deal with loss-making smaller enterprises.

Loss-making enterprises

The Chinese authorities are taking special measures to deal with loss-making enterprises according to the nature of their losses, and bearing in mind the current low level of development of the social safety net. It is estimated that about 70 per cent of the losses of SOEs are policy induced, mainly arising from price control. These enterprises are mainly concentrated in the transportation and energy sectors. If these enterprises are to be financially independent, it is necessary to liberalize the prices of the goods and services they produce. It is intended to liberalize the prices of coal and other energy products over the next three-to-five years to avoid major disruption to the rest of the economy.

In the interim before profitability, or reduced losses, is ultimately achieved, the policy-induced losses of those enterprises will continue to be subsidized through the budget. For remaining enterprises that are experiencing losses because of poor management, the authorities are providing fiscal and financial incentives for them to restructure or move into other lines of production. Several thousands of smaller enterprises have been either closed or merged with profitable ones to rationalize their operations. In some cities experiments are being carried out to allow foreign investors to buy into and restructure existing loss-making SOEs. Finally, the authorities are cautiously applying the bankruptcy law to the enterprises.

In the following section the reform experience of other transition economies with respect to their large SOEs is analyzed and inferences with respect to their applicability to China identified.

3.4 Alternative approaches to SOE reform in other Transition economies

The literature on economic transition from a planned to market economy focuses upon the need to implement changes that will: impose financial discipline upon enterprises by eliminating access to soft finance in the form of bank credits on easy non-commercial terms, and the accumulation of inter enterprise arrears; lead to the opening-up of markets to competition; enable the entry of new firms and exit of non-viable firms to and from such markets; and bring about decentralized ownership change (World Bank, 1995). Such changes would encourage the necessary conditions for enterprise restructuring, especially amongst state enterprises. As a means of increasing competition in markets and improving the performance of enterprises, decentralization of ownership, in particular, is seen as being a key ingredient. In the context of the Central and Eastern European transition economies, as well as the Newly Independent States of the former Soviet Union, most have made the unambiguous decision to move to decentralized ownership under majority private-sector control. This has been achieved through the privatization of state assets and, for many, the most important way, through the entry of new private businesses both domestically and foreign-owned.

The imposition of financial discipline, as well as the intensification of competition in markets for the products of SOEs in these transition economies, has forced them to restructure, with the objective of improving their efficiency and profitability. This resulted in major labour shedding and a fall in real wages, or a combination of the two. For example, in the three leading transition economies of Central Europe, the Czech Republic, Hungary and Poland, their largest 150 to 200 SOEs reduced their work forces by 32, 47 and 33 per cent respectively between 1989 and 1993 as their sales fell by 40 to 60 per cent on average. Evidence from the transition economies also suggests that once SOEs are subject to financial discipline they show a more aggressive attitude toward the collection of receivables, a much stronger link between profitability and investment, a re-orientation of goals from output targets to profits, and a more managerial focus on marketing and product quality.

A key question of concern for the transition economies, and of particular interest to China, is whether privatization is essential for imposing financial discipline on enterprises with the objective of stimulating their restructuring and enhancing their competitiveness. Could such favourable developments also be achieved with public or mixed ownership? The empirical literature, primarily from the 1980s for industrial market economies, concludes in general, although not uniformly, that private firms exhibit higher productivity and better performance than public enterprises. In the transition economies of Central and Eastern Europe and the Newly Independent States, judgement on the impact of privatization has only recently emerged. The first signs are encouraging in many cases, but less so in others. Evidence from Hungary, Poland, Russia and Slovenia suggest that newly privatized firms behave differently from, and better than, state firms, exhibiting more dynamism and generating higher profits. Of course, this may in part be a reflection of the fact that only the more productive and profitable state firms were the first to be privatized.

While the evidence suggests that private ownership can make a difference in terms of enterprise performance, the urgency and speed with which it has been conducted has varied significantly across these transition economies. While it may not represent an optimal solution, a slower process of privatization is likely to be more feasible in an economy where the authorities, or workers, are able to exercise enough control over state enterprises to prevent managers from absconding with state assets, and where domestic saving and growth in the non state sector are high. Such conditions would be representative of the situation in China and to a much more limited extent in Vietnam. On the other hand where enterprise managers are strong but the authorities and workers are weak, and where available funds are insufficient to meet restructuring needs, it is likely to be the case that privatization will be more urgent. This is more representative of the situation arising from the fall of Communist governments in Europe in the late 1980s and early 1990s. In a number of these European countries, this led to the undesirable development of 'spontaneous' privatization in which managers purchased state assets very cheaply or simply absconded with them, and often in collusion with the former nomenclature elite. This occurred in countries such as Belarus, Bulgaria, Hungary, Russia and the Ukraine, creating much resentment in the process.

The transition economies' experience with privatizing large enterprises

For many of the European transition economies, the primary objective of the economic reforms was to bring about market economies, with predominant private ownership, as rapidly as possible. This was especially the case for the Czech Republic, Hungary and Poland who have been at the forefront of the transition process. The initial predominance of SOEs in their economies inevitably required moves towards their privatization. However, each country has found that privatizing large and medium-sized enterprises has been more difficult than originally anticipated. The process has not been easy due to: policy makers having to weigh up complex and often competing goals; the need to satisfy a multitude of competing stakeholders; coping with the administrative difficulties involved in privatizing thousands of firms in a relatively short time; and the lack of mature and functioning domestic capital markets.

A number of alternative approaches toward privatization by transition economies have been adopted including sales to strategic owners, insider buy-outs, and voucher programs involving the creation of new financial intermediaries. These efforts are often complemented by extensive programs of restitution to pre-transition owners and by smaller programs of debt equity conversions or public offering of shares on newly emerging stock markets. As summarized in Table 3.3, these approaches create trade-offs among the various objectives set by government from the process of privatization. The major objectives include: improving corporate governance and the efficiency of asset usage; de-politicizing firms by cutting their links to the state; rapidly establishing new ownership; increasing firms' access to capital and expertise; generating government revenue; and ensuring a fair distribution of benefits. The various transition economies adopted an approach to privatization which best suited their own priorities and urgencies. In the case of Hungary, for example, with its sizeable foreign debt the need to generate government revenue, particularly in the form of hard currency, was viewed as of critical importance. For the Czech Republic this has been of considerably less significance. For the Russian authorities priority was given to the need to break rapidly from the past while fairness was seen as being more important in the case of Poland. The Czechs have consistently stressed the significance of

Table 3.3   **Trade-offs Among Privatization Routes for Large Firms**

	Objective				
Method	*Better corporate governance*	*Speed and feasibility*	*Access to capital and skills*	*More government revenue*	*Greater fairness*
Spontaneous privatization	?	?	–	–	–
Sale to outside owners	+	–	+	+	–
Management-employee buyout	–	+	–	–	–
Equal-access voucher privatization	?	+	?	–	+

– negative impact

+ positive impact

Source: Taken from World Bank, *World Development Report*, 1996, p. 52.

privatization in breaking the link between an enterprise and the government, while Estonia's privatization program sought out 'real' owners capable of bringing new money and management skills to bear. Table 3.4 presents a summary of the major methods of privatization of medium-sized and large enterprises which have been adopted in seven transition economies as at the end of 1995.

Table 3.3 provides only a partial view of the trade-offs arising from the alternative approaches to privatization. An additional objective is each options' ability to achieve long-term institution building in the context of an economy in transition. The process of privatization in general can stimulate the development of fundamental market institutions such as capital markets, legal systems, and business related professions. However, each approach to privatization sets off a complex process of institutional and ownership change whose long-run results may differ considerably from the shorter-run picture. For example, mass privatization may not produce the best owners in the short run but it might lead to a better corporate governance in the long run if it promotes

Table 3.4 **Methods of Privatization for Medium-size and Large Enterprises in Seven Transition Economies (% of total)**

Country	Sale outside owners	ment-empl. buyout	Equal-access voucher privatiz-ation	Restit-ution	Other[a]	Still in state hands
Czech Republic						
By number[b]	32	0	**22**[c]	9	28	10
By value[d]	5	0	**50**	20	3	40
Estonia[e]						
By number	**64**	30	0	0	2	4
By value	**60**	12	3	10	0	15
Hungary						
By number	**38**	7	0	0	33	22
By value	**40**	2	0	4	12	42
Lithuania						
By number	<1	5	**70**	0	0	25
By value	<1	5	**60**	0	0	35
Mongolia						
By number	0	0	**70**	0	0	30
By value	0	0	**55**	0	0	45
Poland						
By number	3	14	6	0	**23**	54
Russia[c]						
By number	0	**55**	11	0	0	34

Note: Bold numbers show the dominant method for each country. Data are as of the end of 1995.
a. Includes transfers to municipalities or social insurance organisations, debt-equity swaps, and sales through insolvency proceedings.
b. Number of privatized firms as a share of all formerly state-owned firms. Includes parts of firms restructured prior to privatization.
c. Includes assets sold for cash as part of the voucher privatization program through June 1994.
d. Value of firms privatized as a share of the value of all formerly state-owned firms. Data for Poland and Russia are unavailable.
e. Does not include some infrastructure firms. All management buyouts were part of competitive, open tenders. In thirteen cases citizens could exchange vouchers for minority shares in firms sold to a core investor.

Source: Taken from World Bank, *World Development Report*, 1996, p. 53.

the development of capital markets, and subsequent rearrangements of ownership, and of intermediary monitoring for the economy as a whole.

Privatization options for medium and large SOEs

A brief elaboration of the potential advantages and disadvantages of each of the previously identified methods of privatization is now conducted.

Spontaneous privatization

This is most likely to occur early on in the transition process, during the period of time of transfer from Communist government control to the establishment of a democratically elected government. During this turbulent period, state enterprise managers can acquire state assets very cheaply by selling the assets they control to themselves, or simply abscond illegally with them usually in collusion with members of the former nomenclature elite. This occurred extensively in Hungary and Russia and resulted in widespread resentment about its unfairness, which ultimately led to its abandonment. There are major ambiguities over its benefits in terms of better corporate governance and its feasibility and desirability. It is also unlikely to improve enterprise access to capital and skills, and because such enterprises are sold off so cheaply do not generate much revenue to government. This is an approach to privatization which should, overall, be avoided.

Sales to outsiders

In the early days of transition, most of the Central and Eastern European countries hoped to privatize by selling state enterprises as going concerns on a case by case basis, based upon the experiences of the UK and other middle-level income countries like Chile. Sales to 'outside' or 'core' investors were also favoured since they would bring in revenue and turn the firm over to 'real' owners possessing the knowledge and incentives to govern the company efficiently, as well as having the necessary capital to restructure it. Although sales to outside investors have largely achieved expected performance improvements, they have proved to be disappointing in that they have been costly and slow, more difficult to implement than anticipated, and relatively few in number. The latter is primarily due to the limited availability of domestic capital, as well as political concerns arising from a large dependence on foreign capital. Even where domestic capital is sufficient, insiders, managers and other employees have been able to block sales. More generally the process is held back by the sheer enormity of the task of evaluating and negotiating deals one by one, and then of following up to be sure that the buyers fulfil contract provisions. For example, in Germany it was at one time reported that 20 per cent of the thousands of privatization contracts signed by the Treuhandanstalt, the privatization agency, were in dispute. Other difficulties relate to: problems with placing a value on firms to be offered for sale; appraising and assigning responsibility for past environmental damage; its perceived unfairness. Many ordinary citizens cannot participate and find the process non-transparent and arbitrary, if not corrupt. Among other transition economies only Hungary and Estonia have privatized a significant share of their enterprises through direct sales. In Poland the power of workers to block privatization considerably slowed progress. The conclusion is that such sales, although a useful element in the privatization process, cannot in most circumstances be the sole or even the primary method.

A second form of sale to outsiders involves floating shares on public stock exchanges. The infancy of stock exchanges limits this approach in all the transition economies. Furthermore, the method works only for firms with good financial prospects and strong reputations. Even Poland, which has had the most success with this approach, privatized fewer than thirty firms in this manner. Hungary has had no greater success. Initial public offerings are clearly not the answer to the need for rapid large scale privatization, although at the margin they can help develop capital markets and share trading.

Management–employee buyouts

Management–employee buyouts were a widely used alternative to sales, notably in Croatia, Poland, Romania and Slovenia. Many of the firms privatized through Lithuania's and Mongolia's voucher programs effectively became management–employee buyouts, as employees and their families used vouchers and cash to buy major stakes in their own firms. Such buyouts are relatively fast and easy to implement both politically and technically. In theory they could also be better for corporate governance if insiders have better access to the information needed to monitor managers. However the risks and disadvantages are many, particularly in large-scale buyout programs that include many unprofitable firms in need of restructuring. One disadvantage is that the benefits are unevenly distributed, since employees in good firms get valuable assets while those in money losers get little or nothing of value. Another is that governments typically charge low prices to insiders and thereby realise little revenue. In addition management-employee buyouts may weaken corporate governance, particularly in transition economies, where controls on managers are less developed than in a fully fledged market economy, and product and capital markets cannot be counted upon to enforce discipline. Insiders are generally unable to bring in new skills and new capital, yet may deter outsiders who can from investing. Managers or employees may simply prevent outsiders from buying shares, or outsiders may hesitate to invest in firms with significant insider ownership because of potential conflicts of interest between inside and outside owners. Management–employee buyouts can, therefore, lead to managerial and worker entrenchment that blocks further reform. Russia's mass privatization program of 1992–94, although it used vouchers, was basically a management-employee buyout program because of its preferential treatment of managers and workers. In the end insiders acquired about two-thirds of the shares in the 15 000 privatized firms. Outsiders obtained 20 to 30 per cent, about 10 to 15 per cent each went to investment funds and individual investors, and the rest remained in government hands.

Equal access voucher privatization

The final form of privatization to be discussed distributes vouchers across the population, and attempts to allocate assets approximately evenly among voucher holders. Such programs have proven to excel in terms of both speed and fairness. On the negative side they raise no revenue for government, and have unclear implications for corporate governance. Mongolia, Lithuania and the former Czechoslovakia were the first to implement this form of privatization. Albania, Armenia, Kazakstan, Moldova, Poland, Romania, in its 1995 program, and Ukraine have followed, and Bulgaria recently completed such a program. Some countries, such as Georgia and Russia, have used vouchers but gave strong preference to insiders. A few countries – Estonia and Romania in its 1991 program – used vouchers to transfer only minority stakes in certain firms. Hungary, FYR Macedonia and Uzbekistan are among the few transition economies that have specifically rejected the use of vouchers in privatization.

The Czech Republic's mass privatization program is widely accepted as being one of the most successful to date (Claessens et al., 1997). In two successive waves, the first while part of Czechoslovakia, the Czechs transferred more than half the assets of state enterprises into private hands. Citizens were free to invest their vouchers directly in the firms being auctioned. However, to encourage more concentrated ownership and so create incentives for more active corporate governance, the program allowed the free entry of intermediary investment funds to pool vouchers and invest them on the original holders' behalf. More than two-thirds of voucher holders chose to place their vouchers with these competing funds. The ten largest obtained more than 40 per cent of all vouchers in both waves, about 72 per cent of all vouchers held by such funds, leading to concentrated ownership of the Czech industrial sector by these large funds. This is in stark contrast to the experience of Mongolia which forbade the entry of intermediary funds and ended up with heavy inside ownership.

Such intermediary investment funds are represented on company boards where they can demand better financial information and impose financial discipline on the firms they own. They trade large blocks of shares among themselves or sell them to strategic investors. As a result a moderately active share market has developed on the Prague stock exchange. However, patterns of ownership in the Czech Republic are still in a state of flux. Some observers hope that the intermediary funds, together with banks, will become the cornerstone of the financial infrastructure, which is essential for capital allocation and corporate governance in a market economy. Others expect the investment funds' influence to dwindle rapidly as strategic investors pick up controlling blocks of shares. In either case the longer-term goal of institution building is operating well by this approach to privatization. Hence the Czech experience illustrates how a well-designed voucher privatization program can overcome many problems. It can depoliticize restructuring, stimulate development of capital markets, and quickly create new stakeholders with an interest in reform. A critical determinant of the longer-run success of any reform program is the extent to which ownership rights can evolve into more efficient forms. Programs that stimulate the growth of capital and asset markets, such as the Czech Republic's privatization program, have a distinct advantage. In addition, governments need also to implement complementary reforms, for example, regarding the supervision of financial intermediaries and the regulation of natural monopolies. In this context the voucher privatization model is one which could be given serious consideration by the Chinese authorities should they wish to take the next step of privatizing many of their large SOEs.

The lessons from enterprise reform are quite clear and applicable across the range of transition economies. Firms surviving from the era of central planning need major restructuring of their production and reorientation of their incentives. Entities that face strict financial discipline and competition and have clear owners are most likely to undertake the needed restructuring or to exit, leaving room for new and better firms. In the short run, financial discipline can be fostered through stabilization and liberalization measures, but in the longer run decentralized ownership, preferably private, clearly defined property rights and supporting institutions are needed to sustain financial discipline, to respond to market-oriented incentives, and to provide alternative forms of corporate finance and governance. This, in conjunction with the desire for long-term institution building appropriate for a market economy, would suggest that China could learn a great deal from the equal access voucher approach to privatization should, or when, this becomes politically expedient.

3.5   Summary and conclusions

Despite the reforms initiated in the mid-1980s, the performance of the SOEs remained weak, and further reform was required. The stated goal of the government in 1992 of attaining a socialist market economy spurred a renewed phase of SOE reform. Emphasis was given to the corporatization of SOEs through an intensification of the shareholding experiment begun in the 1980s, the establishment of enterprise groups along the lines of Korea's chaebols, and small and medium-sized SOEs were to be sold, leased or, in the case of loss-making enterprises, allowed to go bankrupt.

The experience from other transition economies is that the imposition of financial discipline, in conjunction with an opening up of markets and increased competition, is the best way to bring about an improved performance of SOEs. Decentralization of ownership, also seen as essential, has been achieved in most of the other transition economies through both the privatization of SOEs and the entry of new private businesses. In the case of China, decentralization of ownership has been occurring primarily through the expanded significance of the non-state sector as well as limited 'privatization' of large SOEs and the selling off of small and medium-sized SOEs. In China, however, public ownership of the pillar industries of the economy will remain for the foreseeable future at least. However reforms in terms of corporatization, the development of stock exchanges, standardization of accounting practices suggest that a framework for the future privatization of large SOEs is being put in place.

A number of privatization methods adopted in the other transition economies were outlined. Some of these could be utilized in the context of China's large SOEs at a future date. The evidence suggests that spontaneous privatization should be avoided. Sales of large SOEs to 'core' investors may be politically possible in China, as long as they were to domestic rather than foreign owners. Management–employee buyouts may be difficult at the large SOE level, but more practical at the medium to small SOE level. The benefits of equal access voucher privatization, as implemented in the Czech Republic, indicate it is a model that fits well with China's attempt to build a socialist market economy. The model achieves the objective of greater fairness of access, with the potential to improve enterprise performance and to create value for investors. The voucher system also requires significant financial development, which also fits well with China's attempts at financial intermediation institution building.

Notes

1 See Naughton (1996).
2 At the beginning of 1998 the authorities announced the phasing out of the credit plan.

References

Asian Development Bank. (1995), *Key Indicators of Developing Asian and Pacific Countries*, Vol. 26, ADB, Manila.

Asian Wall Street Journal (AWSJ) (Various issues), Dow Jones & Company Inc., Hong Kong.

Bell, M.W., H.E. Khor and K. Kochhar (1993), *China at the Threshold of a Market Economy*, IMF Occasional Paper 107, IMF, Washington.

Bonin, J., and P. Wachtel (1997), *Towards Market-Oriented Banking in the Economies in Transition*, New York University Salomon Centre, Working Paper Series, S-97-2.

Claessens, S., S. Djankov and G. Pohl (1997), 'Ownership and Corporate Governance: Evidence from the Czech Republic', Policy Research Working Paper 1737, World Bank, Washington.

Department of Foreign Affairs and Trade (1996), *Country Economic Brief – China*, Canberra, February.

Dyck, I.J.A., and K.H. Wruck (1998), *Organization Structure, Contract Design and Government Ownership: A Clinical Analysis of German Privatization*, Harvard University Graduate School of Business Working Paper, 1/22/98.

Jefferson, G.H., T.G. Rawski and Y. Zheng (1994), 'Enterprise Reform in Chinese Industry', *Journal of Economic Perspectives*, Vol. 8, No. 2, pp. 47–70.

Grossman, S., and O. Hart (1986), 'The Costs and Benefits of Ownership: A Theory of Vertical and Lateral Integration', *Journal of Political Economy*, Vol. 94, pp. 691–719.

Naughton, B. (1996), *Growing Out of the Plan – Chinese Economic Reform 1978–1993*, Cambridge University Press, Cambridge, UK.

Perkins, D. (1994), 'Completing China's Move to the Market', *Journal of Economic Perspectives*, Vol. 8, No. 2, pp. 23–46.

Rawski, T.G. (1994), 'Chinese Industrial Reform: Accomplishments, Prospects, and Implications', *American Economics Association, Papers and Proceedings*, Vol. 84, No. 2.

Shleifer, A., and R. Vishny (1986), 'Large Shareholders and Corporate Control', *Journal of Political Economy*, Vol. 94, pp. 461–88.

—— (1997), 'A Survey of Corporate Governance', *Journal of Finance*, Vol. 52, pp. 737–83.

Tisdell, C.A., and J.C.H. Chai (1997), *China's Economic Growth and Transition – Macroeconomic, Environmental and Social/Other Dimensions*, Nova Science, New York.

Tseng, W., H.E. Khor, K. Kochar, D. Mihajek, and D. Burton (1994), *Economic Reform in China, a New Phase*, IMF Occasional Paper 114, IMF, Washington, November.

Vickers, J., and G. Yarrow (1988), *Privatization: An Economic Analysis*, MIT Press, Cambridge, Mass.

Williamson, O. (1985), *The Economic Institutions of Capitalism*, New York: Free Press.

World Bank (1996), *World Development Report 1996 – From Plan to Market*, Oxford University Press, New York.

World Bank (1995), *Bureaucrats in Business*, Oxford University Press, New York.

Xu, X., and Y. Wang (1997), *Ownership Structure, Corporate Governance and Corporate Performance*, Amherst College Working Paper.

4

Business Alliances, Organizational Change and Township and Village Enterprises

Charles Harvie

This chapter identifies the contribution which the Township and Village Enterprises (TVEs) have made to the Chinese economy during the period of economic reform. While the economic literature suggests that the success of the TVEs has arisen due to special circumstances, this chapter argues, to the contrary, that they are likely to remain a significant feature of the Chinese economy, albeit in new organizational and ownership forms, for some time. Their demonstrated flexibility in terms of organizational structure, delegation and incentive design, in conjunction with their evolving strategic business alliances in the form of joint ventures with foreign companies and, increasingly, alliances with science-based research institutions, it is argued, will make this possible.

4.1   Introduction

One of the most striking outcomes during China's period of economic reform since 1978 has been the rapid growth of the non-state sector. This consists of four broad types of business entities: township and village enterprises (TVEs); urban collectives; private and individual enterprises; and joint ventures and wholly foreign-owned enterprises which together are called foreign funded enterprises (FFEs). The sector has attained major outcomes in terms of output, employment, and export growth as well as in technology upgrading, profitability and gains

71

in total factor productivity. By the mid-1990s the non-state sector produced two-thirds of industrial output and over 70 per cent of total national output, as both agriculture and the personal-services sectors are largely privately owned. The industrial output share of state-owned enterprises (SOEs), as indicated in Chapter 3, and collectives has dropped, while that of the more dynamic TVEs and local private and foreign enterprises has grown rapidly. Indeed the highest growth rates more recently have been recorded by the privately owned enterprises and FFEs. A similarly radical shift has occurred in industrial employment patterns. While in 1980 SOEs employed more people than all other forms of enterprises combined, by the mid-1990s the non-state sector's contribution had increased substantially and the TVEs had become the single largest source of employment for industrial workers. TVE employment, overall, more than quadrupled between 1980 and 1995.

The non-state sector dominates light industry and has generated about three-quarters of total export growth since 1978. It also produces over 80 per cent of industrial output in the coastal provinces. In fact the pre-eminence of the non-state sector in these provinces is one of the main sources of dynamism of the coastal region. In the past the non-state sector confronted discriminatory tax and other policies, and, even today, still has some concerns regarding security of property rights. Difficulties remain in accessing bank finance, upgrading technology, obtaining access to skilled labour and management personnel, dealing with government interference in the management of some enterprises, and securing product transport and distribution. However, legal and regulatory reforms and political developments in the 1990s have greatly improved the position of non-state sector firms, contributing to the sector's dramatic growth.

The dynamism of the industrial sector during the period of reform has been primarily provided by that of the TVEs, which have achieved a remarkable performance. Their output increased by 25 per cent a year from the mid-1980s to the mid-1990s, resulting in their share of GDP increasing from 13 per cent in 1985 to over 30 per cent by the mid-1990s. During the past fifteen years they have also created over 100 million new rural jobs. A comparison of their performance with that of the SOEs is also remarkable. Although the capital-output ratio in collective industry, of which the TVEs are a crucial component, in China is only 25 per cent of that in the state sector, labour productivity (output per capita) is close to 80 per cent of that in state enterprises and rising at more than 10 per cent a year. Total factor productivity in TVEs is also considerably higher than in the state sector, and is growing at 5 per cent a year. This is more than twice the rate in state enterprises.

The factors behind this remarkable performance, and its sustainability within the framework of the TVE organizational and ownership form will be emphasized.

The chapter proceeds as follows. Section 2 conducts a brief review of the TVEs in terms of: their development; their unique organizational form; the issue of property rights and the TVE performance paradox; and the prospects for their sustainable development. The TVEs' contribution to the economy in terms of output, employment and exports as well as their performance in terms of profitability, total factor productivity and upgrading of technology is identified in section 3. The reasons behind the success of the TVE organizational form is discussed in section 4. Section 5 focuses upon the evolving business alliances involving TVEs, including those with publicly funded research institutes and universities, as well as organizational and ownership changes which will be required if the TVEs are to sustain their development within China's rapidly evolving market economy. Finally, section 6 presents a summary of the major conclusions from this chapter.

4.2   TVE background and contemporary issues

Background

The origins of the TVEs can be found from the agricultural collectives, or communes, established at the time of the Great Leap Forward in 1958, and which were held responsible for establishing and promoting rural industry. So called 'commune- and brigade-run enterprises' were the outcome from this process. These remained in place until the end of the 1970s when the household contract responsibility system gradually replaced the people's commune system, and commune- and brigade-run enterprises began to enjoy greater autonomy. In this new environment they had an incentive to increase production, improve productivity, and develop new businesses. In addition, the government implemented various policies encouraging their development such as loans on favourable terms, tax reduction or exemption, and technical assistance. All these measures laid the foundations for the further development of rural industries. With the effective demise of the agricultural collectives by 1983 the responsibility for the commune- and brigade-run enterprises was transferred to local government industrial departments, which contributed start up funds, appointed managers, and were ultimately involved in strategic decision making.

In 1984 commune- and brigade-run enterprises, of which there were approximately 1.4 million, were officially renamed as village and township enterprises (TVEs), but it was also decided that the label would apply to individual rural enterprises and those based on farm cooperatives. This meant that the number of TVEs suddenly increased five fold to about 6.1 million in 1984. Hence four types of ownership structures involving TVEs, as defined by a government document in 1984, existed: county- and township-run enterprises; village-run enterprises; farmers' cooperatives; and individual- or family-run businesses. The first two categories are owned collectively by townships (formerly communes) and villages (formerly brigades). The cooperatives are owned by households/farmers who pool their resources together for production. The latter category consisted of enterprises owned by individuals. Many of the first two types, that is county-, township- or village-run enterprises, followed on from the commune and brigade enterprises. The additional farmers' TVEs were mostly very small. Because of the family quota contract system, farmers produced an agricultural surplus and found themselves with some free time. They were encouraged and supported by the government to use this time to develop certain new businesses. Unlike SOEs, TVEs' finance, supplies, sales, production, and personnel were not subject to state planning, though they became intimately linked with local government.

TVEs and their contribution to promoting rural industrial development

The impetus for the initial growth of the TVEs arose from the success of China's agricultural reforms of the late 1970s and early 1980s, which greatly expanded rural savings, freed millions of workers to seek non-farm employment and increased rural demand for consumer goods, as well as the decentralization of fiscal revenue raising in the mid-1980s. The importance of the TVE form of industrial enterprise in the context of promoting rural industrial development in China has been due to the following features. Firstly, the TVEs allowed rural communities to translate control over assets and resources into income, despite the absence of asset markets. The growth of product markets provided rural communities with the opportunity to realize value from locally controlled resources. Secondly, TVEs provided a way to convert assets into income without solving the difficult problem of privatization. The Chinese government then, and reconfirmed in 1993, was unwilling on ideological grounds to permit mass privatization. The administrative difficulties involved with privatization would have been immense due to the sheer size of China and the lack of administrative apparatus. The difficult problems associated with privatization were probably insoluble in China during the 1980s. Hence the TVEs circumvented this difficulty while contributing importantly to competition and the opening up of markets. Thirdly, with well-functioning markets urban firms would have purchased land and hired suburban labour. In the absence of such institutions TVEs represented an alternative solution. Urban SOEs could sub-contract to TVEs providing in the process technology and equipment, or rural governments could take the initiative in this regard themselves. Many TVEs grew up as complements to state-run industry. The majority of TVE growth has been concentrated in advanced periphery-urban regions. For example, in 1988 in the three provinces of Jiangsu, Zhejiang and Shandong, which produce half of all TVE output, linkages with urban firms were central to TVE growth.

Finally, TVEs facilitated access to capital on the part of start up firms. In China local government ownership played a key role in the process of financial intermediation. Local governments could better assess the risks of start up businesses under their control, and were diversified and able to act as guarantors of loans to individual TVEs. By underwriting a portion of the risk of entry, local governments enabled start up firms to enter production with a larger size, starting with some mechanization, and exploiting economies of scale. With local governments playing an important role in the flow of capital to rural enterprises, such firms were able to take advantage of China's relatively abundant household savings. In return, the profitable opportunities and reasonable risk levels in the TVE sector kept real returns high and contributed to the maintenance of high savings rates.

TVEs and local government

Township and village leaders are typically appointed from above by county administrators, who in turn designate the managers of TVEs. They in effect possess all the key components of property rights: control of residual income; the right to dispose of assets; the right to appoint and dismiss managers; and assume direct control if necessary. Local residents possess no 'right of membership' in the TVEs, nor do TVE workers possess any rights to participate in TVE management. Township and village officials' compensation is determined by a 'managerial contract' with explicit success indicators covering economic and social objectives. TVE output and sales value, profits, and taxes enter into the compensation schedule, as well as family planning, maintenance of public order and education. However there are strong pressures to stress profits since the township or village as a unit is subject to a fairly strong hard budget constraint. The successful township official maximizes his own career prospects by producing economic growth during his term as a community leader, and this is likely to crucially depend upon maximizing net revenue from the TVEs. Managers of TVEs not performing in a satisfactory fashion in accordance with such criteria can be dismissed.

The role of China's TVEs is unique in the context of an economy in transition. In no other such economy has public ownership played such a dynamic role. However, the collective ownership form, which TVEs are classified as being, does not have a precise definition in the country, leading to uncertainty about ultimate ownership rights. The literature would suggest that public ownership combined with vague ownership rights would present a recipe for economic disaster (Weitzman and Xu, 1994). However the performance of the TVEs in terms of output growth, employment creation, profit rate and growth of total factor productivity (TFP), indicates to the contrary that the TVEs have accomplished a good record in comparison to its private counterparts and much better than that of the SOEs (Svejnar, 1990; Pitt and Putterman, 1992). Under a collective ownership with an unclear delineation of property rights, the success of TVEs therefore seems to pose a paradox for the standard property rights theory which states that a well-defined private property rights system is a precondition for eliminating disincentive and free-rider problems as well as other opportunistic behaviour (Alchian and Demsetz, 1972; Demsetz, 1972; Furubotn and Pejovich, 1974; and Cheung, 1982). Weitzman and Xu (1994) attempt to reconcile this by arguing that the success of the TVEs has arisen from their internal institutional form, which facilitates cooperation through implicit contracts among community members.

Naughton (1994) argues on the other hand that the success of the TVEs has been largely due to a set of external conditions to which they have been an effective adaptation. They have been an effective response to a distinctive feature of the Chinese transition process that saw the early development of product markets, without well-developed markets for factors of production and assets. The latter in fact only developed gradually, such that even in the 1990s it was still at a very early stage of development. Naughton therefore argues that the TVEs were a flexible and effective but basically ordinary adaptation to this environment. Such a view would suggest that TVEs may not represent an enduring organizational form, and that as underlying economic conditions change rural industry will lose ground to large domestic firms, enterprise groups, and joint-venture companies during the course of the 1990s and beyond.

However, although predominantly owned by local government, an increasing number of TVEs are now privately owned. Many are involved in joint ventures with SOEs and foreign companies and a high proportion incorporate a complex network of affiliations and alliances involving scientists, engineers, academics and business entrepreneurs. This has enabled them to gain access to technology and to become competitive.

These evolving alliances will be essential to the sustainability of the TVE form of enterprise, and are discussed further below.

4.3 TVEs' performance and contribution to the economy

Greater autonomy, financial support, freedom from bureaucracy and entrepreneurial drive resulted in a stunning rate of growth for the TVEs during the period of economic reform, contributing significantly to the rapid growth of the Chinese economy during this period. Major progress was made by the TVEs on a number of fronts including that of output, employment, export growth, as well as improvements in efficiency as measured by both labour productivity and total factor productivity, an upgrading of technology, and sustained profitability

Output

Table 4.1 shows the output value, number of establishments and employment level of the TVEs during the period of economic reform. The output value of TVEs increased from 49.3 to 6,891.5 billion yuan

Table 4.1   **Basic Statistics of China's TVEs, 1978–95**

Year	Number of Enterprises (Million)	Workers Employed (Million)	Gross Output Value (Billion Yuan)	Current Prices Growth (%)
1978	1.52	28.27	49.3	—
1980	1.43	30.00	65.7	—
1984	6.07	52.08	171.0	—
1985	12.23	69.79	272.8	59.5
1986	15.15	79.37	345.1	29.8
1987	17.50	88.05	476.4	34.5
1988	18.88	95.45	649.6	36.4
1989	18.68	93.66	742.8	14.3
1990	18.50	92.65	846.2	13.9
1991	19.09	96.09	1162.2	37.3
1992	20.79	105.81	1797.5	54.7
1993	24.53	123.45	3154.1	75.5
1994	24.95	120.18	4258.9	35.0
1995	22.03	128.6	6891.5	61.8

Source: State Statistical Bureau, *China Statistical Yearbook 1996*, Tables 11-29, 11-30, 11-31, pp. 387–89.

over the period from 1978 to 1995. In line with this rapid expansion in output TVE numbers also increased rapidly from over 1.5 million in 1978 to 22 million by 1995. The latter figure, however, being almost three million less than for 1994. In 1995 the GDP (value added) of the TVEs accounted for 25.5 per cent of the national total, and in 1994 they contributed some 30 per cent of gross industrial output (see Table 4.2). Between 1979 and 1991 the average growth rates of GDP and industrial output in TVEs were 30 per cent and 26 per cent respectively, while those at the national level were 10 per cent and 12 per cent respectively. Table 4.2 indicates that by the mid-1990s TVEs were contributing over 30 per cent of industrial output, over 40 per cent if urban collectives are included, which compared with a figure of 22 per cent in 1978. In conjunction with these developments the SOE share of industrial production has fallen steadily during the period of reform, from 78 per cent in 1978 to around one-third by the mid-1990s, as already identified in Chapter 3. There has also been a rapid expansion in the contribution of privately owned and foreign-funded enterprises, whose share of industrial production increased from a negligible level in 1978 to over 25 per cent by the mid-1990s. The latter represents a rise almost as spectacular as that of the TVEs themselves, and

Table 4.2   **Gross Industrial Output by Business Type, 1990–94 (billion Yuan)**

Year	1990	1991	1992	1993	1994
Total	2 392.4	2 824.8	3 706.6	5 269.2	7 690.9
SOEs	1 306.4	1 495.5	1 782.4	2 272.5	2 620.1
Per cent of total	54.6	52.9	48.1	43.1	34.1
Urban collectives	368.7	414.9	514.4	626.3	801.1
Per cent of total	15.4	14.7	13.8	11.9	10.4
TVEs	483.5	593.5	895.7	1395.0	2342.3
Per cent of total	20.2	21.0	24.2	26.5	30.5
Privately owned	129.0	160.9	250.7	440.2	885.3
Per cent of total	5.4	5.7	6.8	8.4	11.5
Other (mainly FFEs)	104.8	160.0	263.4	535.2	1042.1
Per cent of total	4.4	5.7	7.1	10.2	13.6

Source: *TVE Statistical Yearbook* (1995 and previous years).

potentially has important implications for the future evolution of the TVEs in terms of their organizational as well as ownership form. Although growth of the TVEs continued apace during the 1990s (see Table 4.1), more recent developments during 1996 and 1997 suggest a slowdown in their growth. The reasons for this are discussed in section 5.

As indicated in Table 4.3, most of the TVE output, some 84 per cent in 1994, is produced in the coastal region which consists of China's most dynamic economic provinces. In no small measure the dynamism

Table 4.3 **Gross Output Value of Industrial Enterprises by Region, 1990 and 1994 (Yuan '00 million)**

	Year	SOEs	Urban Collectives	TVEs	Private	Others	Total
Coastal Region							
	1990	6 570	9 313	4 072	626	978	21 559
% of total		30	43	19	3	5	100
	1994	13 262	16 430	22 323	4 584	8 180	64 778
% of total		20	25	34	7	13	100
Central Region							
	1990	3 930	3 392	1 172	388	36	8 917
% of total		44	38	13	4	0	100
	1994	7 500	4 166	2 277	426	843	15 212
% of total		49	27	15	3	6	100
Western Region							
	1990	1 563	1 149	385	145	21	3 262
% of total		48	35	12	4	1	100
	1994	4 220	1 766	1 819	1 017	631	9 453
% of total		45	19	19	11	7	100

Note: The coastal region consists of Shanghai, Beijing and Tianjin municipalities and Jiangsu, Zhejiang, Fujian, Shandong, Guangdong Hebei, Liaoning, Guangxi and Hainan provinces. The five dynamic provinces are Jiangsu, Zhejiang, Fujian, Shandong, and Guangdong. The central region consists of Shanxi, Jilin, Inner Mongolia, Heilongjiang, Anhui, Jiangxi Henan, Hubei and Hunan. The western region consists of Sichuan, Guizhou, Yunnan, Shaanxi, Gansu, Qinghai, Ningxia, Tibet and Xinjiang.

Source: State Statistical Bureau, *China Statistical Yearbook*, 1996

is due to the rapid growth of the TVEs, whose share of industrial production increased from 19 per cent in 1990 to 34 per cent in 1994.

Employment

In terms of employment creation, the contribution of TVEs to the rural economy has been truly spectacular. TVEs employed some 28.3 million workers in 1978, this figure rising to 128.6 million by 1995 and to 135 million by 1996 (see Figure 4.1 and Table 4.4). This has made a major contribution to the employment of surplus labour in rural China, in a cost-efficient way, as well as raising rural incomes. These are two essential tasks in the development of China's rural economy. Table 4.4 indicates that the TVEs are the largest employers of industrial labour. Indeed over the period 1978–96 they provided an additional 100 million jobs in the rural sector.

While the output growth of TVEs has remained at a high rate concern has, more recently, arisen from the fact that expanded TVE employment has increased at a much slower rate (see Figures 4.1 and 4.2). For example, the net output of TVEs increased by 125 per cent at fixed prices from 1991 to 1995 but employment expanded by only 27 per cent. There is a general concern by the authorities that the non-state sector as a whole may not be able to expand sufficiently to absorb unemployed labour in both the rural and urban economies.

Exports

Until 1984, exports from TVEs were negligible, but starting from 1985 they increased rapidly. In 1986 TVEs' exports of US$5 billion accounted for one-sixth of China's total exports. In the same year about 20 000 TVEs specialized in production for export, 2 400 TVEs were involved in

Table 4.4   Employees by Business Type ('000 People)

Year	SOEs	Urban Collect- ives	FFEs	TVEs	Private	Indiv- idual
1980	80 190	24 250	—	30 000	—	810
1985	89 900	33 240	60	69 790	—	4 500
1990	103 460	35 490	620	92 650	1 700	11 050
1995	112 610	31 470	2 410	128 620	9 560	46 140

Source: State Statistical Bureau, *China Statistical Yearbook*, 1996 and previous years.

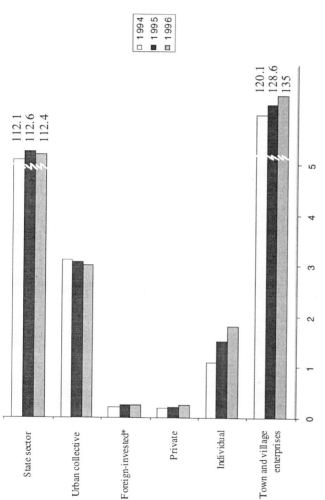

* Inclusing investment from Hong Kong, Taiwan and Macau

Source: State Statistical Bureau, *China Statistical Yearbook*, 1997

Figure 4.1 **Employees by Sector 1994–96 (millions)**

equity and cooperative joint-ventures, and about 10 000 were engaged in compensation trade and production according to clients' requirements or samples. In 1987 China's new policy of accelerating the economic development of coastal regions gave 14 cities the status of coastal open cities, with extra freedoms and tax breaks for foreign trade and investment and gave a further impetus to the development of TVEs. From the second half of the period 1988 to 1991, both central and local governments put great emphasis on the development of export-oriented businesses to acquire capital, technology and raw materials from western companies and international markets. Although during the same period the central government was tightening money supply and

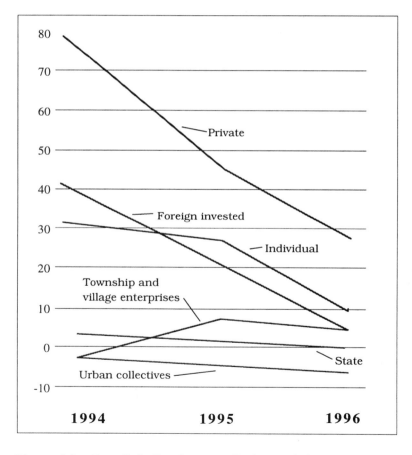

Figure 4.2   Growth in Employment By Sector (%)

controlling investment in domestic markets, export-oriented TVEs began to take off. They succeeded because of their operating flexibility and customer-oriented approach. The position of TVEs in China's foreign trade became increasingly important thereafter. From 1987 through 1992 TVEs' exports and imports grew by an average of 60 per cent per year. Their exports of US$20 billion in 1992 accounted for a quarter of China's total exports (US$85 billion). By the mid-1990s about 80 000 TVEs were engaged in export-oriented production, accounting for over 40 per cent of China's total exports and over 30 per cent of China's GDP.

Profitability

Table 4.5 compares the profit rates between TVEs and state-owned industrial enterprises (SOIEs) during the period of economic reform. This suggests that for most of the years from 1978 to 1994 the pre-tax and after-tax profit rates of the TVEs have been higher than that of the SOIEs, except for the years from 1986 to 1989. However, to obtain a more accurate picture of their respective performances, the profit rates of the SOIEs must be discounted by the subsidies provided by the central government. These budget subsidies increased from 11.7 billion yuan in 1978 to 36.6 billion yuan in 1994, and for most of the years this accounted for a share of more than 10 per cent of total government revenue. Therefore if the profit rates of the SOIEs recorded in Table 4.5 are discounted by this factor, their performance has lagged considerably further behind that of the TVEs which operate in the absence of government subsidy.

Upgrading of technology

During the period 1991 to 1995, the capital stock of TVEs increased by 142 per cent and was the primary factor behind the rapid growth in TVE output during this period. This expansion of capital intensity of TVE production is confirmed from Table 4.6, which clearly indicates an upgrading of the technology employed by TVEs. The vast majority of the funds for which has come from bank loans and retained earnings, with the latter becoming of increasing significance during the period of the 1990s (see Table 4.7). While this is of benefit to some TVEs, as they move to increasingly higher value products, it does present a strange paradox in a labour surplus economy, and explains the slowdown in labour absorption in rural China as previously indicated. Why has labour been substituted for capital in this way? Recent research (see Liu, 1997) suggests that in the coastal provinces the reason for this is that most of the surplus labour has already been absorbed, and that further production is being achieved by increasing relatively cheap

Table 4.5   Profit Rates of TVEs and SOIEs, 1978–94 (%)

Year	TVE Pre-tax	TVE After-tax	SOIE Pre-tax	SOIE After-tax
1978	39.8	31.8	24.2	15.5
1979	35.4	29.1	24.8	16.1
1980	32.5	26.7	24.8	16.0
1981	29.1	22.3	23.8	15.0
1982	28.0	20.2	23.4	14.4
1983	27.8	18.5	23.2	14.4
1984	24.6	15.2	24.2	14.9
1985	23.7	14.5	23.8	13.2
1986	19.7	10.6	20.7	10.6
1987	17.0	9.0	20.3	10.6
1988	17.9	9.3	20.6	10.4
1989	15.2	7.1	17.2	7.2
1990	13.0	5.9	12.4	3.2
1991	12.7	5.8	11.8	2.9
1992	14.3	4.8	9.7	2.7
1993	19.0	11.6	9.7	3.2
1994	14.8	9.0	9.8	2.8

Source: ZGTJNJ (1992: 391, 431; 1993: 436–37; 1994: 366: 1995: 403–6)

Note: Profit Rate = Pre or After-tax Profit/Fixed Capital + Working Capital

capital for increasingly costly labour. In the poorer inland provinces with surplus labour the marginal productivity of labour is already low, and hence expanded production could come about more easily through an expansion of capital rather than labour. This, Liu concludes, has important policy implications for labour migration and training, and for the allocation of capital, to improve labour absorption in rural China across its provinces. Labour should be encouraged to move to the coastal provinces, and capital to the poorer inland provinces.

Efficiency

There is strong empirical evidence to support the proposition that TVEs are more efficient than SOEs. Weitzman and Xu (1994) compared the growth rates of output (Y), capital (K), labour (L) and total factor productivity (TFP) of the SOIEs and the TVEs from 1979 to 1991 (see

Table 4.6 **The Capital Intensity of TVEs and SOEs**

Year	TVEs' Capital to Labour Ratio	SOEs' Capital to Labour Ratio
1985	1 362.8	10 434.6
1986	1 636.5	11 488.7
1987	2 034.2	12 830.2
1988	2 522.5	14 283.3
1989	3 148.6	16 459.6
1990	3 633.6	18 529.9
1991	4 110.1	21 259.4
1992	5 022.3	24 292.6
1993	6 532.9	29 571.9
1994	8 808.9	35 867.1
1995	11 780.9	39 741.0
1985–95 growth % p.a. (nominal)	24.1	14.3
1985–95 growth % p.a. (deflated)	12.2	2.4

Source: *TVE Statistical Yearbook* (1995 and previous years)

Table 4.8). They found that the growth rates associated with the TVEs were much higher than that of the SOIEs. It is particularly evident for the growth of TFP, which grew three times faster for the TVEs in comparison to that of the SOIEs. Similar results were derived by Jefferson and Rawski (1994, see Table 4.9), who found that the collective form of enterprise performed better than that of the state sector both in terms of labour productivity and more importantly in terms of TFP. The outstanding performance of the TVEs, however, is most noticeable. These results reflect that TVEs have achieved a considerable level of technological progress as previously mentioned, and particularly relative to both the SOIEs and collective industries in urban areas.

The reasons behind the phenomenal success of the TVEs during the period of economic reform, as well as outstanding problems, are discussed in the following section.

4.4 Reasons for the success of the TVEs

A number of reasons have been advanced in the literature to explain the phenomenal growth and superior efficiency record of TVEs relative to that of the SOEs in particular. The major ones include the following:

Table 4.7   **Sources of Enterprises' Investment Finance (% of Total), 1980–93**

	SOEs	Urban Collectives	TVEs	JVs[a]	WFOEs[b]
Plan allocation					
1980–84	12	0	0	0	0
1985–89	9	0	0	0	0
1990–93	12	0	0	0	0
Bank loans					
1980–84	82	80	na	25	na
1985–89	72	67	81	24	37
1990–93	76	78	53	47	27
Retained earnings					
1980–84	6	20	na	75	na
1985–89	18	33	19	74	63
1990–93	9	22	47	47	73
Share/bond issues					
1980–84	0	0	na	0	na
1985–89	1	0	0	0	0
1990–93	3	0	0	6	0

Notes: a   Joint ventures
          b   Wholly foreign-owned enterprises
Source: Perkins and Raiser (1994, Table 12) from a survey of 300 coastal province enterprises.

- *Small, flexible and market driven.* From the outset TVEs had to rely on markets for sourcing supplies and selling products. Many TVEs positioned their businesses in areas where there were severe shortages, or where SOEs were weak. Most were small and autonomous compared with SOEs, and thus had flexibility to respond to market changes quickly. Their management was also more market-oriented.

- *Appropriate production technology.* The TVEs faced cheap labour and expensive capital and natural resources, causing them to choose appropriate production technologies. As the reform process progressed prices were gradually liberalized, reflecting

Table 4.8   **Comparison of Growth and Efficiency of the SOIEs and TVEs, 1979–91**

	National Industry	SOIEs				TVEs			
	Y	Y	K	L	TFP	Y	K	L	TFP
Growth Rate	13.3	8.4	7.8	3.0	4.0	25.3	16.5	11.9	12.0

Source: Weitzman and Xu (1994, p. 28).

Table 4.9   **Estimated Rates of Annual Productivity Growth in Chinese Industry (% change)**

	1980–84	1984–88	1988–92
A. Total Factor Productivity			
State sector	1.8	3.0	2.5[a]
Collective sector			
Urban and township	3.4	5.9	4.9[a]
Township-Village	7.3[a]	6.6[a]	6.9[a]
B Labour Productivity (real terms)			
State sector	3.8	6.2	4.7
Collective sector			
Urban and township	8.6	7.0	13.8
Township-Village	5.8	14.4	17.7

a   Preliminary results.
Source: Taken from Jefferson and Rawski (1994, p.56).

more relative scarcity values, and the SOEs found themselves at a competitive disadvantage because of inappropriate capital and resource-intensive technologies.

• *Distortions, market opportunities and rural saving.* The TVEs were highly profitable because of the distortions carried over from the formerly planned system. At the beginning of the reform process in 1978, the average rate of profit on TVE capital was

32 per cent (capital being defined as depreciated fixed capital plus all inventories). Most of the new TVEs were in manufacturing, where state price controls kept profitability high so that the state could obtain high revenues from the SOEs. In addition, due to past biases in the planned system against light industry and services, the TVEs could enter market niches for which the SOEs had either failed to produce or failed to innovate and improve quality control. The resulting high profits achieved by TVEs attracted further investment and rapid growth. This was further strengthened by high rural saving and demand following the agricultural reforms of 1978, in conjunction with the limited scope for emigration from rural areas.

- *Low taxation.* Taxes on TVEs were low, requiring them to pay only 6 per cent of profits as tax in 1980, climbing to 20 per cent after 1985. Such low tax rates in China were primarily due to a policy-driven desire to foster rural industrialization.

- *Decision making.* Information channels between the TVE managers and local government authorities tended to be both shorter and simpler compared to that for the SOEs, encouraging greater efficiency. Further, this greater flexibility and autonomy in management has meant that inter-firm alliances and technological alliances with universities and research institutes has produced a 'networked' approach to innovation and industrial production.

- *Decentralization plus financial discipline.* In 1984 a decentralization of fiscal power took place in China which allowed lower levels of government to retain locally generated revenues, creating a strong incentive for the development of local industry. A non-performing TVE in this system would become a drain on limited resources. Therefore local government officials and TVE managers had to focus more upon financial objectives, profit plus local tax revenues, since local governments lacked the borrowing capacity of higher levels of government. Hence the TVE enterprises under their jurisdiction faced harder budget constraints than SOEs, and were more likely to fall into bankruptcy if persistent losses were made. This focused upon the need for TVEs to be efficient, competitive and profitable in a period of a rapid opening up of markets. Meanwhile managers of SOEs, having responsibility for housing and other social services as well as industrial operations, faced a more complex set of objectives and state obligations.

- *Kinship and implicit property rights.* A number of researchers have suggested that, despite the absence of well-defined property rights, the demographic stability of China's rural communities promoted the emergence of 'invisible institutions' to provide a 'moral framework for rights' or a 'cooperative culture' that served to reduce problems of shirking and monitoring found in most public enterprises (see Byrd and Lin, 1990; Yusuf, 1993a, 1993b; and Weitzman and Xu, 1994). The incentives facing TVEs are similar to those of private firms in that residual profits are dispersed among a small group, consisting of a stable local community and in particular its local government and TVE manager. Studies have shown the importance of TVE profits in local government budgets and the close links between local economic performance and the status, income and career prospects of local officials.

- *Links with the state enterprise sector.* The state sector also represents an important, and not sufficiently recognized, component in the successful development of TVEs and other non-state firms. The TVEs and collectives in general rely on the state sector as a source of capital, materials, equipment, specialized personnel, technology, sub-contracting arrangements and sales revenue. For example, in southern Jiangsu province more than two-thirds of TVEs have established various forms of economic and technical cooperation arrangements with industrial enterprises, research units and higher educational institutions in larger cities. Local government officials attempting to develop industry in poor localities are encouraged to pursue joint operations with scientific research organizations or large and medium-scale enterprises.

- *Market entry and competition.* The continual reduction of entry barriers associated with China's industrial reform created a domestic product cycle in which new products, materials and processes introduced by innovative state firms were adopted by TVEs and other non-state enterprises. They could then use their cost advantages to erode state-sector profits and force state industry toward fresh innovations. In addition there has been intense competition for investment, including that for foreign investment, among communities with TVEs. The ability to attract such investment is strongly influenced by the reputation of the TVEs as well as local economic performance. TVEs themselves are increasingly subject to competition from the even more dynamic but smaller private and foreign invested sectors. An issue developed further in the following section.

- *Dedication to human resources, innovation and quality.* Many TVEs put special emphasis on human resources, innovation and product quality. With their autonomous and flexible systems it is their usual practice to recruit highly competent engineers and technicians from SOEs, to pay them attractive salaries and actively pursue innovation. At the beginning of the 1980s they mainly targeted and sought retired technicians and engineers from urban areas. Since the mid-1980s their attention has shifted to scientists and technicians working in research institutes and SOEs, who are discontented with their working conditions. Currently they are competing with large and medium-sized SOEs for talented staff and trying to attract foreign experts. TVEs maintain close links with research institutes. About 60 per cent of inventions and innovations developed by China's scientific and technological institutions have been put into production by TVEs.

- *International orientation.* Many TVEs, particularly those in coastal provinces, are actively pursuing cooperation and joint ventures with SOEs, with other TVEs, and with foreign companies. By developing joint ventures and sub contracts with foreign firms, TVEs have gradually upgraded their technology and many have become involved in foreign direct investment (FDI). Joint ventures between TVEs and foreign companies have grown rapidly in the last few years.

- *Lower cost structure.* TVEs have lower cost structures than SOEs, and they pay less tax. Because their managers historically had to rely on retained earnings and loans instead of government grants, they constantly pressured local authorities to give them tax breaks. Wages in rural areas are also significantly lower than in cities where most SOEs are found. They also do not have thousands of retirees on their books. The TVEs also do not have to offer welfare benefits like health care and social security insurance. Workers at TVEs work long hours, and the quality of their production has improved towards the SOE level. Where simple technology is required this represents a big advantage. Particularly in light industries like textiles and electrical appliances,

Despite these favourable characteristics, a significant number of TVEs still suffer from a number of difficulties, including the following:

- *Limited funds and supplies.* The growth of TVEs has had to rely chiefly on re-investment of any surplus. Although the Chinese government has implemented favourable loan and taxation policies to support TVEs, it has not directly invested in TVEs as it has with SOEs. Nevertheless, state bank loans have played an important role in sustaining the rapid development of TVEs. Another difference between TVEs and SOEs is that the former never benefited from supplies, at low cost, through the central plan.

- *Obsolete technology.* Many TVEs are still using obsolete technology, partly because their businesses are small and newly established and partly because their managers and employees have only recently stopped working on the land. In fact some still work part-time as employees and part-time as farmers. Hence, they are incapable of pursuing R&D activities and developing new products. Apart from some TVEs in the southern coastal provinces, most still rely on mechanical or semi-mechanical technology and quite a few on manual work. Many are too small to invest in R&D and keep up with the latest technology, making them vulnerable to competition from financially stronger foreign-invested ventures.

- *Low level of employees' education.* One of the major problems in TVEs is the employees' very low level of education. In the early 1990s only about 200 000 employees in TVEs had a degree or higher education, and only 420 000 held a medium-level technical qualification. These two figures come to less than 1 per cent of employees.

- *Profitability not clear.* Many foreign investors partnering TVEs sometimes discover that much of their profitability is based purely on preferential tax policies.

- *Vague property rights.* Growing conflicts of interest may arise from their historically vague ownership status. Because employees theoretically own everything collectively and nothing individually, they often act more like employees than owners, seeking to increase their salaries rather than cut costs and maximize company profit. Vague ownership rights and reliance on special privileges could cloud their future.

4.5   Evolving business alliances, organizational and ownership change

For the TVEs to maintain their remarkable performance, they will be required to evolve into enterprises capable of being competitive within the context of China's increasingly market-oriented economy. This will require making further advances in a number of key areas including that of: management control; clarification of property rights; expanding access to finance; access to developments in science and technology; enhancing the human capital of its employees and managers; ensuring access to input supply; and improving the efficiency of their distribution and marketing systems. Those TVEs unable to make such advances are unlikely to survive within the new economic environment evolving in China. Successful TVEs are likely to be those able to develop into new organizational forms based upon business alliances with other enterprises, involving cooperation and joint ventures between TVEs, SOEs, private domestic and foreign enterprises, and also with research institutes and universities in order to gain access to advances in science and technology. This will enable them to compete in both domestic and international markets, as well as to invest overseas. The gap between the developed coastal and backward inland regions is likely to widen since TVEs in the coastal region attract and introduce far more FDI than inland regions[1]. This process will encourage more and more TVEs to turn to exports, including processing and manufacturing based on clients' samples and specifications, processing clients' raw materials, and direct export. Joint ventures between TVEs and foreign firms will increase. TVEs in the coastal region will gradually develop their own R&D capacity. More and more capable technicians will be attracted to TVEs in the coastal region, where they enjoy a higher living standard than inland areas and have autonomy and funds to pursue research. Additionally, the intensification of competition, particularly with the rapidly developing private sector, is likely to result in the traditional collective ownership structure of the TVEs no longer being viable. Some of these key issues are now discussed further.

Evolving business alliances and partnerships involving TVEs

For foreign firms TVEs can be appropriate business partners or sub-contractors to pursue a global sourcing strategy and to penetrate China's domestic market, and this process can also bring major benefits to the TVEs in the form of access to finance, technology, managerial expertise, and international markets. The development of joint ventures with TVEs, in comparison with that of SOEs, can bring numerous benefits to foreign companies:

1. TVEs can provide greater commercial focus and are more flexible in comparison with the SOEs, and hence they can respond rapidly to changing market circumstances;

2. they are more sensitive to market signals and are more conscious of the need for efficiency;

3. Joint ventures with ailing SOEs, even in more dynamic provinces, may be too costly, as many of the better ones already have business links with foreign companies. Foreign companies may find that those available have poor potential. Such SOE joint ventures may require excessive investment by foreign partners with long payback periods;

4. TVEs operate much more independently from state bureaucracy. Such bureaucracy may wish to participate in SOE joint venture hiring and pricing policies;

5. There is a willingness of local party officials at the village level, who sometimes see themselves as patrons of TVEs, to help a TVE/foreign company joint venture with daily problem solving;

6. TVEs have the ability to hire labour as needed without being required to hire unnecessary or unsuitable workers;

7. In most cases TVEs face an absence of financial burdens, such as surplus labour, weak distribution systems, excessive factory space, obsolete equipment, high welfare benefit obligations to current and retired workers;

8. Many TVEs are now able to produce goods which are acceptable in international markets;

9. TVEs are eager to develop partnerships with foreign enterprises;

10. In many cases local governments encourage, support, and reward those TVEs which have developed cooperation or joint ventures with foreign firms;

11. Land and labour costs are lower for the TVEs than in urban areas. Salaries in TVEs can be 20–30 per cent lower than in SOEs. Thus by developing a partnership with TVEs, foreign firms' products are able to achieve competitive cost advantages in China and in international markets. TVEs have also attained higher productivity in comparison to SOEs;

12. The sense of pressure to make profits is felt more by TVE managers and employees than by those in SOEs, and thus hard work and greater entrepreneurship are often the norm.

For these reasons, foreign companies that want to have products manufactured to their own designs and specifications, and to source supplies/components, may find TVEs ideal partners. Products which require frequent changes in design and specifications and whose product batches are relatively small would be particularly suitable for TVEs.

However, a large number of TVEs may not be suitable for the establishment of a business alliance with a foreign company, for a number of reasons:

1. they may have limited financial, technological and human resources;

2. they may be in locations away from major urban areas and without essential amenities;

3. they may receive less support from senior political leaders in provincial or central governments, possibly leading to problems of resource allocation and utilities supply; or

4. there is the possibility of weaker legal protection for a TVE partner if the political climate of the non-state sector deteriorates.

Technology

In order to maintain their competitiveness, TVEs have not only been developing relationships with industrial partners but also R&D relationships with research institutes, universities and government agencies. As indicated previously a number of TVEs are rapidly upgrading their technology, relying heavily on retained earnings to do so. It is this horizontal connection between TVEs and science-based institutions which is likely to provide the organizational capabilities for their sustainable development. There appear to have been three important areas of reform that have contributed to these developments. Firstly, state-driven economic reforms have contributed to an environment that has encouraged TVEs to move into new areas of industrial production and trading. Secondly, science-policy reforms have steered technological alliances with public research institutions toward TVEs rather than toward SOEs. Thirdly, reform at the local government level created an environment conducive to the formation of horizontal alliances among TVEs and other enterprises. As future reforms in the state-owned sector deepen, it is likely that the long-term survival of the

TVE sector will rest even more on their capacity to build and maintain scientific and industrial organizational networks.

Through the 1980s China progressively implemented a series of Science and Technology development programs with specially designed objectives. These included the 'Spark Program', intended to direct science and technology towards the development of township enterprises and the promotion of rural and local economic development; the '863 Program' intended to promote China's high-tech R&D; the 'Prairie-Fire Program' designed to guide agriculture technology training; the 'Harvest Program' aimed at diversifying agriculture, animal husbandry, and fisheries; and the 'Torch Program' directed towards promoting new technologies in industry (China State Science and Technology Commission, 1991). At the same time research institutes and universities, many with well-established manufacturing capabilities, have been permitted and encouraged to trade independently. In 1992, for example, the China State Science and Technology Council issued regulations enabling research institutes, engaged in basic or applied research, to engage independently in export and trade, providing they have industrial capacity to innovate, are internationally competitive, and are export-oriented, earning at least US$500 000 (China State Science and Technology Commission, 1993). A consequence of the reforms has been that research institutes and universities in China have become embedded in new alliances that have produced not only new and economically powerful corporations, but have also led to the establishment of new institutions directed solely toward the production of trained technicians for the new enterprises. These science-policy reforms, in the context of broader economic reforms, have stimulated the development of new technological alliances between research institutions and the rapidly growing TVE sector.

These cooperative arrangements between TVEs and other firms, as well as science-based institutions, have produced organizational alliances with the capability to compete successfully with the larger and more powerful SOEs. However a major issue is whether this development will also enable the TVEs to compete successfully with the rapidly developing and highly efficient private sector in the future. This may require a change in ownership structure from the collective to private form. This option has been given major impetus arising from decisions made at the 15th Communist Party Congress during September 1997, which encouraged an expansion of other ownership types including that of private ownership. The issue of privatization has therefore clearly appeared on the agenda for China's small and medium-sized SOEs under the control of local governments, and is increasingly being applied to TVEs under their control.

Privatization

As discussed in Chapter 1, during the period 1993–96 the Chinese authorities implemented an austerity program with the objective of reducing inflationary pressure within the economy while maintaining a high, but more sustainable, rate of economic growth. With a so-called soft landing achieved in 1996, it was anticipated that the economy's growth rate would once again pick up. However, in 1997 the economy slowed further to a GDP growth rate of 8.8 per cent, and this was largely due to the collective sector's sluggish 11.7 per cent expansion in 1997 which was down from 17.7 per cent in 1996. During 1998 there were signs of a further slowing in the economy arising from the Asian financial crisis. This general slowdown in the economy has contributed to excess capacity and production in most sectors of the Chinese economy. With China planning to lay off millions of SOE workers in urban areas over the next few years, policymakers treat with considerable concern a slowdown in the rural economy as well. Rural unemployment pressure has been increasing, with surplus rural labour totalling approximately 130 million people at the end of 1997. Slowing labour absorption and prospective lay-offs by TVEs is likely to result in rural dissatisfaction and workers migrating to China's cities in search of jobs. In response to these recent developments, as well as increasing competition from the private sector, there have been many cases of privatization of TVEs with the objective of reviving sluggish rural industry. The success or failure of these efforts will have important implications for the Chinese economy, and a key issue is whether this process is temporary or inevitable.

More recently, many of the TVEs have experienced a decline in market share and profits. The slowing economy and excess capacity, arising from many domestic and foreign companies' expansion of production in the first half of the 1990s, has resulted in a surplus of many commodities and especially the low value-added labour-intensive items that TVEs produce. In this intensively competitive environment, only the best managed and most efficient companies will survive. While some TVEs have made the necessary changes to remain contenders, as identified previously, many have not. Highlighting the limitations of the TVE form of business entity.

For many TVEs low-skilled labour, unsophisticated management, capital shortages, inability to attract business partners and engage in alliances with research institutes have made it difficult to upgrade quality, move into higher value types of manufacturing, and increase their scale of production. At the same time, local government ownership can make it hard for company managers to make their own decisions.

On the other hand many managers of local government-owned TVEs are not held responsible for failures. During periods where profits are being made this may be acceptable, but during periods of declining profits and possible losses, as has occurred more recently, local governments are left with the debts, unsold inventories and workers who need jobs. This is one reason why some township and village governments are considering privatizing their companies, selling them wholly or partially to private citizens whether former factory managers or outsiders. If such enterprises go bankrupt thereafter, it then no longer becomes a problem for the local government. Shrinking tax receipts for local government has also been another motivation for privatization. Without good TVE results, local governments cannot collect enough tax revenue to build more roads, schools, houses and other community services.

Privatizing TVEs, however, has become popular not just for loss-making TVEs. Increasingly local government officials appear to be convinced, particularly in the richer coastal provinces where most of the successful TVEs are located, that private ownership is the appropriate form of ownership to ensure that organizational developments, essential for sustained competitiveness, take place even for profitable TVEs. TVEs are also being privatized simply because they can be. Ideological objections to private ownership have been relaxed over the past few years, and this was formally sanctioned at the Party Congress in September of 1997. Many local governments have taken advantage of such a development.

4.6 Summary and conclusions

The success of China's TVEs was largely an unanticipated outcome from the process of economic reform, attaining a major market niche in the production of consumer goods for both domestic and international markets. The former arose as a legacy of the central planning system and the SOEs' lack of consumer goods production. Their rapid rate of growth during the reform era has contributed significantly to the absorption of surplus rural labour, the generation of higher rural incomes and saving, assisted more generally in the economic development of local rural communities, and generated revenue for local governments. These developments contributed to reducing the extent of migration to urban areas, and is an outcome that should not be underestimated.

While there are many aspects of the TVEs that are specific to China, they can still provide important lessons for other economies in transition.

Most notably the significance of liberal market entry, the benefits of competition, the need for enterprises to operate under a hard budget constraint, the benefits of appropriate fiscal incentives for local governments, and the gains to be had from access to science and technology. However, to maintain competitiveness in China's rapidly developing market economy will require changes in their organizational form, through the development of both business and scientific alliances. The rapid rise of China's privately owned and foreign-funded enterprises suggests that the major source of competition will no longer simply be with the SOEs, over which the TVEs' performance has been superior, but rather with these alternative forms of business entities. The pressure for change will be intense, and may ultimately require a change of ownership form of the TVEs themselves.

While the literature in general suggests that the longer-term growth of TVEs in their present form is unsustainable, there is much evidence to suggest that many TVEs are already transforming themselves into complex interconnected networks involving science, industry and local government. The status of firms in China is highly dynamic in the present environment. Hence the key issue is not whether the TVEs will be able to maintain their industrial momentum in the light of deepening reforms, but rather the organizational and ownership form that will enable them to do so.

Note

1   See also Chapter 10.

References

Alchian, A.A., and H. Demsetz (1972), 'Production, Information Costs, and Economic Organisation', *American Economic Review*, Vol. 62, No. 5, pp. 777–95.

Bell, M.W., H.E. Khor and K. Kochhar (1993), 'China at the Threshold of a Market Economy', IMF Occasional Paper 107, IMF, Washington, September.

Byrd, W.A., and Q. Lin (1990), 'China's Rural Industry: An Introduction', in W.A. Byrd and Q-S. Lin (eds), *China's Rural Industry: Structure, Development, and Reform*, Oxford University Press, New York.

China State Science and Technology Commission (1991), *White Paper on Science and Technology No. 4*, International Academic Publishers, Beijing.

China State Science and Technology Commission (1993), *China S&T Newsletter*, No.13, December.

Christerson, B., and C. Lever-Tracy (1996), The Third China? China's Rural Enterprises as Dependent Subcontractors or as Dynamic Autonomous Firms?, paper presented to *The Asia-Pacific Regional Conference of Sociology*, Manila, 28–31 May 1996.

Demsetz, H. (1967), 'Towards a Theory of Property Rights', *American Economic Review*, Vol. 57, No. 2, pp. 347–59.

Furubotn, E.G., and S. Pejovich (1974), 'Introduction: the New Property Rights Structure:1-9', in E.G. Furubotn and S. Pejovich (eds), *The Economics of Property Rights*, Ballinger, Cambridge.

Jefferson, G.H., T.G. Rawski and Y. Zheng (1992a), 'Growth, Efficiency, and Convergence in China's State and Collective Industry', *Economic Development and Cultural Change*, Vol. 20, No. 2, pp. 239–66.

—— (1992b), 'Innovation and Reform in Chinese Industry: A Preliminary Analysis of Survey Data (1)', Paper delivered at the annual meeting of the Association for Asian Studies, Washington DC, April.

Jefferson, G.H., and T.G. Rawski (1994), 'Enterprise Reform in Chinese Industry', *Journal of Economic Perspectives*, Vol. 8, No. 2, pp. 47–70, Spring.

Liao, S-L. (1995), The Development of Township Enterprises in Rural Fujian Since the Early 1980s, paper presented to the *International Workshop on South China*, Nanyang Research Institute, Xiamen University, PRC, 22–24 May.

Liu, Y. (1997), Labour Absorption in China's Township and Village Enterprises, paper presented at the *International Conference on the Economies of Greater China*, Perth, Australia, July.

Naughton, B. (1994), 'Chinese Institutional Innovation and Privatization from Below', Amercian Economcs Association, *Papers and Proceedings*, Vol. 84, No. 2, pp. 266–70, May.

Perkins, D. (1994), 'Completing China's Move to the Market', *Journal of Economic Perspectives*, Vol. 8, No. 2, pp. 23–46, Spring.

Perkins, F.C., and M. Raiser (1994), 'State Enterprise Reform and Macroeconomic Stability in Transition Economies', Kiel Working Paper, No. 665, Kiel University, Kiel.

Pitt, M., and L. Putterman (1992), Employment and Wages in Township, Village, and other Rural Enterprises, mimeo, Brown University.

Rawski, T.G. (1994), 'Chinese Industrial Reform: Accomplishments, Prospects, and Implications', American Economics Association, *Papers and Proceedings*, Vol. 84, No. 2, pp. 271–75, May.

Research Centre for Rural Economics (1995), 'Case Study on Technology Transfer and Development of Township and Village Enterprises (TVEs)', Report to UNESCO, Beijing.

Svejnar, J. (1990), 'Productive Efficiency and Employment', in W.W. Byrd and Q. Lin (eds), *China's Rural Industry: Structure, Development, and Reform*, Oxford University Press, New York.

Tseng, W., H.E. Khor, K. Kocharm, D. Mihajek and D. Burton (1994), 'Economic Reform in China, a New Phase', IMF Occasional Paper 114, IMF, Washington, November.

Wietzman, M., and C. Xu (1994), 'Chinese Township Village Enterprises as Vaguely Defined Cooperatives', *Journal of Comparative Economics*, Vol.18, No. 2, pp. 121–45.

Yusuf, S. (1993a), The Rise of China's Nonstate Sector, unpublished manuscript, World Bank.

—— (1993b), Property Rights and Nonstate Sector Development in China, unpublished manuscript, World Bank.

5

Financial Sector Reform

Martin Hovey

Tony Naughton

This chapter focuses upon China's process of financial reform. While major changes have taken place, it is generally recognized that China still has a long way to go. The financial system remains dominated by banks, particularly state-owned institutions that retain many of the features of a repressed financial system. Experiments in developing other financial sectors have not been overly successful. Attempts are being made to free the major banks from the cycle of directed lending to inefficient state enterprises, resulting in non-performing loans. The quality of the loan portfolios, supervision and regulation of the banking sector is a hindrance to progress. On the positive side, the growing influence of Hong Kong and the greater freedom permitted to foreign institutions is likely to provide a much-needed stimulus to the domestic market.

5.1   Introduction

A fascinating aspect of the recent history of the reform process in China has been the willingness of authorities to embrace aspects of Western financial market practices such as stock and derivative markets. The process of reforming the financial sector had its origins in the late 1970s, but it was not until the Third Plenum of the Fourteenth Central Committee met in 1993 that finance was raised to the status of a key area for attention. The Chinese authorities recognized that the achievement of the goals of a socialist market economy depended on a financial system that did not represent a bottleneck, but rather directed finance towards efficient utilization of capital. The allocation of resources within the economy was therefore set to adopt a market decision-making process, within a system of state-controlled macroeconomic policy. This chapter examines this process of transition in the Chinese financial system using a financial development theory framework.

What emerges from this analysis is a somewhat cloudy view of the financial reform process. At one level we observe policy pronouncements that indicate a shift towards a market-based decision-making process in the allocation of funds, while in practice state control remains tight and inconsistent in its application. Bonin and Wachtel (1997) argue that successful reform of the financial system can be achieved in transition economies, even with state ownership of financial institutions, provided government disengages from direct involvement but establishes a strong regulatory framework. This is essentially a market economist's view of economies in transition, a central issue in the reform of the financial sector in China. What remains unresolved is how China should progress towards this still imprecise notion of a socialist market economy. This chapter tackles this issue by initially exploring traditional views of financial development within the context of China. We then track the most significant aspects of the recent financial reform process and attempt a forecast of likely future developments.

5.2   Financial development theory

The links between economic development and financial development are well established in the literature. Financial development refers to the expansion and increasing sophistication over time of a country's financial structure comprising institutions, instruments and markets (Drake, 1980). Financial development theory emerged as a distinct branch of economic thought in the late 1960s. At the centre of the debate is the objective of achieving financial efficiencies so that economic rents and the cost of capital can be effectively identified. This can be modelled in the form of the q ratio: the market value of productive assets as a ratio to their replacement cost. The ratio represents, theoretically, a comparison of the marginal efficiency of capital and the financial cost of capital (Tobin, 1969 and 1978). Financial efficiencies depend on the efficient functioning of bank intermediation and capital markets.

Early writers concentrated on broad structural and institutional measures of financial development. Goldsmith (1969) proposed that the structure and extent of financial development of a country could be determined by comparing the aggregate market value of all financial instruments to the value of national wealth. Goldsmith also proposed that the level of institutional development be measured by a ratio of financial assets held by financial institutions to the aggregate financial assets in the economy. The focus of the early work was, therefore, on the creation of financial assets and the expansion of holdings of these assets by financial institutions.

McKinnon (1973) and Shaw (1973) argue that developing countries suffer from financial repression that creates weak and inefficient financial markets. A repressed financial system is one in which financial prices are distorted, typically through interest rate ceilings set below market equilibrium rates. Combined with directed lending, repression creates credit subsidies for preferred creditors who are likely to invest in poor quality projects. Holders of financial assets are inadequately rewarded for risk taking and potentially high quality investment projects are starved of funds. The solution, often referred to as the McKinnon–Shaw hypothesis, is a program of liberalization of both real and financial sectors of the economy. Liberalization creates the environment in which financial development occurs. Empirical studies have identified significant links between financial development and economic growth. Gupta (1984), for example, found that financial liberalization and financial development causes economic development with improvements in savings and capital formation. However, it has become generally accepted that the prerequisites for financial sector development are macroeconomic stability and sound prudential supervision of the banking system (Fry, 1988).

5.3   An overview of China's financial sector reform

The McKinnon-Shaw financial repression analysis has been extended to socialist countries and their transition to market economies. In the case of China there are mixed opinions as to whether there was clear evidence of classic financial repression. Writers such as Byrd (1983) and Tam (1986) argue that China was not a classic case of repression. However, Li (1994) argues that China has experienced financial repression since the early 1950s. His analysis extends some of the traditional concepts of repression. Interest rate ceilings can, for example, be extended to other price ceilings. He also argues that many of the classic consequences of repression, such as low marginal productivity of loans, were clearly evident. Financial rigidity and vague policy making in the early years of reform only reinforce the observation of repression. Li proposes that the financial repression model is the most suitable framework for the reform of China's financial sector. Relatively simple in conception, it focuses on institutional arrangements that are well developed elsewhere. In the early years of the reform process, China was well placed to tackle financial development. There was no shortage of financial resources during this period. The problem has been, and still is, largely to do with the productivity of financial resources. However, despite this reservation, the gradualism of Chinese financial reform has avoided many of the problems of the 'big-bang' approach adopted in many other former socialist economies (Benziger, 1998).

The process of financial reform in China has also been praised for being closer to the models adopted in Asian emerging economies than to the reform in former Soviet and European transition economies (Mehran et al., 1996). China followed policies directed towards macroeconomic stability and achieved a high savings ratio, as did many Asian countries. This has provided a solid foundation to reform in the pragmatic political environment since 1978. In several Asian nations market controls were removed slowly in the early stages of reform, while the financial sector remained highly regulated. Korea and Japan, for example, have long retained tight control of the financial sector during the process of developing their economies. Such models have inspired China to move slowly in the process of developing the financial sector. Financial sector reform has not followed a rigid or comprehensive blueprint, but has been pragmatic and gradual. As will be discussed below, many of the major developments have evolved from small-scale experiments that took place in an environment of decentralized decision making in the early stages of reform. The size and diversity of the country has also played a part in the financial reform process. The emergence of local secondary markets for government securities in the mid-1980s was the forerunner to the establishment of stock exchanges in Shanghai and Shenzhen. The creation of localized interbank markets in selected cities in 1986 is another example of experiments that were subsequently adopted on a wider scale. The creation of Special Economic Zones (SEZs) is a striking example of this form of gradual and experimental reform. Foreign bank branches are permitted in the SEZs and domestic banks are permitted greater flexibility in application of credit quotas and in setting interest rates when operating in the zones. The spectacular economic growth of the SEZs is an indication that greater flexibility and decentralized decision making is paying rewards.

While reform of the financial sector to date has been impressive, major progress has still to be made. The primary focus of attention has been on institutional development. The creation of markets, including the liberalization of the operations of financial institutions, has received less attention. The reason lies in the status of the financial sector at the commencement of the reform process. The monetary sector was at the heart of the macroeconomic control system within the planned economy. The emergence of market-based financial activity was regarded as complementary to this core role. In effect, the authorities sought to retain the reformed financial sector as an essential element in the continued interventionist economic development model. While the political ideology may differ, this is another example of the similarities between China and other Asian nations in the process of financial sector reform. Control overpricing and the granting of credit remains a vehicle for financial allocation in line with government priorities.

The reforms to date have not changed the fact that China remains a bank-dominated financial system. Underdeveloped financial systems are characterized by a dominance of the banking sector (Drake, 1980). However, central bank regulation and supervision of the banking sector in China remains weak. This coupled with government controls and directed lending, has resulted in a large build up on non-performing loans. Much of Asia can also be classified as having bank-dominated financial systems. However, China's banking sector accounts for a much larger share of intermediation than elsewhere in the region, with 90 per cent of all financial intermediation between savings and investment being accounted for through the banks (Lardy, 1998). The absence of a well-developed capital market means that there is little competition for the banks. Bank dominated financial systems also suffer from a tendency to systematically under-price loans and to lend excessively to government preferred firms. The authorities are in a stronger position to control and direct lending in a bank-dominated system compared to borrowers accessing funds through capital markets.

5.4   The banking sector

During the Cultural Revolution all banks in China were incorporated into the People's Bank and, as such, they were protected from competition from both external sources and among each other. Thus, they lacked the necessary incentives that drive the banking sector in free market economies. One of the primary aspects of the reform process to a market system is that most of the responsibility of financing the economy moves from the government budget to the banking system. As such the reform of the financial system, and especially the banking sector, is critical to the overall reform of financial markets and the economy as a whole.

The Banking System

From Figure 5.1 it can be seen that the core of today's banking sector is the central bank, the People's Bank of China (PBOC). Secondly, there are the policy banks administering the state-directed loans, followed by the four enormous state specialized commercial banks, along with thirteen smaller commercial banks. On the periphery, the non-bank financial institutions act as pseudo-banks. The total number employed in China's entire banking industry has been estimated at three million (Hanes and Lindorff, 1998).

The PBOC is responsible for monitory policy and supervision of the financial system of China. The PBOC develops and implements the National Cash Plan, the National Credit Plan, and the National Foreign Exchange Plan. Other important areas include research and draft financial legislation, formulating monetary policies regarding money supply and interest rates, supervising specialized banks and other financial institutions, distributing government bonds, and regulating the securities markets.

The other key players in the banking sector are the four state specialized commercial banks: The Industrial & Commercial Bank of China (ICBC), The Agricultural Bank of China (ABC), the Bank of China, and The People's Construction Bank of China (PCBC). Collectively the four banks employ around 1.7 million people in a network of more than 130 000 branches, hence, in these terms, they are the world's largest. Overall, they control over 10.76 trillion renminbi (US\$1.3 trillion), or 88 per cent of banking assets (Hanes and Lindorff, 1998) (see Table 5.1). Hanes and Lindorf (1998) argue that the sheer size of the four big banks is a measure of large-scale inefficiencies. Whilst this may well be so, Yang (1996) nevertheless argues that having been set up to serve distinct sectors of the economy, they have fulfilled a significant strategic role in China's development. They have helped the government to manage huge investments, and have done so with relatively favourable outcomes – few projects being unsuccessful.

A critical strategic move in banking reform is to free the huge specialized commercial banks from the policy-based, state-directed loans. The formation of the three state council-forged policy banks was aimed at achieving this. In 1993 and 1994 these banks were established with the function of financing long-term projects, import and export, and agricultural infrastructure at subsidized rates. The three were: the State Development Bank (SDB), which is the largest; the Agriculture Development Bank of China (ADBC); and the Export and Import Bank of China (EXIM). Their establishment was meant to liberate the existing four large specialized banks by taking over responsibility for state-directed loans. For example, the State Development Bank is divided into seven business areas: energy, forestry, agriculture, raw materials, transportation, infrastructure, and technology. It advances for purchases of grain, cotton, edible oil, pork, sugar and other farm products. The Agricultural Development Bank has taken over the policy-based affairs of the Agricultural Bank of China, the Bank of China, the Industrial and Commercial Bank of China, and the People's Construction

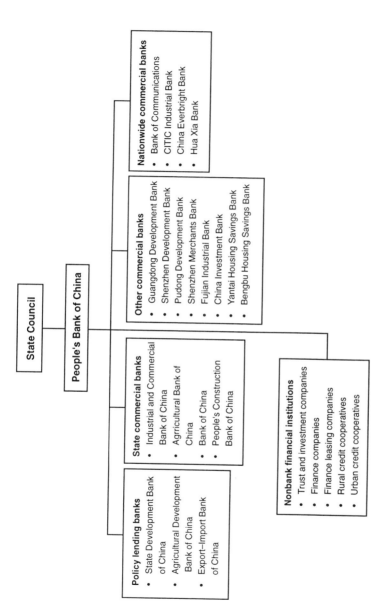

Figure 5.1 **Structure of the Financial Sector**

Bank of China. The Export-Import Bank advances long-term loans for the importing and exporting of machinery and equipment. The move has released state commercial banks to concentrate entirely on commercial banking business. Consequently, the one-time policy lenders now form the hub of a network of state-owned commercial banks overseen by the PBOC.

In addition to the four large state-owned banks, there are thirteen smaller commercial banks – most formed since the late 1980s. Those with national coverage are the Bank of Communications, the CITIC Industrial Bank, the China Everbright Bank, and the Hua Xia Bank, plus a number of regional banks. Recently non-banking financial institutions have entered the fray, including thousands of both rural and urban credit cooperatives that often, in reality, operate like banks. Trust and investment corporations, finance companies and leasing companies have also emerged (Kennedy, 1995; Lake et al. 1994; Girardin, 1997a).

Credit quotas and controls have undoubtedly been a catalyst for the upsurge of informal financial intermediaries – the non-banking financial institutions. The 1980s saw a surge in formation of non-bank and non-state financial institutions. In China, non-bank financial institutions (NBFIs) play an important role in that they provide a service otherwise not available to local communities, individuals and businesses. They developed in response to inflexibilities, inadequacies, and controls in the state-banking sector. These bodies were supported by local authorities and provincial governments who draw funds from them, which is easier than getting loans from specialized banks (Girardin, 1997b). There is no doubt that NBFIs have seen rapid growth, yet their market share is minute in comparison to the immense state banks (Girardin and Bazen, 1998).

The five main types of non-bank financial institutions are trust and investment corporations, finance companies, leasing companies, rural credit cooperatives, and urban credit cooperatives. As they mainly financed the non-state sector, they did not initially compete directly with the banks. However, the most significant recent characteristic of non-bank financial institutions, as identified in a survey by Caprio (1995), is that they now compete with state banks in the loans market, thus, to some degree, they have broken the monopoly of the state banks. NBFIs also suffer from a deficiency of backing from the government in attracting deposits. In addition, the credit plan of the central government and the PBOC does not extend to NBFIs. In this regard, state banks and governments often established NBFIs to sidestep the credit plan.

Many NBFIs are therefore controlled by banks and often make use of the same information, funds and personnel. Consequently, they face

Table 5.1   Top Five Chinese Banks, December 1996 (Rmb million)

	Tier One capital	% change	Total assets	% change	Cap-ital/ assets	Pre-tax profits	% change	Profit/ capital %	Staff	Branches	BIS ratio %
Bank of China	113 992	10.9	2 427 672	7.1	4.7	18 945	22.5	16.62	197 079	15 337	12.5
Industrial & Commercial Bank of China	92 711	10.8	3 629 570	16.8	2.55	5 810	24.4	6.27	560 000	38 000	na
China Construction Bank	45 500	13.7	2 125 302	23.4	2.14	4 833	-21.7	10.62	387 000	11 663	8.15
Agricultural Bank of China	40 052	3.1	1 466 947	19.2	2.73	4 681	8.8	11.69	538 800	65 866	na
Bank of Communications	21 629	7.3	397 883	18.7	5.44	5 782	2.8	26.73	43 357	89	11.25

$ = 8.29 Rmb (12/96). Average inflation 1996 = 8.3%

Source: The Banker, March 1998.

considerable moral hazard, especially as NBFIs are frequently utilized by the controlling organizations to elude supervision and regulation. In all respects there are few laws and regulations pertaining to NBFIs, and those that do are not enforced effectively and not as well as regulation pertaining to state-owned banks (Girardin and Bazen, 1998). Finally, being controlled by less regulation, NBFIs have greater autonomy than banks, and thus they have increased motivation to maximize returns.

During the 1980s, the Trust and Investment Corporations (TIC) came into being. They approximate a cross between a trust company and a development bank. TICs can accept deposits, with a maturity greater than one year, from state-owned enterprises or state banks comparable to a trust company, and invest the funds in approved projects like a development bank. They are not part of the credit plan and thus have no credit ceiling (Girardin, 1997a).

At the end of 1998 there are around 240 TICs in existence, with a little less than 10 per cent of the assets of the financial sector. There were as many as 700 but recent moves to disassociate them from specialized banks has reduced their number. The largest is The People's Construction Bank of China, the biggest non-banking securities house in China. TICs have become one of the most important parts of China's NBFI sector, offering services and financing not offered by the state-owned banks. They are permitted to raise foreign capital, and invest in long-term projects such as infrastructure, power stations, roads, and so forth, but, in the quest for quick returns, have also ventured into riskier investments including property and equities. TICs have had poor oversight and have generally failed to operate on sound commercial terms. Consequently, many have liquidity and asset-quality problems. In October 1998 the second largest, Guangdong International Trust and Investment Corporation, was shut down by the central bank, and the Bank of China was instructed to take over its liabilities. Two smaller operations were closed earlier in the year (*The Economist*, 10 October 1998, pp. 80–4; *Wall Street Journal*, 1998, p. A18).

The thousands of Rural Credit Cooperatives (RCC) have grown in popularity and market share in rural communities. They receive 80 per cent of deposits in rural areas and 25 per cent of savings deposits in urban areas (Girardin, 1997a). Urban credit cooperatives (UCC) have gained acceptance in urban communities in the 1990s. Whilst UCCs are still small compared to the giants represented by the state banks, by the end of 1994 there were 5 229 urban credit cooperatives in China. Their outstanding credit of 132.3 billion renminbi was 3.2 per cent of the total, whilst deposits of RMB 235.3 billion (US$28.42 billion) amount to 5.81 per cent of the whole. They are thus large in number but small in market share. Furthermore, the quality of loan portfolios is generally better than that of state-owned commercial banks (Girardin and Bazen, 1998).

There are a total of three private sector banks that have also commenced operations in recent years in China, the China Minsheng Banking Corporation, the China Merchants Bank and Huaxia Bank. The first public-held bank, China Minsheng Banking Corporation, commenced operation in 1996 in Beijing. The bank is looking to serve the niche market of small to medium-sized businesses, overlooked by the state banks. It is the smallest bank with assets of around RMB 8.2780 million (US$1 million) and is regarded as another experiment in the reform process (Hanes and Lindorff, 1998).

The unified interbank market of China was set up in early 1996. It enables financial institutions and local banks to accept or lend short-term deposits of one day to four months. The combined effect of interest rate stability and development of the interbank market system will facilitate the establishment of a yield curve that in its turn provides the means for a renminbi forward market to be established (*The Banker*, February 1996).

5.5   Banking sector reform in progress

The authorities favour a measured approach to reform concurrently across sectors. They espouse the notion that in the long run measured reform maintains stability. Thus, in a desire to provide a sound banking sector in China, reform has been carried out in a restrained and judicious manner. The policy has been largely successful in maintaining stability. However, it has to be conceded that since the beginnings of general reform in 1978 it has indeed taken a very long time to achieve the measured result of efficiency improvements. The commercialization of the banks is expected to take at least another three-to-five years. In March 1998, Zhu Rongji, former central banker and premier, gave a three-year timeframe for them to be operating independently and to open the banking and financial sectors to the outside world (Rongji, 1998).

Undoubtedly motivated by the Asian crises of 1997–98, which thus far has had little impact on China, the National Financial Work Conference was convened in November 1997 for only the second time since 1949. It is the clearest indication yet of the increased resolve to the commitment and timetable of reform that Rongji and the other leaders attending have made – they agreed on the urgency and importance of financial reforms (do Rosario, 1998).

The undertakings of China's financial reforms in light of the current situation are: to develop new financial institutions and clarify the responsibilities of existing institutions; to replace direct administrative economic controls with macroeconomic levers; and to develop efficient financial markets. Certainly, the banking system has a way to go and needs full and thorough reform. To achieve these objectives the banking sector must dissociate itself from state and political influences and be fully subjected to market forces and competition. Ultimately, China should direct its approach toward free private markets, not regulated and controlled socialist markets.

To accomplish reform in China sound support channels must be in place. Firstly, a dependable, independent, uncompromising, and non-discriminatory legislative system should be assured; secondly, foreign exchange availability and currency convertibility must be implemented; and thirdly, a sound pricing system based on macroeconomics must be designed. Given the general awareness of these obstacles in the administration, it is considered that they will be overcome. A clear step in the right direction was achieved when Chinese banks gained the right to be independent of government and Communist Party officials' interference with the enactment of commercial banking legislation in July 1995. Before this a bank had no power to refuse a local government official who ordered the bank to make a loan to an enterprise even if it were not viable (Roell, 1996). They now have the authority to reject applications for high-risk projects that lack adequate collateral or strong repayment ability. Time will tell as to whether they have the will to do so.

The PBOC must be determined to have a banking system that is competently supervised, with prudential regulations and proper accounting standards and systems for reform to be successful. Nevertheless, the Ministry of Finance is not keen to grapple with the non-performing loan dilemma presently, as it could necessitate a huge rescue package for the banks (this is discussed further under 'Non-Performing Loans').

A dilemma for the central bank is that one of the primary aspects of reform to a market system is that most of the responsibilities of financing the economy move from the government budget to the banking system. Yang (1996) argues that the PBOC may not necessarily have the wherewithal to control the banks effectively. The power to control and allocate funds within the centrally planned economy has moved from the budget to the banking system. If there is an ineffective interest rate policy, and if the bureaucratic power of government is disregarded, the central bank may face control problems.

With legislative and central bank reform presently proceeding, the next requirement is for currency convertibility. Unfortunately, however, it is not universally accepted by the Chinese government that the renminbi must be fully convertible as a pre-condition for project financing (Lake et al., 1994).

Reform must continue, albeit even at a steady pace. As Dorn (1998, p. 131) argues, 'Without free markets and widespread private property, investment decisions necessarily become political decisions'. For reform to continue, the institutional, legislative, legal and financial infrastructure that will support private markets should be fostered. The banking sector must move from making political decisions to making commercial decisions on commercial terms.

Non-performing loans

The Chinese people have a high level of savings with deposits of 4.6 trillion renminbi (US$552 billion) in 1995, providing a cheap source of funds for the banks. The problem is that a high proportion is provided to state-owned enterprises as non-performing loans. Overall, they lack the necessary incentives that drive the banking sector in free market economies. Consequently, a hallmark of this sector of the centrally planned economy in China is a lack of prudent investment management and subsequently the deterioration in the quality of loan portfolios. Investment in collective or private enterprise yields twice as much as do investments in state enterprise, yet, despite this, 75 per cent of the state-bank loan portfolio is invested in state-owned enterprises (Tanzer, 1997). They have a huge bad-debt problem, and a high ratio of non-performing loans. Yang (1996) proposes that the bottom line is not really known. There could be hundreds of millions of non-performing loans – Tanzer (1997) estimates more than US$200 billion and Hanes and Lindorf (1998) US$275 billion. The official figures suggest that such loans account for approximately 20 per cent of total bank credit, other estimates are as high as 40 per cent (Tanzer, 1997). Hanes and Lindorf (1998, p. 1) put it at 30 per cent of last year's GDP and four times the banking industry's entire capitalization'. Furthermore, Girardin (1997b) argues that the state banks are typically poor at resolving the difficulties of asymmetry of information and at monitoring the performance of their borrowers, the state-owned enterprises. They also suffer from some shortcomings in their development. From 1985 to 1994 the equity of the four commercial banks grew at an average annual rate of 13 per cent, which was lower than the growth of their loan portfolio over the same term.

China's central bank branches face interference from government and Communist Party officials in enforcing supervision and setting monetary policy, particularly at a district level. Although the PBOC has maintained relatively tight credit controls to ensure credit flows to deserving or policy projects, district power brokers, through the 2 400 local bank branches, have tended to override the policies of the PBOC and focus on alternate favoured projects. Thus undermining the policies and enforcement of the PBOC. Party officials and local government have held considerable ascendancy over PBOC offices in their districts.

To overcome the non-performing loan predicament could require an enormous bail-out of the banks by the Ministry of Finance. For example the Bank of China, as a state-owned bank, will apply to its owner, the state, to advance the necessary capital to meet the shortfall. There is also concern that the specialized state banks, rather than single-mindedly focusing on efficient and prudent banking business, tend to focus on gaining and advancing credit for their particular sector. This may lead to unnecessary expansion in a sector simply because it is favoured by policy or has pressure applied to it for credit by local power brokers, and thus capital allocation has become inefficient (Yang, 1996).

To unravel the situation will take significant expertise, commitment and resolve, and the development of the appropriate personnel skills and experience to be able to accurately assess loan applicants' ability and willingness to make and maintain loan payments and the quality of relevant collateral offered. This also requires that the borrower can furnish, and that bank personnel are able to properly analyze, meaningful and accurate financial statements and indicators. It may also include a major commercial culture change if there were to be the necessary resolve to thoroughly investigate loan applications. This will require a genuine desire and also support for the necessary shift in culture. A mechanism is needed to ensure that non-performing loans do not recur. Borrowers need to be committed to pay back loans, and lending offices to take loan decisions seriously.

Related to the loan quality issue is the relatively poor performance of the major banks in terms of capital adequacy. The ratio of equity to assets of the four major state banks at the end of 1997 ranged from 2.14 per cent to 4.7 per cent (do Rasario, 1998). This was well below accepted international standards of around 8 per cent.

Credit control

Traditionally the PBOC has strictly administered the state credit control system via the credit quota plan, through which Chinese authorities directed state-credit controls to establish the amount of credit to be prescribed for particular provinces through the four specialized banks, as related to the planning objectives set by government. For example, traditionally the PBOC has relied on direct credit controls to restrain inflation (Cashmore, 1997). To a large extent the system has added to the almost insurmountable problem loan scenario presently faced by the nation.

The formal credit plans and control reduces productivity and allocative efficiency by extending efforts to control credit tightly. Rather than responding to demand, governments seek to enforce, by varying degrees, their priorities in an autocratic, centrally planned environment. For the present, the non-performing loans may be restrained by the relatively high levels of economic growth and the measures of ongoing restrained credit controls. Allowing the economy to grow could also progressively reduce doubtful loans, while increased consumption in rural sectors and increased low-cost housing commerce via reformed mortgage schemes could facilitate lending to more productive sectors (Davies, 1998).

Nevertheless, Schoenberger (1996) maintains that the current credit quota system is damaging for China as it channels 'capital' blindly to state-owned enterprises by way of non-performing loans, forming backdoor subsidies. The decentralized allocation of credit allows the 2 400 local branches of the central bank to extend further loans to SOEs, which brings about greater financial distress.

Significantly, in a bid to overcome the influence of power brokers and local government undermining PBOC policies, as mentioned previously, the central bank has started to remove the responsibilities of the 2 400 local branches of China's 31 provinces and regions. Nine central bank branches representing broad economic regions will be given considerable powers of oversight, beginning November 1998 with the opening of the first in Shanghai. As these branches will represent broad economic regions, the goal is to circumvent the local power barons. (Reuters, 18 November 1998; *The Economist*, 21 November 1998, p. 76).

5.6   Foreign investment

China supposedly encourages foreign financial institutions. However, restrictions are imposed and deprivation occurs through rigorous regulatory control. For example, until recently, no licences were issued to foreign banks to trade in local currency, thus effectively barring them from what is considered an enormous and lucrative market. In late 1997 licenses were issued, but only to four foreign banks. Certainly, despite any political risk that may be involved, foreign banks are keen to get their hands on the billions of dollars in deposits held by the state-owned banks and non-banking institutions. This would undoubtedly supply a cheap source of funds traditionally pegged to the US dollar (Gilligan and Blayney, 1998; Dobson, 1997).

Nevertheless, the permission in December 1997 to conduct renminbi business in Shanghai was a major breakthrough for foreign banks. The initial four that met the prerequisite requirements and named by the People's Bank of China were: Citibank, Hong Kong and Shanghai Banking Corporation, Bank of Tokyo–Mitsubishi and Industrial Bank of Japan. The licenses permit local currency deposits; loans; settlements; security for lending, that is, primarily giving guarantees; bonds issued by the state; and any other business that a bank may have special approval to enter upon. However, as at late 1998, doing renminbi business with domestic local enterprises continues to be prohibited.

Recently new measures were introduced to give foreign banks greater access to the domestic banking sector. These included: the opening of Shenzhen as the second city for renminbi transactions, where twenty-five foreign bank branches have been established; the granting of more licences to foreign banks to conduct local currency banking; and the relaxation of restrictive regulations for renminbi operations of the licensed foreign banks (*Crossborder Monitor*, 1998). Shenzhen was chosen for its close proximity to markets such as Hong Kong, and because the PBOC Shenzhen branch has experience in the oversight and regulation of foreign banks (*Asia Pulse*, 1998).

August 1998 figures indicate that, in total, foreign banks and insurance companies from twenty countries have established 544 offices and 173 branches in China (*Asia Pulse*, 1998). The Peoples' Bank of China data identified 178 foreign operational bodies, six joint-venture finance companies, five wholly owned banks, seven joint-venture banks and one joint-venture investment bank in China. Total capital amounts to 309.6 billion renminbi (US$37.4 billion) and outstanding loans to 226.82 billion renminbi (US$27.4 billion), representing 25 per cent of the market. Furthermore, there are additional representative offices waiting for licences. For example, foreign banks keenly awaiting the further freeing up of the markets include giant US banks Citibank and Bank of America (Qing and Genliang, 1998).

A few years ago Beijing had no foreign financial branches; today 220 foreign financial institutions have offices and fourteen banks are offering services in the capital (*Asia Pulse*, 1998). Shanghai, arguably China's most dynamic city, has sound infrastructure that stands it in good stead to serve as a primary financial hub and has the most liquid financial market in China. The dream is for Shanghai to become a regional centre for international finance to rival Hong Kong, restoring it to its pre-1949 place as the country's financial capital. On the other hand, Dalian is touted as the financial hub for northeast China. Its primary strategic benefit is that it is close to Japan. However, it has seen disappointingly poor acceptance and slow growth for the ten mainly

Japanese foreign banks set up since 1995. To combat the poor acceptance, authorities are suggesting strongly to foreign banks interested in licensing in China that an office in Dalian will be a primary prerequisite to consideration (Yatsko, 1996; Morarjee, 1997).

5.7   The interest rate regime

The traditional policy relating to interest rates aimed to maintain artificially low rates to facilitate the expansion of capital-intensive industries, in particular heavy industry. In a capital-deficient economy – the strategy is known as the heavy industry-oriented development strategy (HIODS). Consequently, the government increased both the savings rates and the loan rates after the commencement of the reform process. The complex framework of rigidly imposed low interest rates is so ingrained in the conventional wisdom and ideals of contemporary Chinese politics and culture, that political leaders are treading carefully. Contrary to conventional economic theory, political leaders see a distorted macro-policy environment in the form of a low interest-rate policy as being absolutely essential. Thus, it is probable that central intervention in the financial market will continue for the foreseeable future (Lin et al., 1996; Girardin, 1997a).

The overall effect of these economic policies and rapid economic growth was brisk money supply growth, with inflation reaching 18 per cent in 1988. Interest rates could have been deregulated at this point but the 'planned system' was reinstated and the central control of credit and the direct control of projects returned, consequently a 'boom-and-bust' cycle followed. Furthermore, because interest rates are below market prices, non-price allocation and other distortions continued unrestrained in the apportionment of credit (Lin et al., 1996).

Currently China faces high real interest rates of around 7 per cent (Joseph, 1998). Over the past couple of years, in an attempt to motivate increased spending and reduced savings, interests rates have been adjusted downward, as can be seen in Figure 5.2. The move is aimed at reducing enterprise financial distress through the reduction of interest charges and to invigorate their investment demand (*Asia Pulse*, 1998). To stimulate lending, in mid-1996 interest rates were reduced for the first time in ten years and the long-term deposit interest-rate subsidy was removed.

The interest rate regime also put pressure on state banks to provide 'value guarantee' accounts, which afforded inflation-protected returns on three-to-eight-year bank deposits. In 1996 the PBOC abolished these accounts (Goldie-Scot, 1996).

The next phase in the reform of the commercial banks' lending

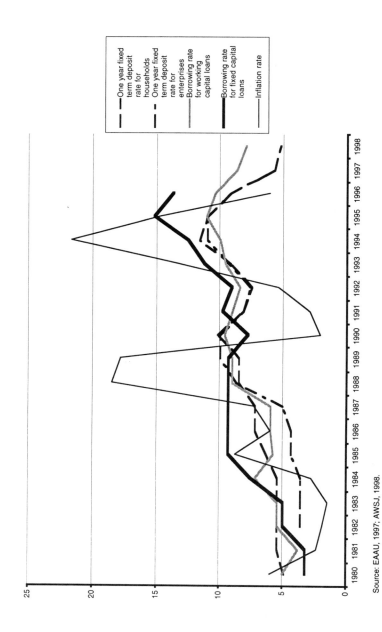

Figure 5.2 **Inflation Adjusted Borrowing Rates: Interest Rates for Term Deposit and Bank Loans and Inflation, 1980–98 (%)**

Source: EAAU, 1997; AWSJ, 1998.

system was announced by the PBOC in October 1997. The maximum term for general working capital loans was extended from one to three years. In addition, the one-year lending rate tumbled from 10.08 per cent to 8.64 per cent. At the same time the one-year deposit rate also dropped from 7.47 per cent to 5.67 per cent. Again in March 1998 the lending rate was lowered from 8.64 per cent to 7.92 per cent and the deposit rate reduced to 5.22 from 5.67 per cent. Furthermore, the government reduced the reserve requirements of the banks from 13 per cent to 8 per cent (*South China Morning Post*, 14 October 1997; *AWSJ*, 25 March 1998). This move appears to have been made in an effort to arrest retarding growth and to support distressed banks by extending their returns.

The complex structure of rigidly set interest rates is aimed at minimizing the cost of savings deposit collection by state banks and to subsidize selective production and investment in the state sector. At the same time interest rates have the capacity of providing a means of indirect monetary control. They appear to be a serviceable instrument for controlling the apportionment of savings and have no real sway on investment. Indeed, whilst bank supervision and loan-loss provisions are deficient, the liberalization of interest rates could well give rise to more risks than benefits. It is also most likely that portfolio quality would plunge acutely if the banks attempted to pass on escalating interest rates to borrowers (Girardin, 1997a).

The People's Bank of China at present decides on the interest rates for loans and deposits, and some commercial banks can lend their money at rates within a certain range. A vital element of the reform dynamic is the move toward purely market interest rates. Interest rates fundamentally need deregulation to stimulate the state banks to conduct their affairs commercially, and to enable the central bank to use open market mechanisms to manage monetary supply.

5.8 The foreign currency regime

In 1949 the government first introduced the renminbi, also known as the yuan inside China. Since that time, foreign exchange and the foreign-exchange rate have been strictly controlled by the PBOC, and has been non-convertible on capital account. The central government sets the official exchange rate, currently essentially pegged to the US dollar. In December 1996 it was first made convertible on current account (DMG, 1997).

Before 1979 China strictly controlled foreign exchange. A quota system was in place that allocated foreign exchange to the state-owned banks. In 1979 foreign trade and foreign exchange started to be decentralized and a foreign-trade retention system also introduced. It gave the right to buy back previously surrendered quotas of foreign-exchange earnings at the official exchange rate. The official exchange rate was roughly 1.5 renminbi per US dollar during 1979–80 (see Figure 5.3), which could not cover the costs of exports as the typical cost of obtaining a US dollar was approximately 2.5 renminbi (Lin et al. 1996).

Furthermore, the Bank of China facilitated foreign-exchange swaps between enterprises that were allowed to swap their entitlement at rates higher than the official exchange rate. The beginning of 1981 saw a dual-rate system adopted. Commodity trade was settled at the internal rate of 2.8 renminbi per US dollar and the official rate of 1.53 renminbi per US dollar continued to apply to other transactions. Restrictions were further relaxed on trading foreign exchange when the 'foreign-exchange adjustment centre' was establishment in Shenzhen in 1985, where enterprises could trade foreign exchange at negotiated rates. By the late 1980s many centres were established and through the centres over 80 per cent of the foreign-exchange earnings were swapped (Sung, 1994).

Finally, China established a managed floating system on 1 January 1994. Consequently, the renminbi devalued from 5.8 to 8.7 per US dollar. Essentially, the unification of the dual-rate system formed a vital step in the reform process. Fortunately, the unification of the rates did not cause major upheaval as most of the trade had been at the higher rate (Huang et al., 1996). The climax of foreign exchange-rate policy reform came in December 1996 when it was first made convertible on current account (DMG, 1997).

Interestingly, until 1993, China essentially had two currencies in circulation: renminbi (RMB) and foreign exchange certificates (FEC). They were introduced to allow foreigners to purchase merchandise in stores that were licensed to conduct transactions in them. FECs sold at a premium of up to 30 per cent on the black market as they gave locals the opportunity to purchase these particular goods also. Even after they were abolished in 1986 they continued in circulation in Beijing until 1993. Finally, in 1994 they ceased to circulate when authorities replaced the official rate with the market rate as previously mentioned (Cheung, 1998).

Foreigners may hold foreign currency in a domestic bank and may transact in foreign currencies with Chinese. However Chinese themselves cannot trade in foreign currencies. Domestic firms who receive foreign direct investment must convert to renminbi, thus increasing the domestic money supply. Hence, the foreign-currency transfers to the government have consequently accumulated from about US$20 billion in 1993 to approximately US$140 billion in 1998.

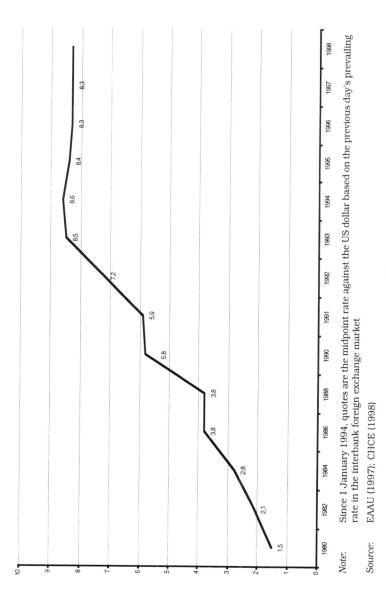

Note: Since 1 January 1994, quotes are the midpoint rate against the US dollar based on the previous day's prevailing rate in the interbank foreign exchange market

Source: EAAU (1997); CHCE (1998)

***Figure 5.3* Exchange Rates, 1980–98 (Rmb per US$1)**

There is strong domestic pressure on Beijing to devalue the renminbi due to the devaluation of other currencies in the region as a result of the Asian crisis, as discussed in Chapter 1. Devaluation will tend to keep exports competitive, as export growth plays an important role in the economy and growth has slowed in most industries. On the other hand, a devaluation could undermine Chinese citizens' confidence in the financial and banking system. Furthermore, it could also spark another round of currency devaluations across Asia. Despite speculation fuelling rumours, as at the end of 1998 Beijing has held on resolutely, and analysts predict it will continue to do so. Beijing has assured the International Monetary Fund that it has no intention to devalue.

As evident from the above discussion, the foreign exchange-rate regime is in a transition stage. By China's own admission, before the convertibility of renminbi can be fully realized, major improvements to the supervisory and regulatory functions of the market are necessary (Rongji, 1998).

5.9   The bond market

China has a small bond market, at less than 5 per cent of the overall money supply. According to ING Barings total outstanding Treasury bills at the end of 1996 amounted to only 300 billion renminbi (US$36.24 billion). Furthermore, there is very little trading and the participants are primarily commercial banks. Today, bond trades are conducted by a computerized system on the Shanghai Stock Exchange, where over 80 per cent of Chinese government bonds are traded, and thinly traded on the Shenzhen Stock Exchange (Roell, 1996).

Bonds proved to be a popular form of investment in recent years. There is a continuing and growing need for government debt financing as infrastructure demands are increasing dramatically, and state-owned enterprises move to restructure and finance capital requirements. As can be seen in Table 5.2, there is plenty of room for growth; China had a ratio of government debt to GDP of 23 per cent in 1995, made up of 5.7 per cent in the form of Treasury-bonds (T-Bonds), and 17.2 per cent external debt. In contrast the next lowest ratio on the list in 1996 was the United Kingdom at 59 per cent (Chen, 1998).

Development of the fixed income market

The first issue of bonds was by the Ministry of Finance to State employees and Chinese institutions in July 1981 as part of an obligatory purchase plan. Purchases did not become discretionary until 1991. This first issue was a modest 4.86 billion renminbi (US$0.59 billion). The Central Promotion Committee for T-notes, chaired by the Finance Minister,

Table 5.2   **Ratio of Government Debt to GDP, 1996**

Country	%
China	23.0
United Kingdom	59.1
Germany	59.9
United States	63.0
Japan	90.1
Canada	97.3
Italy	124.0

Source: Chen, 1998

was responsible for allocation of T-notes to local levels. The trading of bonds was illegal, thus there was no official secondary market. There was, however, limited trading on black markets at discounts to the par value. There were no set instruments and bond interest rates differed depending on who the purchaser was. For example, 5–9 year bonds issued at that time had rates of 8 per cent for individuals, yet institutions received only 4 per cent (Chen, 1998, and Bei et al.,1992).

Before the inception of the secondary market the demand for government bonds was very low. Consequently, bondholders found that notes issued between 1981–87 were not redeemable at their maturity dates and had to be reinvested in new T-bonds. Eventually the secondary market was launched in April 1988 when the State Council approved trading of T-bonds issued in 1985 and 1986 to commercial banks in seven cities. Government-approved over-the-counter markets were developed throughout the country. T-notes were traded at a significant discount, with large price differences across regions. The variation in demand and supply profiles in the two main markets of Shanghai and Shenzhen meant that the same bond traded at different prices in each market. A major problem was that, though the PBOC and the Ministry of Finance published regulatory guidelines in 1988 for the T-bond secondary market, there are no unified regulations in the regional markets.

The trading of all T-notes was approved in early 1990 and secondary trading extended in December when all T-bonds became freely tradable in commercial banks in major cities. In October the Trading Automated Quotations System (STAQS), a computerized trading system linked by satellite, was launched. Finally, in December, the Shanghai Stock Exchange formally opened. With these developments trading suddenly became more active. The volume increased 220 per cent in 1990 and as a result of the increased liquidity prices also gradually increased.

Primary dealers are the main players in the market, now totalling 30, and include both banks and securities houses. Their counterpart in other markets are market-makers. However, at the moment they are really just a central government-approved group of underwriters. Financial institutions have therefore become the underwriters of government securities, replacing the forced allocation method.

Up until 1996 interest rates have been set by the Ministry of Finance, usually at 1 or 2 percentage points higher than the bank deposit savings rate. However, in 1996 limited auctioning was introduced in the primary market-based on the issuing price, where the Ministry of Finance set the coupon, or on the interest rate, where bonds are issued at par. The advantage of the T-bill market is that the PBOC will now get some feedback on market interest rates. As can be seen from Table 5.3, there are a variety of notes issued. However the market is relatively thinly traded and the diversity limited in comparison to markets elsewhere.

A concern of large traders is that there are no bond derivatives available as the bond futures market in Shanghai closed in February 1995. However in the secondary market all conventional transaction types are available. Spot transactions are settled immediately: futures transactions are available (a contract to purchase or sell a bond at a certain future date at an agreed price); and through repurchase agreements, in which an investor sells a bond on a given day and agrees to buy it back in the future at a negotiated price (Chen, 1998).

Table 5.3   **Securities Issued**

Securities Issued by the:

Ministry of Finance	**Enterprises**
Fiscal Notes	Local Enterprise Notes
State Construction Notes	Stocks
Key Construction Notes	Short-term Enterprise Bills
Inflation-adjusted Notes	Internal Enterprise Notes
State planning Commission	**Specialized Banks**
Basic Construction Notes	Key Enterprise Notes
Banking Notes	Negotiable CD

Current problems in the fixed income market

There are a number of problems associated with the bond market at present. Firstly, the market is relatively new and lacks experienced traders. Secondly, the market does not have a fully functioning auction method for issues. Thus, the issuer and not the market effectively sets the rate. There has been an imbalance in the schedule of bond issues and maturities, causing a lack of liquidity as investors cannot necessarily match investment timing. Along the same lines there is a need for standardization, as mentioned earlier. An indication of the volatility of the market at times is the 'Postponement' of enterprise-held bonds.

Recently, more favourable conditions for debt issuance have become apparent in China. This has been largely brought about by improving investor confidence as the country successfully weathered the storm of the Asian crisis. The Ministry of Finance has been working hard to establish benchmarks in dominant international markets and, thus far, it has been the specialized Chinese banks and investment arms of provincial governments involved in the bulk of offshore borrowing. Essentially, the next step in the reform process of the bond market will be to allow enterprises to offer debt instruments directly to the market.

5.10   The role of the derivatives market

Overall, the derivatives market of China has had a bumpy ride since the first commodity exchange was established in Zhengzhou in 1990. In the early to mid 1990s a further 14 opened their doors along with 30 unofficial trading houses dealing in futures contracts and trading 'on everything from government bonds to mung beans,' (*The Economist*, 1995, p. 70). The enthusiasm of speculators was such that the market reached similar volumes as a sluggish day on the Chicago Board of Trade.

Given the lack of experience and sophistication, it is understandable that the Chinese authorities became nervous. Consequently, on 18 May 1995 the T-Bond futures market in Shanghai was closed down, after Wanguo Securities crashed because of excessive speculation. Shortly after dealings in mung-bean futures, both the Zhengzhou and Beijing exchanges were greatly restrained. This lulled the whirlwind trade and the country's experiment in derivatives (Roell 1996). This bout of derivative speculation has been blamed for a rapid rise in commodity prices and consequent upturn in inflation (*The Economist*, 1995, p. 70).

Currently, the largest domestic futures exchange is the China Commodities Future Exchange (CCFE) with about 25 per cent of the market. The government established the CCFE in November 1993 as a pilot program in Hainan. It spanned 29 provinces and had 430 members at July 1997. Initially it listed contracts on white sugar, plywood, natural rubber, palm oil, coffee, cocoa and Chinese government treasury bonds. As at July 1997 there were five contracts listed: natural rubber, palm oil, coffee, cocoa, and malting barley. Cocoa is the most actively traded at present.

China needs a well-run derivatives market

The role of the derivatives market in China is relatively small. Especially limiting is the lack of futures in T-Bonds as discussed above. Nevertheless, derivatives are vitally important to the stability of the financial markets. For example, futures, or forwards and other derivatives for that matter, can be used to fix future prices on commodities, exchange rates or interest rates ahead of the delivery date. Traders can therefore fix in advance the rate of interest they will have to pay, the cost of the raw materials, and how much currency they will receive on their exports. Thus, as China moves toward a free-market economy, derivative markets must therefore become an important focus of future reform efforts. China needs a well-run derivatives market with enforceable regulation and alert, competent supervision. It also needs strong and vigorous clearing-houses to act as the counter-party to transactions, especially given that many of the enterprises have doubtful creditworthiness. As mentioned previously, the combined effect of the development of the interbank market system and interest rate stability will make possible the establishment of a yield curve that will then provide the means for a renminbi forward market to be established.

5.11   The stock market

A well-functioning stock market open to international investors is a common feature for emerging economies in Asia, and is increasingly featured as part of the development strategy of transition economies. But why should this be so, and is this accepted wisdom still dominant in view of the recent Asian crisis? Market economists argue that an open market reduces the cost of capital for economic development and increases market efficiency and hence allocational efficiency. A stock market fulfils two basic functions. The primary function is to provide large-scale direct finance to productive units within the economy. The second function is to facilitate a secondary market in shares, thereby enabling holders of shares to achieve liquidity when desired, or to acquire shares without having to subscribe to new issues. The two functions are not exclusive, but are closely linked. A deep secondary market clearly facilitates the primary function. The lessons of the Asian crisis are still to be interpreted. However, recent actions by Malaysia, for example, suggests that the policy of encouraging large-scale foreign portfolio investment is beginning to be challenged.

The early writings of the development economists placed little emphasis on security market development, but instead emphasized interest rates, banks and money markets (Fry, 1988). The McKinnon-Shaw model that guided much of the development finance literature was developed at a time when security markets in developing countries were generally either very small or non-existent. The increasing importance of stock markets was perhaps underestimated at that time. However, writers such as Drake (1980) and Samuels and Yacout (1981) recognized that fostering a stock market is only part of a wider scheme of reform that is not necessarily restricted to the financial sector of the economy. The regulatory and other factors that impaired the growth of stock markets have gradually been eroded in the process of deregulation. That has been a feature of international financial markets in recent years. China was perhaps slow at security-market development, taking at least ten years from the beginning of the reform era to the establishment of formalized stockmarket trading.

As discussed above the decision to implement formalized stock market trading was the result of a process of experimentation. The first steps towards trading securities were essentially a black market. In the early 1980s the central authorities commenced the issue of Treasury bills that could not legally be traded, but which formed the basis of a black market where the securities were traded at substantial discounts. In the mid-1980s the first issues of bonds and shares by state-owned enterprises appeared. This gave rise to officially sanctioned over-the-counter markets. These developments took place within a background of major ideological debate concerning the acceptability of the ownership and trading of enterprise securities. The pragmatists won through and the Shanghai stock exchange, closed by the authorities in 1949, was reopened for formalized trading in all forms of securities in 1990. This was rapidly followed by the opening of the Shenzhen stock exchange in 1991. Both were opened with technology and trading systems comparable to the most advanced markets in the region. However, the immaturity of the markets and the lack of experience of investors and brokers meant that both exchanges went through a long period of assimilation.

Shares issued by Chinese enterprises take a number of different forms. While all are essentially equity or common stock, there are restrictions on trading and transfers of ownership in certain categories.

State shares are owned by the government and are not listed on the stock exchange, or traded in any other manner while in government ownership. Enterprise shares are owned by other corporations and are also not listed, but can be transferred to other Chinese corporations. Such shareholdings derive from trading and other organizational relationships, as is common in the cross-shareholding system in Japan. Like Japan, these cross-holdings create problems of interpretation and comparison of market capitalization and certain performance measures. The remaining types of shares are termed 'individual shares'. These can be held by the investing community and traded freely when listed on a stock exchange. Individual shares are further categorized as 'A shares' and 'B shares'. 'A shares' are available only to domestic investors and have been the most actively traded securities in the markets. Chinese small-scale investors have taken to the stock market with fervour. A popular image of the Chinese stock markets in the early years were of near riots outside the stock exchange buildings when subscription forms became available for initial public offerings of shares. 'B shares' are available only to foreign investors. A further category is 'H shares' issued by Chinese enterprises, but listed on the Hong Kong stock exchange. The jargon of Chinese markets includes a number of other terms for shares. 'Red Chips' are stocks issued by Hong Kong registered firms which have received significant backing from Chinese institutions. 'China Plays' is another term used for firms from Taiwan and Hong Kong that are listed on their home exchanges but have substantial business interests in China. Both Red Chips and China Plays are not Chinese firms, but rather have significant exposure to China.

Since the opening of the markets, 'B share' activity has been somewhat subdued. Initially it was assumed that foreign investors were waiting to learn what was really involved in holding shares in enterprises that, in many instances, remained majority-owned by the Chinese government. This reluctance to invest existed despite the routine approval for entry to and exit from the markets for foreign investors with trading conducted in Hong Kong dollars in Shenzhen and in US dollars in Shanghai. The failure of the B market is '...one of the bigger flops of China's reform era and a drag on current efforts to reform state-owned enterprises by selling state assets to investors' (*AWSJ*, 29 June 1998, p. 17). The intention of the 'class B' share market was to expose selected Chinese enterprises to the discipline of international capital market activity. This included preparation of accounting reports in accordance with international accounting standards. However, the better firms were permitted to list in New York and Hong Kong, resulting in a less than appealing selection of domestic firms available for foreign investors in China. The lack of appeal of this sector has also created problems for Chinese firms selected for listing in the B market. Price earnings (P/E) ratios of 'B shares' are typically much lower than those of 'A shares'. The P/E ratio is the multiple of the latest earnings per share reflected by current share price. In June 1998 the estimated P/E ratio of A shares was 35, while 'B shares' were as low as seven. Firms raising funds through the B market therefore receive a much lower price compared with firms in the A market.

The problems of the B market are not reflected in overall market activity. The Chinese stock market was the second most liquid market in the world in 1997, as measured by turnover ratio. The turnover ratio measures the value of annual turnover as a percentage of market capitalization. The ratio indicates, on average, how many times each share changes hands in a given period. For 1997 China achieved a ratio of 231 per cent, second only to Taiwan with a ratio of 462 per cent. A typical developed country stock market has a ratio in the region of 50 per cent (IFC, 1998). This suggests that the enthusiasm for share trading in Taiwan has spread across to the mainland. The demand for shares in the domestic market has even resulted in local investors resorting to loopholes in regulations to acquire shares in the B market.

As can be seen in Table 5.4, the number of listed firms in the Chinese markets increased dramatically in recent years. The number of stocks more than doubled in the last two years. This has been matched by a corresponding increase in market capitalization, which almost doubled in 1997. However, given the size of the economy, the number of listed firms is small and the capitalization to GDP ratio remains low. Other emerging markets of the region, such as Malaysia, Thailand and Taiwan, have in recent years reported capitalizations in excess of their GDP. The return on the IFC Chinese market index for 1997 was an impressive 33 per cent. The strength of the market in 1997 is remarkable given the turmoil in Asian equity markets in the latter half of the year. However, the market has had a turbulent history. Major corrections and recoveries in the index has resulted in a very risky environment for stock investors. The annual index returns shown in Table 5.4 and Figure 5.4 range from a loss of 33 per cent in 1994 to a gain of 91.5 per cent in 1996. These figures do not reveal the major swings that have occurred within each year. The volatility of the market may be another factor inhibiting foreign investors from enthusiastically embracing the B market. This is despite the potential diversification benefits that accrue to foreign investors because of the low correlations between the Chinese market and international stock markets (Naughton, 1996).

Table 5.4 China Stock Market Data 1991-98

	1991	1992	1993	1994	1995	1996	1997
Number of Listed Companies	14	52	183	291	323	540	764
Market Capitalization							
In yuan	11 019	105 000	352 934	367 585	349 791	943 981	1 708 630
In US dollars	2 028	18 255	40 567	43 521	42 055	113 755	206 366
Trading Value							
In yuan	4 366	92 177	375 571	840 775	415 580	2 128 478	3 063 656
In US dollars	820	16 715	43 395	97 526	49 774	256 008	369 574
Turnover ratio	–	158.9	164.0	235.2	115.9	329.0	231.0
IFC Global Index							
Number of stocks	–	61	81	117	149	180	195
Share of market cap. (%)	–	91.3	47.3	44.2	58.5	51.8	38.9
P/E ratio	–	–	57.3	20.1	16.7	27.8	34.5
P/BV ratio	–	–	4.8	1.3	1.0	2.1	3.9
Dividend yield (%)	–	–	0.2	2.3	3.2	0.8	1.3
Change in index (%)	–	–	-7.3	-33.0	-12.4	91.5	33.0
Economic Data							
Gross domestic product (US$)	376 617	418 181	431 780	540 925	697 647	815 412	–
Change in consumer price index (%)	3.5	6.3	14.6	24.2	16.9	8.3	–
Exchange rate	5.4342	5.7518	8.7000	8.4462	8.3174	8.2984	8.2796

Source: IFC, 1998

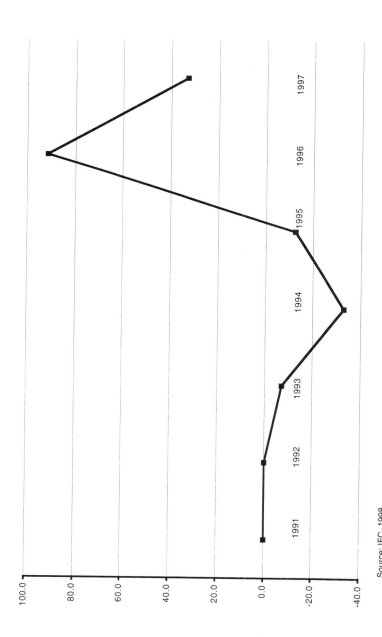

Source: IFC, 1998

Figure 5.4   **Stock Market Data, 1991–98: Change in Index (%)**

5.12　Discussion and conclusions

The bank-dominated financial sector of China has undergone major reform in recent years. The gradualism and willingness to experiment has earned the Chinese authorities much respect. However, it is clear from the discussion above that continued and significant changes remain to be implemented. While considerable development has occurred in the capital market, the financial sector remains dominated by banks. These banks are inadequately supervised by the central bank, which is far from being an independent institution. The financial reporting by major banks is generally regarded as well below international best practice. This is particularly so in relation to the classification and reporting of non-performing loans. In addition, fraud and corruption in banking, while difficult to measure and detect, is generally regarded as being on the increase. The central bank appears unable or unwilling to deal forcefully with this issue, nor the continued practice of inefficient directed lending. The weakness of the central bank may reflect the reluctance of powerful political figures, particularly at provincial and local levels, to relinquish their authority to channel funds to favoured projects and enterprises.

During the transition period, when faced with some of the extremes of inflation, rent seeking, derivative speculation or institutional reform, the authorities often turn back the clock to historic wisdom and reassert controls or autocratic administrative mechanisms to overcome the difficulty. This has the tendency to put the brakes on the reform process, inhibiting vigorous growth and transition effectiveness. In such circumstances any ground gained can be quickly lost.

The state-owned commercial banks face the difficulty that their experience is built around operating and lending in a political environment, and consequently not on commercially viable terms. As a result they generally lack the managerial expertise for a smooth transition to burgeoning commercial banks. In addition to the lack of necessary expertise the banks have the awesome predicament of non-performing loans particularly to SOEs, and while competition is limited there will not be the motivation to develop the technical ability or the incentive for commercially viable operations.

On the positive side, the role of Hong Kong in the future direction of the financial sector reform of China is also important. Increasingly Hong Kong is a significant financial intermediary for China. While direct banking links between the two economies remain limited, it is estimated that as much as one-quarter of Hong Kong's currency is in circulation in Southern China (Hussain, 1997). Most large-scale syndicated loans directed towards mainland enterprises are arranged through Hong Kong, and, as outlined above, the Hong Kong stock exchange is increasingly used as a vehicle for launching successful enterprises into the international capital market.

References

Asia Pulse (1998), 'Profile: China's Financial Services Industry', Asia Pulse Pty Ltd, (commercial intelligence wire) Sydney, August.

Asian Wall Street Journal (AWSJ), Various Issues, Dow Jones Publishing Company (Asia) Inc., Hong Kong.

Asian Wall Street Journal (AWSJ) (1998), 'China Combats Slowing Growth with Cut in Rates', Dow Jones Publishing Company (Asia) Inc., Hong Kong, 25 March.

Asian Wall Street Journal, 25 March 1998.

Australian Department of Foreign Affairs and Trade (1997), *China Embraces the Market: Achievements Constraints and Opportunities*, East Asia Analytical Unit (EAAU), Canberra.

The Banker (1996), 'China's Market Launch', *The Banker*, Vol. 146, No. 840.

Bei D., A. Koontz and L. Lu (1992), 'The Emerging Securities Market in the PRC', *China Economic Review*, Vol. 3, No. 2, pp. 149–72.

Benziger, V. (1998), 'Can China's Gradualist Reform Strategy be Applied in Eastern Europe?', *Journal of Asia Pacific Economy*, Vol. 3, No. 1.

Bonin, J., and P. Wachtel (1997), 'Towards Market-Oriented Banking in the Economies in Transition', New York University, Stern School of Business, Salomon Center Working Paper Series, S-97-2.

Byrd, W. (1983), 'Enterprise-Level Reforms in Chinese State-Owned Industry', *American Economic Review*, Vol. 73, No. 2, pp. 329–32.

Caprio, G. Jr. (1995), 'The Role of Financial Intermediaries in Transitional Economies', *Carnegie Rochester Conference Series on Public Policy*, Vol. 42, pp. 257–302.

Cashmore, N. (1997), 'Work in Progress', *Asiamoney*, Vol. 8, No. 5.

Chen, K. (1998), 'China Closes Two financial Houses, Signaling Resolve to Clean Up Sector', *Wall Street Journal* (Eastern Edition), 24 June, p. A14.

Crossborder Monitor (1998), 'Better Than Nothing', *Crossborder Monitor*, 9 September.

Davies, B. (1998) 'Dinosaurs Lumbering Towards the Real World', *Asiamoney*, Vol. 8, No. 10, pp. 20–8.

Deutsche, Morgan Grenfield (DMG) (1997), 'The 1997 Guide to Emerging Currencies', *Euromoney*, July Supplement, p. 2.

Dobson, R. (1997), 'World Economic Analysis: Country Risk Rankings', *Euromoney*, September; Supplement: World Economic Analysis.

Dorn, J.A. (1998), 'China's Future: Market Socialism or Market Taoism?', *Cato Journal*, Vol. 18, No. 1, pp. 131–46.

doRosario, L. (1998), 'Defusing a Time Bomb', *The Banker*, March, Vol. 148, No. 865, pp. 51–2.

Drake, P.J. (1980), *Money, Finance and Development*, John Wiley & Sons, London.

The Economist, Various issues, London, 335 (7916).

Fry, M.J. (1988), *Interest and Banking in Economic Development*, Johns Hopkins University Press, Baltimore.

Gilligan, P., and S. Blayney (1998), 'How to Establish Joint Venture Banks in China', *International Financial Law Review*, Vol. 17, No. 3, pp. 12–14.

Girardin, E. (1997a), *Banking Sector Reform and Credit Control in China*, OECD Development Centre Studies, Paris.

—— (1997b), *The Dilemmas of Banking Sector Reform and Credit Control in China*, OECD Development Centre Studies, Paris.

——, and S. Bazen (1998), 'An Empirical Study Of Urban Credit Cooperatives In China', *International Review of Applied Economics*, January, Vol. 12, No. 1, pp. 141–55.

Goldie-Scot, D. (1996), 'Promises, Promises', *The Banker*, Vol. 146, No. 843.

Gupta, K.L. (1984), *Finance and Economic Growth in Developing Countries*, Croom-Helm, London.

Hanes, K., and D. Lindorff (1998), 'Can Zhu Rongji Save China's Banks?', *Global Finance*, Vol. 12, No. 5, pp. 22–7.

Huang, Y. (1996), *Inflation and Investment Controls in China: The Political Economy of Central-Local Relations during the Reform Era*, Cambridge University Press, NY?.

Hussain, A.M. (1997), 'Hong Kong, China in Transition', *Finance & Development*, Vol. 34, No. 3, pp. 3–6.

International Finance Corporation (IFC) (1998), *Emerging Stock Markets Factbook*, IFC, Washington.

Joseph, G. (1998), 'A Giant to Stumble?', Reuters News Service, 9 September.

Kennedy, S. (1995), 'Beijing Sheds Some Weight', *The Banker*, Vol. 145, No. 829.

Lake, D., C. Ming and J. Cossette (1994), 'Profile: State Development Bank', *Euroweek*, No. 381.

Lardy, N.R. (1998), 'China and the Asian Contagion', *Foreign Affairs*, July/August, 78-88.

Li, K.W. (1994), *Financial Repression and Economic Reform in China*, Westport, Praeger.

Lin J.Y., F. Cai and Z. Li (1996), 'The Lessons of China's Transition to a Market Economy', *Cato Journal*, Vol. 16, No. 2, pp. 201–31.

McKinnon, R.I. (1973), *Money and Capital in Economic Development*, Brookings Institute, Washington.

Mehran, H., M. Quintyn, T. Nordman and B. Laurens (1996), *Monetary and Exchange Reforms in China: An Experiment in Gradualism*, IMF Occasional Paper 141, Washington.

Morarjee, R. (1998), 'A Financial Hub In The Making?', *The Banker*, Vol. 147, No. 861, p. 96.

Naughton, A. (1996), 'A Factor Analysis of Equity Market Relationships in Asia', *Applied Economics Letters*, Vol. 3, No. 11, pp. 725–8.

Qing, P., and Z. Genliang (1998), 'China Pushing Forward Financial Reform', Xinhua News Agency, 11 August.

Reuters (1998), 'China Opens First Branch of Stronger Central Bank', Reuters News Service, 18 November.

Roell, S. (1996), 'Bank of China's Cultural Revolution', *Euromoney*, London, April 1996, Vol. 324, p. 148.

Rongji, Z. (Premier) (1998), Press Release, Zhu Xinhua News Agency, 19 March.

Samuels, J.M., and N. Yacout (1981), 'Stock Exchanges in Developing Countries', *Savings and Development*, Vol. 4, pp. 217–32.

Schoenberger, K. (1996), 'China's Boomtown is a Bust for Investors, Chicago', *Fortune*, Vol. 134, No. 2, p. 90.

Schwimmer, A. (1993), 'China's Hidden Risks', *Investment Dealers Digest*, Vol. 59, No. 50, pp. 12–17.

Shaw, E.S. (1973), *Financial Deepening in Economic Development*, Oxford University Press, UK.

South China Morning Post, various issues.

Sung, Y.W. (1994), 'An Appraisal of China's Foreign Trade Policy, 1950–1992', in T.N. Srinivasan (ed.), *The Comparative Experience of*

Agricultural and Trade Reforms in China and India, International ICS Press, San Francisco, pp. 109–53.

Tam, O.K. (1986), 'Reform of China's Banking System', *World Economy*, Vol. 9, No. 4, pp. 427–40.

Tanzer, A. (1997), ,Will China Bite the Bullet?', *Forbes*, Vol. 160, No. 14.

Tobin, J. (1969), 'A General Equilibrium Approach to Monetary Theory', *Journal of Money Credit and Banking*, Vol. 7, No. 1, pp. 15–29.

—— (1978), 'Monetary Policies and the Economy: The Transmission Mechanism', *Southern Economic Journal*, Vol. 44, No. 3, pp. 421–31.

Yang, H. (1996), *Banking and Financial Control in Reforming Planned Economies*, Macmillan, UK.

Yatsko, P. (1996), 'Field of Dreams', *Far Eastern Economic Review*, Vol. 159, No. 29, p. 69.

6

Labour Market Developments

Greg O'Leary

This chapter focuses upon labour market developments during China's transition to a market economy. It is suggested that the rationalization of state enterprises and the continued transfer of labour from rural to urban areas, will be the major features shaping China's labour market development. The former will result in increased urban unemployment and the loss of traditional benefits to urban workers, while the latter will add to job pressure in urban labour markets. These suggest the prospect of major social unrest. Several barriers remain to the operation of a flexible labour market, and changes to basic labour institutions will be required. In particular, the transition to a market economy will require industrial relations and trade union institutions appropriate to a market economy. However, reform in these areas has not been successful to date due to the retention by the central government of tight political control.

6.1   Introduction

Labour remains one of the most central aspects of China's transition to a market economy. Without major reform to develop an operational labour market and industrial relations institutions in which employers, employees and the state are appropriately represented, the broader economic reforms, as well as those to industry in particular, remain compromised. Not surprisingly, serious reform of labour institutions, both formal and informal, has gradually gained the attention of Chinese policy-makers, academics, as well as the media. While the delayed attention of the Chinese authorities is explicable in terms of the profound social consequences of serious reform to labour markets, industrial relations and trade unions, the costs of delay have become increasingly obvious in recent years as the social unrest which these tensions have long threatened become more apparent. Developments of late, including: the increased rate of structural change to state-owned enterprises and the massive employee stand-downs which have accompanied them; the rapid expansion of the non-state or '*min ying*' economy; the return of Hong Kong; and the continued outflow of labour from rural areas, have intensified both the social significance of employment issues and government interest in the area. In addition, the slowdown induced by the Asian economic crisis has jeopardized continued robust economic growth, which was expected to provide an increasing demand for labour.

This chapter proceeds as follows. Section 2 conducts an overview of developments in the labour market arising from the process of economic reform, such as that taking place in China. Section 3 conducts an analysis of recent developments in China's labour market. Section 4 outlines how China's industrial relations structures have been evolving in the midst of rapid economic reform. Section 5 focuses upon China's trade unions and the prospects for the development of independent trade unions capable of looking after the interests of workers in the rapidly developing market environment. Section 6 presents the major conclusions from this chapter.

6.2   An overview of economic reform and its impact on labour markets and institutions

The changes taking place in labour issues in China are part of, and central to, a much larger transition, which is reshaping labour throughout Asia. Wherever industrialization has taken place, from the European Industrial Revolution in the eighteenth and nineteenth centuries to Asia in the late twentieth, the role of labour and its relationships to the state and employers has been central to the character and rate of the industrialization concerned. The industrialization in Asia, while different in important respects from its antecedents most notably in terms of its larger scale, faster pace and the technological advantages of 'late industrialization', shares many of their central features, including the imperatives of incorporating those responsible for the production, distribution, servicing, marketing, administration and other aspects of the industrial economy into a new political order which reflects its changed economic underpinning. In Asia, the previous political regimes concerned, based on their agricultural economies, generally allowed for little political expression from their uneducated rural producers. Like most of their western antecedents Asian governments have generally sought to maintain absolutist regimes during the industrialization process, attempting to impose political authority on their industrial workforce as they had on their agricultural predecessors. Like their western counterparts, Asian governments have been accepting that such measures are incompatible with sustained efficiency, rapid technological development and international competitiveness. This process of accepting political change and realignment of political authority is an inescapably fraught one, undertaken with more or less disorder and over a longer or shorter period of time.

As was the case with their European antecedents, the political elites of the industrializing countries in Asia have sought to retain their economic power, which derived initially from their control over agricultural production. Their generally high levels of political authority have secured access for the leadership to the spoils of industrialization, and the central social role played by the family in much of the region has meant that family members of those managing these transitions have also been enriched.

Factors such as cultural homogeneity, political continuity and levels of institutional legitimacy, among others, play a part in determining the ease and pace of this transition to less autocratic political and economic regimes. New political philosophies emerge and aspects of old ones are revived and reinterpreted to assist the management of change and the stability of a new order. The debate over 'Asian values' has been central to the philosophical discussion of these issues in the region. But whatever the impediments to change, similar transitions to societies in which the workforce is more urbanized, educated, mobile, socially resourceful and with higher living standards and greater political independence have had to be undertaken. Conscious recognition of the nature and significance of the transition on the part of those in power is perhaps essential to the process, if major social and political upheaval is to be avoided.

Industrial revolutions have all involved major structural changes not only to the patterns of social and political authority, but also to the relationship between the interests of labour and those of the state. In all cases a stable social order has been underpinned by labour institutions, to a greater or lesser extent, able to articulate the independent interests of the workforce, and to reach an accommodation with the interests of employers and the state.

China's proclaimed ideology during the period of Communist power has expressed the traditional socialist belief that the interests of the workforce and those of the socialist stateemployer are identical. In fact the latter institutionalizes and expresses those of the former (Walder, 1988). With the development of a significant private sector and the marketization of much of the public sector, such a relationship in China is no longer sustainable; nor, without major changes, are institutions such as China's trade unions and industrial relations mechanisms. The difficulty faced by the Chinese government in dealing with these matters is that it continues to retain exclusive political authority, including an oversight of labour institutions, while divesting itself of sole economic authority. The tensions in this very basic dichotomy, tensions which generate discussion of the need for democratic change across a range of issues in China, have continued to mount in the labour area in recent years.

To understand the nature of the transitions affecting labour in China, it is necessary to situate them within this broad context, as a simple recounting of labour-market developments may well obscure the significance of the patterns into which they fall. The mixture of social characteristics that China brings to the process of industrialization, makes its situation particularly significant. Many of the characteristics of China's recent past make its transition more difficult than most. Its vast rural population, authoritarian government traditions, limited international exposure, suspicions surrounding its long-term national intentions and the like have all been suggested as antagonistic to the process. However, its huge resources, its renowned ability to concentrate them for designated national interests, its capacity to generate entrepreneurial activity and the potential of its population to work hard are clearly in its favour.

In the 1990s, Chinese government, party and trade union policy activity and institution-building have gained considerable momentum in attempts to control the existing labour difficulties in most areas of the economy and to prevent more damaging breaches of the industrial order and ultimately of the political order. Labour remains central to the official, but decreasingly pertinent, ideology, since the Communist Party officially rules in the name of the workers. Their tacit support, at least, is required for the maintenance of Communist Party authority. That was a straightforward matter in the past, since the officially defined concept of 'worker' was limited in scope to those in state-owned enterprises (SOEs). The favourable remuneration, tenure, social welfare entitlements and retirement provisions these workers have enjoyed in the past is now increasingly tenuous as the 'iron rice bowl' is being withdrawn and capitalist-like conditions established in these enterprises.[1]

This political balance is also being shifted by the increasing percentage of workers employed outside the SOE system who have a different set of relations to Party, state, employers and trade unions than their SOE counterparts, and whose interests are less obviously enhanced by the existing political order (O'Leary, 1998).

The long-awaited and much-resisted action to reform SOEs to create competitive capitalist-like enterprises that are neither beholden to the state nor dependent on it, finally reached a point of no return with the decisions taken at the 15th Party Congress in September 1997. Implementation of these reforms is scheduled to be undertaken by the turn of the century. But in many areas they had already begun and licence is now given to a variety of experiments to transform SOE property rights, management, financial and social security arrangements, all of which have major implications for labour. In general terms, the state, while resisting formal moves to 'privatize' the SOEs, will allow disparate forms of ownership, including private ownership, and supply financial support less on the basis of perceived national need than market-oriented risk assessment. Many are being allowed to fail, others are encouraged to merge, to find financial support elsewhere, to acquire joint venture partners and the like.[2]

As the 'Asian meltdown' continues to create financial, economic, social and political problems throughout the region, China's economic institutions, and the labour market in particular, have struggled to minimize damage. Reduced foreign investment, more competitive exports from southern rivals, lower retail sales and lower growth may eventually force China to depreciate, despite denials on an almost daily basis, or allow export growth to slow. These effects, when superimposed on high urban unemployment and a massive rural labour surplus, could well be economically and politically destabilizing as they are proving to be throughout much of Southeast Asia. China's economic management during the reform process has been remarkably adroit to date, but is facing its biggest challenge exactly at the time when the most difficult and central component of domestic reforms, the serious restructuring of SOEs, has finally begun.

6.3   Recent labour market developments

The development of a labour market in China, as in other socialist states that have sought to create a market economy, has proved an extremely difficult exercise. In the Chinese case the exercise has been complicated by a vast rural labour surplus, rapid state enterprise reform, minimal social security arrangements, and an income distribution system that was designed for other social purposes. At present it is estimated that the peak urban demand for labour may well be over. A fact which complicates the absorption of the rural surplus which continues to grow.³ Until the 1980s, the Ministry of Labour and its various branches had virtually sole responsibility for urban labour management. Individual enterprises were the recipients rather than the makers of decisions about employment, as well as industrial relations and human resource management. This included the number of workers to be employed, the wages to be paid and the welfare provisions to be made available to employees. Urban labour decisions, moreover, were completely separate from those of the countryside, where labour allocation was undertaken by commune administrators within collectively owned agriculture. The reforms since then have sought to decentralize many of these responsibilities to enterprise level in the case of urban industry to create a market, which will replace the previous system of labour allocation. The complex legislative and administrative changes which are required, continue to be made in order to operationalize this new approach. The incipient market has also partially broken down the separation of urban and rural sectors by allowing millions of rural labourers to enter the cities, albeit with limited employment rights.

As in other areas of Chinese economic reform, the government has, to date, avoided the 'shock therapy' applied in Eastern Europe to reform labour markets, unfolding new elements of market development only after the assimilation of earlier phases. Thus despite the insistent calls, particularly from agencies abroad, to deregulate the labour market and wage structures more rapidly, the government has moved cautiously in allowing sectors of the population to move away from a state planned and regulated environment.

— The most pressing problems for the creation of a labour market remain the absorption of the surplus from the rural sector on the one hand and that from SOE redundancies on the other. There a is a range of equally intractable associated problems including the development of a housing market and a social security system, which are independent of enterprises, to allow the possibility of labour transfer as well as more genuine enterprise. In recent years there has been a slightly more determined approach to these issues, as exemplified by a flurry of legislation, pronouncements and inducements to hasten their development. The World Bank, the ILO and other multilateral agencies as well as the German Ministry of Labour, have been active in supplying international perspective and advice on such issues.⁴

Against this background there has inevitably been a growth in urban unemployment, a trend that is likely to continue for some time. Were it not for government support of various kinds to enterprises, it is estimated by *Workers' Daily* that urban unemployment would be 24 per cent (Forney, 1997a).

Rural industrialization remains the central mechanism for relieving labour-migration pressures in the countryside, though its capacity to do so is likely to be short term. In the longer-term government policies will need to ensure that the labour rights of rural migrants are protected, that their education and skill levels are enhanced, and that those remaining on the land are not the least effective producers.

Government policies reflect the view that rural immigrant labour supplements rather than competes with urban labour – a view not always shared by urban residents who continue to complain of increased crime rates and other social problems which they consider are exacerbated, if not wholly caused, by the rural influx. Urban employees also frequently consider their difficulties in finding work after being laid off or in entering the labour market for the first time in relation to the rural labour influx.

With regard to the rural labour force, the proportion engaged in agriculture continues to decline, down from 80 per cent in 1979 to 70 per cent of the 700 million rural population now. This shift reflects increased agricultural productivity, a growth in surplus labour and rural industrialization (*Xinhua News Agency*, 1998).

The township and village enterprises (TVEs), which have absorbed over 100 million workers during the economic reform period, continue to have a high growth rate, estimated at 15 per cent per annum and creating some 2.24 million jobs annually.[5] There is expected, however, to be an annual increase of some 6.66 million in the rural labour force between 1997 and 2000, by which time it is anticipated there will be 134 million unemployed rural labourers with some estimates putting the surplus much higher.[6] Despite the urban migration and rural industrialization, there remains some 26 per cent of rural labour which is chronically unemployed (*China News Digest*, 1998). The age profile in the countryside is such that the labour supply will continue to grow for the foreseeable future, unlike the urban labour supply.[7] The absorption of surplus rural labour will remain the greatest labour market challenge for Chinese policy makers for many years to come, one made even greater by the government's understandable drive to modernize agriculture and to rationalize township enterprises (*China Daily*, 1997a) – a process which ensures the TVEs are increasingly less labour intensive (*China News Digest*, 1998). The net result is that the stream of surplus labour into urban areas will continue.

Not all of those who remain on the land will draw all of their income from agriculture, as diversification of rural production has affected a significant proportion of agricultural workers. According to a recent survey, the proportion of rural workers engaged solely in farming has dropped to 62.8 per cent (Xinhua News Agency, 1998). The shifts involved for this large sector of humanity have implications for labour markets elsewhere, as its partial incorporation into the export sector constitutes a challenge to the competitiveness of labour and industry generally in the rest of the world. Already some 120 million labourers have left for urban jobs in the largest labour migration in history – a transfer responsible in no small part for China's 'industrial revolution' (Xinhua News Agency, 1998).

In urban areas recent labour market activities have been dominated by the changes to the SOE-operating environment and internal changes, which are responsible for increasing the highly conservative official unemployment figures to 3.1 per cent, or 7.5 per cent (15 million) if those stood down from SOEs are included.[8] The real extent of the 'laid-off' worker problem is difficult to gauge. It is not uncommon to encounter functioning SOEs such as the one visited by the author in December 1997 in a Guangdong Special Economic Zone, which had 3 260 workers on its payroll, made up of some 1 820 retired workers, 1 260 laid-off workers and 180 actually working.

Since the early 1980s the government has been committed to a process of SOE reform which has involved fundamentally transforming them from economic and administrative arms of government planning, to effective actors within an economy subject to market signals. This extended process has involved many aspects, including the encourage-ment of enterprise competition and management and taxation reform, as well as general attempts to improve their productivity. That trans-formation, much delayed by the formidable difficulties involved, was greatly consolidated in 1997 with the implementation of what has been called the *zhua da fang xiao* ('manage the large and let the small go') strategy, and gave rise to the most serious labour consequences to date. Under this strategy the state intends retaining control of some 1 000 of the largest industrial firms, with the rest, some 117 000, being left to survive in the market.

The reforms have been of numerous kinds and have been discussed at length in the Chinese and western press, as has their relationship to finance, social welfare and labour market reforms. The remarkable growth of the Chinese economy since 1978, averaging almost 10 per cent per year in real terms, has been at the expense of the significance, efficiency and profitability of the SOEs, which produced three-quarters of industrial output at the beginning of the 1980s but less than 35 per cent by the mid-1990s. By 1996 more than half of them reported losses and the sector as a whole made a loss (Australian Department of Foreign Affairs and Trade, 1997, pp. 333–40). In areas such as the northeast, where SOEs are of greater employment significance, some two-thirds were reporting losses (Lin et al, 1996, pp. 16–21), and according to some reports there have been massive industry closures. In Shenyang, Liaoning Province, for example, it is reported that 85 per cent of factories have closed in the last two years (*China Labour Bulletin*, 1997, p. 2). In the steel industry, one of the traditional core SOE areas of major employment significance, 22 per cent of the workforce (730 000) is to be cut by the end of the century (*China Womens News*, 1997). The reforms have also included mergers, with 1997 being referred to as the 'second high tide' of mergers after the spurt of 1988 which was halted in the second half of 1989 along with many other aspects of the reform process (Li, R., 1997, pp. 11–16 and Li, J., 1997, pp. 9–12).

Some have merged with foreign firms, some with others in similar or different industries. Bankruptcies have become both more acceptable and more common, with the problems of corporate and financial linkages of the bankrupting firms creating problems for many other enterprises. Five hundred firms have been targeted for state support to ensure their survival as proto-multinational companies to be launched into global markets. In 1997 a large variety of employee shareholding arrangements became commonplace, transforming the property rights of many smaller SOEs into cooperative and/or privatized arrangements. The process has been widely adopted in small and medium-sized enterprises and in some areas the process appears to have been comprehensive.[9] The government's strategy essentially involves maintaining such basic industries as energy, transport, post and communications, metallurgy, machinery, electronics, and auto and chemicals under a measure of state economic authority, while withdrawing from non-basic industries such as consumer goods.

Such developments may have slowed but did not prevent the continued decline in SOE employment. It is estimated that there are now 10 million laid off workers in towns and cities, a situation which obviously places considerable stress on urban social stability and developmental prospects. In addition, official figures suggest some 15 per cent of workers in SOEs are surplus (Huang ,1997), and unofficial figures suggest there is more than 20 per cent labour surplus (Forney, 1997a). Most of the unemployed are young, according to one survey 90 per cent of them being under 34 and 60 per cent under 24. Social resources are also drained by some 25 million people who are in state institutions.[10]

The distribution of this official and unofficial unemployment is highly uneven. There is less in the flourishing southern littoral areas where workers displaced from SOEs are much more likely to obtain some work in the non-state sector, and worse in the old industrial heartlands such as the north east or areas where state industry was established in the 1950s to compensate for uneven industrial distribution or strategic reasons. Parts of Sichuan are notable in this category. The unemployment is also disproportionately female, and females find re-employment more difficult (*China Daily*, 1997c).

Nearly fifty years of 'the iron rice bowl' has produced reluctance on the part of many laid-off workers to settle for the conditions available in the non-state sector. Reports abound of laid-off workers being uninterested in available non-SOE work, with some 72 per cent rating SOEs their first preference for re-employment.[11] The shift to non-state employment is nonetheless taking place at a rapid pace and non-state urban employment, which contributes over three-quarters of the total profit of all industrial enterprises, now accounts for over two-thirds of the workforce (*China Daily*, 1997d). The unemployment figure also does not take into account the rural underemployed discussed above, nor the largest pool of urban people who are without work or without enough work – the *'xia gang'* (those stood down from SOEs because of insufficient available work). More employees than ever found themselves in this situation in 1997, and the decisions of the 15th Party Congress almost certainly ensured that larger numbers were involved in 1998. Some estimates claimed that 50 million workers would lose their jobs as a result of the 15th Party Congress decisions (Bu and Zhang, 1997), and the Chinese Academy of Social Sciences predicted that in 1998 alone 11 million state employees would lose their jobs (Zhao and Wan, 1998).

Perhaps the largest of all restraints on the reform of SOEs has been their role as providers of social services such as housing, health, education, retirement benefits and insurance. These benefits are not portable and are very considerable in relation to those from the non-SOE sector, ensuring that labour transfer is minimal despite the *xia hai* ('leap into the sea') phenomenon where the individual concerned voluntarily opts out of the security of the state sector into the turbulence of the private sector. While work in the non-SOE sector may have higher pay, and in some cases much higher pay, surveys regularly show, as indicated above, that there are many who are still reluctant to forego the security of the housing, pension, health care and tenure of SOE employment.

Continued legislative and regulatory changes were made in 1997, and a range of experiments conducted to develop a system in which the costs of such services are to be borne by three parties: the state, which in practice is mostly the municipal authority; the enterprise; and the individual. In the author's experience, this central enabling set of conditions for a *bona fide* labour market is as yet unevenly and generally poorly developed. Most benefits of this kind, and notably retirement pensions, are limited to employees of state enterprises, though health benefits tend to be generally available to urban workers. There have been claims made recently, however, that national, rather than enterprise, insurance arrangements are expanding rapidly (Zhu, 1997a).

A commercial housing market for more than a small percentage of the population remains many years away, with direct occupier contributions remaining, for the most part, a small fraction of housing costs. Steps are currently being taken throughout the country, however, to increase rental costs to commercial value over a period of years, to persuade employees to buy the housing they have previously had as an entitlement or seek market alternatives.

In terms of employee skill levels and transfer possibilities, government training and retraining provisions, while much improved, are still at an initial stage and genuine job information centres remain relevant for only a small percentage of their potential customers. The large-scale rationalization of SOEs begun in recent years is thus in advance of the administrative changes, which would ensure the maintenance of social services to those displaced. It is not surprising, therefore, that social unrest has been widely predicted as a response to SOE rationalization, and has occasionally been evident in recent years. It is fortunate that the age profile of the urban population is such that the peak demand for employment has passed (Yang, 1996, pp. 17–19), making rationalization of the urban workforce more feasible now than in recent decades. However the influx of rural labour reduces this advantage. The rights of urban citizens relative to those from the countryside have been asserted by municipal authorities who, in some instances, have removed rural workers from urban jobs if they were considered suitable for the urban unemployed. In Xian alone, where there are reported to be 180 000 unemployed workers, 15 000 were employed in positions from which rural workers were 'discharged' (Ma, 1997).

One new labour market issue that appeared during 1997 arose as a consequence of the Hong Kong handover. The large numbers of foreign workers in Hong Kong, particularly unskilled workers, and especially the 160 000 Filipinas working as maids and nannies, remain vulnerable while so many Chinese are desperate for work. The Chinese Ministry of Labour is keen to export labour in the region generally and Hong Kong is clearly a soft target (Bu and Zhang, 1997). Changes to SOE internal incentive structures and to those of other enterprises under less direct government control are also of labour market relevance. Just as the substitution in the rural sector of individual incentives for collective decision making and distribution led to increased productivity, it is intended that expanded personal incentives, or removing the 'eating

from the one big pot' syndrome which embodied egalitarian principles
in the workplace, will produce similar outcomes in urban industrial
enterprises. As in agriculture, however, considerable labour
displacement results.

Consciousness of rising unemployment has led to policies familiar
in the west to redress their social impact, including increased training
to reduce the numbers and raising the generally very low skill levels of
labour market entrants by a proliferation of training[12] and extended
vocational education.[13] The rapidly increased numbers of unemployed
have exposed the low level of skill and efficiency of the workforce
generally. While the least skilled have been most likely to be stood
down, the quality of the workforce has been recognized as in need of
major upgrading (Ma, 1997). Among the more interesting transitions
under way in the Chinese labour market is that being undergone by
the workforce itself. As its traditional ties to the state, employers, trade
unions and each other are replaced by market-induced relations, the
character of the workforce is changing rapidly. By mid-1997 the number
of urban employed in private or self-employment reached 25 million,
an increase of 1.7 million in the first half of the year, while the numbers
in government-funded 'staff and worker' positions in towns and cities
declined by 187 000 to 146.7 million during the same period (*China
Daily*, 1997f). Altogether, it is estimated there are 113.6 million urban
workers in China's non-state sector (*China Daily*, 1997g). The trend
towards employment away from SOEs is evident in the 1996 figures for
urban employment creation in which only 4.4 per cent of the 11.7 million
new jobs were created in SOEs, while 23.7 per cent were in collectives
and nearly 72 per cent in private business of various kinds (*China
Daily*, 1997b). The numbers are indicative of the arrest, and now decline,
of employment in the state sector, and the shift to collective, private,
foreign-funded, joint-venture and other forms of employment (O'Leary,
1998). Even within SOEs the relationships which previously existed
and reflected the socialist foundations of the society are being changed,
by the introduction of production techniques and management practices
more familiar to capitalist societies. The transition in consciousness of
the workforce has also apparently involved embracing the idea of
unemployment as a normal, rather than a shameful, phenomenon, at
least in Liaoning where over two million workers have been laid off
since 1994 (Zhao and Nichols, 1998).

6.4   Industrial relations

The transition to a market economy and the associated restructuring
of labour markets have exerted profound pressures on China's industrial

relations. They have introduced pressures on existing negotiation mechanisms, dispute-resolution procedures, union roles and organization, management practices and the regulatory environment. In short, all institutions and parties concerned with industrial relations have been challenged in ways that continue to threaten the established order. These challenges have been more obvious in recent years with unprecedented numbers of demonstrations and strikes against employers and state agencies by workers, largely as a result of the pressures generated by stand-downs from state enterprises, as well as employment problems in the non-state sector and increased numbers of personal grievances.[14] While many of these activities arise from the parlous condition of SOEs rather than directly from employer–employee relations, they have a major effect on these relations.

Despite the intense pressure now on industrial relations institutions and practices, there have been only minor changes to the role of existing industrial relations institutions. The official trade union has expanded its activities to adapt to the emerging labour market, but substantial changes to its roles within the enterprise have yet to be made.

Industrial relations changes have proved to be among the most sensitive political issues in the broad transition to a labour market and a market economy generally. Industrial relations within socialism have been understood by the governments concerned, at least since the 1920s in the Soviet Union, to constitute an administrative or management issue rather than one involving fundamentally conflicting interests. Unlike capitalist industrial relations where socialists consider capital and labour meet as adversaries in the workplace and reach temporary unstable compromises out of necessity, socialist industrial relations were to reflect an essential harmony of interests between various groups all seeking to enhance the interests of workers. While these perspectives may have seldom been accurate, they are much less so now as a result of the labour market changes outlined above. Contemporary Chinese employers do not always consider their interests in this light, be they in state or private enterprises, and workers do not necessarily see their employers as having interests identical to their own. The institutions established for the conduct of industrial relations during the 1950s to 1970s in China and the rhetoric which surrounds their operation have, however, remained largely unchanged. The exclusive political authority exercised by the Party government in this area, as in society generally, provides an environment that makes the expression of differing interests problematic. The net result has been a great deal of tension in recent years, leading to an increased strike and grievance rate, the formation of independent trade unions which are considered illegal, the imprisonment of labour dissidents and the like. At least since the

Tiananmen debacle of 1989 where independent proto-trade unions were the recipients of some of the harshest treatment by the state, the government has been conscious of the potential of this issue to have wide-ranging destabilizing effects.

The rapid economic growth and transformation of the economic landscape coupled with the labour market changes have also led to vast changes in the nature and conditions of employment in industry. The problems encountered by labour during rapid industrialization, wherever it has occurred, have been visited upon China in abundance. Low pay, poor conditions, long hours, abusive, unfair and illegal treatment, child labour, high accident rates, lack of representation and bargaining power and the hostility of the state to independent worker organization, have all been present in significant sections of China's modernizing project. Many of these problems have been documented in *The China Labour Bulletin,* published monthly in Hong Kong and edited by the labour dissident Han Dongfan. His role in attempting to develop an independent trade union in the Tiananmen Square events of 1989 resulted in his incarceration and now 'exile' in Hong Kong.

It is, perhaps, the politics of the transition which makes it so distinctive in China's case. Unlike industrial revolutions that have preceded it, China's industrialization is occurring at a time when it is also undertaking the transition from socialism to a market economy while retaining the political apparatus of a socialist state. In preceding industrial revolutions, the workforce has invariably found means to express its collective interests and eventually form stable organizations which represent them politically and economically more or less well. Where democratic political environments have accompanied the industrializing project, accommodation has been made by the state to accept the independence and legitimacy of the organized workforce as one of the myriad, but more significant, social actors. In the Chinese case, the corresponding political changes have yet to be made to ensure the interests of labour can be publicly expressed and represented without attracting state repression. Until these changes are made, as they must be eventually, the difficulties currently experienced in this area will, most likely, be exacerbated.

There has been little progress recently in the difficult transition to a form of industrial relations which represents the new interests created by economic reform. Most public attention in the area has resulted from such events as demonstrations and strikes by workers, accidents at work or mistreatment by employers and the like. Events which have arisen, at least in part, because the transition to a new form of industrial relations has not taken place.[15]

There has been little or no progress towards the acceptance of independent trade unions, and little in the activity of the only officially sanctioned body, the All China Federation of Trade Unions (ACFTU), which suggests it will pursue its interests independently of the Party and government. There has been some evidence of independent trade union activity on a spontaneous and sporadic basis as documented in journals such as *China Labour Bulletin* and *China Rights Forum* (particularly the Summer 1997 issue which concentrates on labour issues). While such activity has now been ongoing for some years, the state's resolve to disallow it a voice, despite international calls for it to do so, remains unchanged.

The changes to the roles of the ACFTU reflect the developments in the labour market and changes to enterprise property rights rather than a shift away from its traditional interests in social welfare and productivity. Thus it has expanded its welfare roles in an effort to mitigate the difficulties of the unemployed and those stood down; it has increased its role in training and education; it has extended its coverage in the non-state sectors; it has been active in developing legislative and regulatory restraints on employer abuses; and it has opened some three hundred employment agencies (*China News Digest*, 1997a). But its leadership, at a national level and at every level below to that of the enterprise, remains funded and dominated by the Party government system. It is still commonly the case that enterprise union chairmen are also senior enterprise managers, with responsibilities which compromise, at least from a western perspective, their capacity to represent worker interests independently.

There have been continuing attempts to graft some of the institutions from capitalist industrial relations, such as collective bargaining, onto the fabric of Chinese society, without transforming the underlying political structures. Genuine bargaining between the independent representatives of workers and management on the basis of labour market realities is not yet possible, despite much discussion in union circles of collective bargaining (O'Leary, 1995).

During 1997 there were numerous events of an industrial relations kind which gained attention, including demonstrations in Sichuan where in three discrete incidents laid-off workers took to the streets in open defiance of authority. The first of these demonstrations, described as 'some of China's worst labour unrest since the 1949 Communist revolution', was in March in Nanchong east of Chengdu, where employees at the city's largest silk factory took the manager hostage and paraded him through the city demanding six-months back pay as the manager and his wife were about to leave for a factory-funded tour of Thailand. Workers from other factories joined in a 20 000 strong demonstration in front of the town hall for thirty hours until they were promised back pay. The government conceded to the workers' demands and those from other factories, by arranging further bank loans for the struggling companies (Forney, 1997a).

In August 1997, also in Sichuan, at Dujiangyan, there were a series of protests by laid-off workers who were supporting themselves by driving pedicabs. When severe restrictions were placed on their activities by the local government they protested. The first demonstration was greeted with relative restraint and understanding by the authorities who agreed to reconsider their decision, but in the second and third some of those taking part were beaten, arrested and their pedicabs seized. Other notable mass demonstrations took place in Taiyuan in Shanxi Province, in Hefei in Anhui Province (*China News Digest*, 1997b) and in Wuhan, where over one thousand cab drivers blocked roads with their vehicles for almost six hours.[16] A reading of *China Labour Bulletin* in recent years suggests the incidence, magnitude, and repression of strikes have all increased considerably in recent years.

There have been numerous reports in recent years of worker mistreatment in the foreign-funded sector, which has been the site of a good deal of international attention as a result of major industrial accidents in the last decade. In 1997 international attention was focused on the Nike and Reebok companies' operations in China and elsewhere in Asia, in an attempt by NGOs and others to oblige the company to adopt improved industrial relations practices.[17] These companies moved from Korea and Taiwan in the late 1980s to China and Southeast Asia because of cheaper labour costs, operating a number of factories including, with other shoe companies, what is reputed to be the largest shoe factory in the world. Despite the 'Nike Code' of employment which stipulates the rights of independent unions, the factory is run in military style with employees frequently working 12 hours a day (Chan, 1996).

American and European toy makers developed a code for improving working conditions in their industry in Thailand and China after much international pressure to stop child labour. Industrial relations interest in the foreign-funded sector continues to be broadly focused. However, reports of breaches of the Labour Law and local regulations remain commonplace[18] in the enterprises wholly or partly owned by overseas Chinese or Korean entrepreneurs, whose industrial relations practices have become notorious (Chan, 1996).

There has been legislative development, impressive in its quantity, undertaken by the Ministry of Labour, with contributions by the ACFTU among others, concerning all aspects of industrial relations, including arbitration of industrial disputes, social security, accident prevention and insurance, trade union activity, bargaining and representation, contractual arrangements, workers' congresses and the like.

Implementation at a local level is generally much less convincing as surveys by the ACFTU demonstrate.[19]

6.5   Trade Unions

Just as the institutions and operation of China's industrial relations have been seriously challenged by the transition to a market economy, so have its trade unions which have been unable to develop the ability to represent their members' interests independently. While the interests of the workforce are less closely tied to those of the state, Party and employers, the official trade union remains closely associated with all of these authorities. The tensions in this situation have led to the kind of unstructured and un-institutionalized responses noted above in the demonstrations by those seeking back pay. They have also led to the formation of illegal trade unions, to the detention of 'labour dissidents' and to sporadic outbreaks of protest and violence.[20]

The current dilemma has arisen from the historical roles which have been ascribed to trade unions within socialist societies. China's trade unions, like their Soviet models, sought to fulfil two conflicting roles, representing workers on the one hand and national or government interests on the other (Walder, 1986). It was considered that the fundamental conflict between workers and their employers/managers in capitalist society had been removed by the advent of socialism, and it was no longer necessary to institutionalize adversarial relations between them. All that remained was the reconciliation of administrative difficulties in the workplace and liaison between the workforce and the Party government, which officially acted in their interests. In practice, where conflict occurred, the interests of workers were more commonly sacrificed – an outcome facilitated by the 'official' character of unions and the fact that the Party government controlled their funding and personnel, particularly those at senior levels.

In both the Soviet bloc and China, it is not surprising that over time a degree of cynicism arose among workers about the role and efficacy of trade unions in many instances. The model, nonetheless, was operable while the 'workers' – that is, those in SOEs – received the preferential treatment they did, were not subject to harsh workplace discipline or supervision, and were secure in their employment. As those benefits have been eroded and the relations between employers and the workforce become less compatible, a challenge has emerged for the trade unions to meet new workplace needs or face competition from alternative organizations. To date their existence and role has been protected, particularly since 1989, when incipient rivals for workers' loyalties advocating greater autonomy were dealt with harshly. Throughout the

1990s this policy has been continually reinforced by legislation and practice, despite considerable pressure from both within China and without to allow more independent worker representation.[21] In the last year the unions have been given specific guidelines for ensuring social order is maintained. The difference between Chinese unions and those of most other countries is perhaps nowhere more evident than in this role. During 1997, the Public Security Bureau (PSB) issued guidelines to unions, which included the following injunctions:[22]

> Trade unions must emphasize their work on politics and ideology in the workforce as well as propaganda education. Contradictions among employees and labour disputes must also be handled in an efficient manner and the unions must assist the enterprise directors and party and government leaders to promote public security systems. The union must also coordinate with the PSB, organize 'public order and prevention teams' to protect the internal security and order of enterprises as well as social order.

From within China, with its developing market for labour, more flexible wage rates, more independent and increasingly private management and a wider range of working conditions, the environment is ripe for an organization of workers which is not beholden to the state to represent their interests, protect them against unfair or unacceptable behaviour of both employers and government authorities and argue individual grievance cases. Many of the worst cases of employee mistreatment occur in areas where local authorities, enthusiastic for development, may have little interest in ensuring compliance by foreign, or even domestic, investors with labour regulations. Widespread corruption can only exacerbate this situation. The ACFTU has been undertaking a massive drive to unionize private, particularly foreign owned firms,[23] in large part, it would seem, to 'stabilize' the employment relations in these enterprises. The ACFTU hoped to unionize 40 per cent of foreign-funded firms by the end of 1997 and eventually to unionize 80 per cent of them. Both 'to protect workers' rights' and to forge 'stable labour relations, and mobilize workers to promote healthy development of the enterprise' (*China Daily*, 1997g). While one aspect of this work is an attempt to ensure the regulatory compliance of employers, another would seem to be the prevention of alternative organizations emerging to champion the workers' cause.

During 1997 there were numerous instances of workers organizing outside official arrangements, and in many cases suffering legal penalties as a consequence.[24] In recent years there have been many such examples from both state and private sectors, but as the reforms to SOEs bite deeper there are many more originating in that sector and public calls have been made by labour dissidents for the creation of independent unions to protect these workers (Bruell and Wan, 1998). There were also continuing cases of worker mistreatment. In one case, for example, attention was attracted to a 23-year-old female worker in a Chengdu nightclub who broke her spine when leaping from a window to escape the advances of her boss (Zhu, 1997b).

One result of China's refusal to allow the existence of unions other than the ACFTU, both legislatively and practically, has been the official ostracism of the ACFTU by much of the rest of the world's official union organizations. Much is made of unofficial visits by overseas unionists,[25] visits by delegations from less-developed countries, and travels abroad by Chinese union officials. But since 1989 official relations with the rest of the world have been strained, especially with the International Confederation of Free Trade Unions and its associated organizations, though relations with the ILO have been normalized and a Beijing office established. 'Close rapport' is claimed with trade unions from more than 140 countries, and China proposes a somewhat grand vision in which trade unions everywhere have the right to choose their own development mode and policies – a right with which no foreign trade union or international trade union should interfere. But it has joined no international trade union organizations (*China Daily*, 1997i).

6.6   Conclusion

In general there has been a heightened resolve at central levels to implement a more flexible and more unified labour market. Labour bureaux around the country, along with other agencies, see their roles as introducing urban workers to enterprises rather than assigning them as they did in the past. Mechanisms have emerged for dealing in more orderly ways with the influx of rural labour to the cities. While there remain serious barriers to the operation of a flexible labour market, its basic institutions and the accompanying attitudes have begun to emerge. The determination of the government to rationalize state enterprises, and the continued transfer of labour from rural to urban areas, will continue to be the major features shaping China's labour market development.

In terms of the transition to industrial relations and trade union institutions, which are appropriate to a market-driven economy, the reforms have been much less successful.

The retention by the central government of tight political control has precluded serious reform of either. Industrial relations institutions retain their socialist trappings as do trade unions and their activities. The resulting tensions may well threaten the social order should China's remarkable economic growth falter. Other pressures generated by the transition process, such as high unemployment, large-scale labour migration and the inadequacies of the social welfare system add to the difficulties of the Chinese authorities.

The ability, or otherwise, of China's leaders to maintain economic momentum in the face of these challenges and economic crisis in much of the rest of East and Southeast Asia will determine, to a large extent, whether the social consequences of its labour transition remain as politically non-threatening as they have been to date.

Notes

This chapter is an updated version of a chapter in J.Y.S. Cheng (ed.), *The China Review 1998*, 1998, Hong Kong University Press, Hong Kong.

1 For an example of the establishment of such conditions, see Zhao and Nichols, 1998.

2 See Chapter 3 for further discussion of these developments.

3 See, for example, the discussion by Yang, Xiushi, 1996.

4 See, for example, World Bank Report, 1996: *China: Reform of State Enterprises*, Report No. 14924-CHA, Washington DC, 1996.

5 See Chapter 4 for a fuller discussion of China's TVEs.

6 Yang (1996) cites estimates of up to 186 million surplus rural labourers at the beginning of the 1990s, p. 19.

7 Yang, Xiushi, 'The Current Status and the Current Trend of Change of the Employed Labor Force in China', in Jingxing Sun et al. (eds) *Dangdai Zhongguo Renkou* (Contemporary Chinese Population), China Census Bureau and State Statistical Bureau, Beijing (1992, pp. 602–12, cited in Yang (1996, p. 19), where a 1990 estimate of 186 million is noted.

8 See, for example, *China Labour Bulletin*, 1997, p. 2.

9 In Jiangsu and Zhejiang, it is reported that township firms with assets less than RMB 5 million have completed 'ownership reforms' (*China Labour Bulletin*, 1997, p. 3).

10 To cite but one example from an interview conducted by the author with the Labour Bureau of a Guandong Special Economic Zone in December 1997, where it was claimed that some 60–70 per cent of workers stood down from SOEs found some kind of work, albeit not necessarily full-time or permanent, in the non-state sector. This would seem a very high figure in light of the figures for Guangdong as a

whole, where the private sector is said to have hired only 21.7 per cent of laid-off workers in 1996 and 12.2 per cent in the first half of 1997, despite government incentives being offered to private firms to do so. The interviewees claimed that in areas such as the northeast a much lower percentage were successful. For Guangdong figures, see 'Private sector hires laid-offs', *China Daily*, 1998a, (Internet edition), 10 January 1998.

11 See, for example, the report of an employment fair in Chongqing where 3 000 jobs were made available to laid-off workers from the state sector. Some 10 000 came to the fair but only 600 signed contracts (*China Daily*, 1997b).

12 The introduction of the 'Labour Reserve System' is one mechanism created for this purpose. It was introduced in late 1997 to address the fact that some 50 per cent of all labourers begin work without any training at all, by offering professional training over an extended period (*China Daily*, 1998a).

13 There are said to be some 400 000 vocational education and training institutions throughout the country (*China Daily*, 1997e).

14 Labour disputes rose 73 per cent in 1995 to 33 000, according to the Ministry of Labour, and in 1996 grew similarly (Forney, 1997a).

15 There continued to be extremely high numbers of people killed at work. In the first eight months of 1997 there were 10 434, which was a drop of 4.6 per cent on the previous year. Mining accidents continued to dominate, claiming 6 304 lives during this period (Wu and Zhang, 1997).

16 Tu Guangwen, the alleged organizer of the strike in October 1997, was sentenced to three years in prison, being found guilty of 'gathering a crowd to disrupt orderly traffic'. According to Hong Kong's Information Centre of Human Rights and Democratic Movement in China, many of the drivers had been laid-off from the state sector and had little other chance for employment as the city government banned the vehicles from the city 'to ease Wuhan's paralyzing traffic problems' (Stephens and Zhang, 1998).

17 See, for example, the report released 23 September 1997 by the Hong Kong Christian Industrial Committee and the Asian Labour Resource Monitor.

18 See, for example, the results of an ACFTU survey in Guangdong, summarized in 'Joint-Venture Survey', *China Labour Bulletin*, No 29, 1996, p. 8, where overtime was regularly worked but not paid at overtime rates, where there was no insurance, threats of dismissal were commonplace as were body searches, over half of women workers

had no maternity leave rights and a third did not have legally acknowledged work contracts.

19 See, for instance, 'Labour Law Ignored', in *China Labour Bulletin*, No. 29, 1996, p. 8, citing an ACFTU survey from *Southern Labour Daily*, 21 May 1996.

20 For instances of this see the regular reports in *China Labour Bulletin*. In Shenyang, for example, where large numbers of workers have been laid-off, it is claimed that 'Pensioners, whose children have been sacked and pensions no longer issued, are often seen outside the town hall hoping to petition the mayor, a traditional form of protest in China. There used to be a lot more people protesting... But the workers don't have a chance to gather in big numbers. There are too many plain-clothes police and armed police all over the city. Anyone who gets near the government is quickly surrounded by police' (*China Labour Bulletin*, Issue No. 37, July–August 1997, p. 2, quoting *South China Morning Post*, 9 September 1997).

21 Pressure from within has been resisted strenuously. There are considerable numbers of people being held in prison for long periods for attempting to organize independent trade unions. For accounts of some of their experiences, see, for example, 'China Workers in Prison', *Prison Activist Resource Centre*, <prisondesk@igc.org> (JusticeNet Prison Issues Desk), 3 July 1996, and Forney, 1997b.

22 *Summary of Comprehensive Guidelines for Managing Social Order*, Masses Publishing House, 1997, p. 146, cited in *China Labour Bulletin*, Issue No. 37, 1997, p. 4.

23 *China News Digest*, 1998.

24 *China Labour Bulletin* records such instances regularly.

25 See, for example, *China Daily*, 1997h, where there is a report of a 12-day conference in Beijing with union leaders from ten French-speaking African countries. The moral drawn from the meeting was the need for international unity.

References

Australian Department of Foreign Affairs and Trade (1997), *China Embraces the Market: Achievements Constraints and Opportunities*, East Asia Analytical Unit (EAAU), Canberra.

Bruell, S., and G. Wan (1998), 'Chinese worker claims police detention to prevent protest', *China News Digest*, 5 January 1998.

Bu, Q., and R. Zhang (1997), 'Chinese labour to replace Hong Kong workers', *China News Digest*, Internet edition), 25 September 1997.

Chan, A. (1996), 'Bootcamp at the shoe factory, where Taiwanese bosses drill Chinese workers to make sneakers for American joggers', *Washington Post*, 'Outlook', November 3, 1996.

China Daily (1997a), (Internet Edition), 27 December 1997.

—— (1997b), 'Jobless need to broaden outlook', (Internet edition), 16 December 1997.

—— (1997c), (Internet Edition), 19 November 1997.

—— (1997d), 'Market Economy Changes Job Patterns', (Internet edition), 24 December 1997.

—— (1997e), (Internet Edition), 6 November 1997.

—— (1997f), (Internet Edition), 1 November 1997.

—— (1997g), 'Union officials vowing to protect workers' rights, (Internet edition), 26 December 1997.

—— (1997h), 'Trade Unions vow unity', (Internet edition), 22 November 1997.

—— (1997i), 'Trade Unions pledge non-interference', (Internet edition), 28 November 1997.

—— (1998a), 'Private sector hires laid-offs', (Internet edition), 10 January 1998.

—— (1998b), 'New system eases labour market pressure', (Internet edition), 10 January 1998.

China Labour Bulletin (1997), July–August, 'Unemployment redefined', Issue No. 37.

China News Digest (1997a), 'Union plans to help laid-off workers', (Internet edition), 30 November 1997.

—— (1997b), 'Laid-off workers protest in the streets of Hefei', (Internet edition), 11 December 1997.

—— (1998), 'Official trade unions pledge to defend private sector employees', (Internet edition) 1 January 1998.

China Womens News (1997), 'China to slash workforce by 22 percent', 24 November, cited by Reuters in *China News Digest*, 20 December 1997.

Forney, M. (1997**a**), 'We Want to Eat', in *Far Eastern Economic Review*, Internet edition, 26 June 1997.

—— (1997b), 'Dissonant Dissent for their beliefs', *Far Eastern Economic Review*, (Internet edition), 5 June 1997.

Huang, Y. (1997), 'Country has to face unemployment challenge', in *China Daily*, (Internet edition), November 1997.

Li, J. (1997), 'Cooperative Shareholding System: Enterprise Ownership with Chinese Characteristics', *Beijing Review*, September 22–28, 1997, pp. 9–12.

Li, R. (1997), 'Second high tide of the merger of enterprises', *Beijing Review*, 22–28 September, pp. 11–16.

Lin, X. et al. (1997), 'Liaoning: guoyou gaige feng-yu jiancheng, (Liaoning: The trials and hardships of SOE reform)', *Liao Wang (Outlook Weekly)*, Vol. 661, pp. 16–21, cited in *China Labour Bulletin*, No. 38.

Ma, L. (1997), 'Xi'an laid-off workers get help', *China Daily*, (Internet edition), 18 October 1997.

O'Leary, G. (1995), *Zhongguo guoyou qiye: Yizhong zhuo you chengxiao de hetong zhedu* (China's state enterprises: One significant result of the contract system) *Guoji Laodong Yanjiu yu Xinxi (Studies in International labour)* Beijing, China, 1995, pp. 18–20. A summary of this article appeared in *Zhongguo Laodong Bao (China Workers' Daily)*, 14 November 1995.

—— (1998), 'The Making of the Chinese Working Class', in Greg O'Leary (ed.), *Adjusting to Capitalism: Chinese Workers and the State*, ME Sharpe, New York, pp. 48–74.

Stephens, P. and R. Zhang (1998), in *China News Digest*, (Internet edition), 22 February 1998.

Walder, A.G. (1986), *Communist Neo-traditionalism: Work and Authority in Chinese Industry*, University of California Press, Berkeley.

World Bank Report (1996), *China: Reform of State Enterprises*, Report No. 14924-CHA, Washington DC.

Wu, L., and R. Zhang (1997), 'Unions plan to help laid-off workers', *China News Digest*, 3 November 1997.

Xinhua News Agency (1998), cited in *China News Digest*, (Internet edition) 4 January 1998.

Yang, X. (1996), 'Labor Force Characteristics and Labor Migration in China', in Gregory K. Schoepfle (ed.), *Changes in China's Labor Market: Implications for the Future*, US Department of Labor, Bureau of International Labor Affairs, Washington, pp. 13–44.

Zhao, H., and G. Wan (1998), 'Forecast 98: High growth, 11 million jobs cut, public deflation', *China News Digest*, 8 January 1998.

Zhao, M., and Nichols, T. (1998), 'Management Control in State-owned Enterprises: Cases from the Textile Industry', in O'Leary (1998).

Zhu, B. (1997a), 'State set to push social insurance across country', *China Daily*, (Internet edition), 28 November 1997.

Zhu, B. (1997b), 'China watches woman's case', *China Daily*, (Internet edition), 1 November 1997.

7

The Interdependence of Trade and Foreign Direct Investment in China During the 1990s

Chung-Sok Suh
Jung-Soo Seo

This chapter focuses upon international trade and foreign direct investment (FDI), which have been the engines of growth for China since the adoption of its 'open door' policy in the late 1970s. With rapid growth of trade during the 1990s China has experienced surpluses in its trade balance, which are structural in nature and primarily accounted for by the coastal provinces. The country has also emerged as a major recipient of global FDI flows. It is argued that both of these are related and should be considered in the context of business strategy adopted by foreign multinational enterprises (MNEs). An analytical framework is provided to show the nature and extent of interdependence between trade and FDI in China.

7.1   Introduction

Since the 'open door' policy was adopted in 1979, international trade and foreign direct investment (FDI) have been the engines of growth in China. Export demand has been an important source of demand, and FDI filled important gaps in technology, management, and marketing networks in the export market. Before the 'open door' policy, China's international trade was 10 per cent of GDP, which was one of the lowest in the world. By 1995, however, it had reached a level above 40 per cent, roughly equivalent to that of other East Asian economies in the early 1980s.[1] This is a remarkable achievement considering the large size of the economy, and that China is a formerly planned economy where self-sufficiency was pursued for almost 40 years. Table 7.1 shows the changes in the trade/GDP ratio in China.

The increase in trade and FDI inflows in China in the 1990s has generated considerable global interest, including that of scholars in the field and policy makers. No other developing economy's growth has resulted in such an impact relating to world trade and FDI flows. In 1993 China became the second largest host country of FDI in the world, and by the year 2020 China's share in world trade is estimated to reach 10 per cent (World Bank, 1997, p. 31). The effects of such increases in trade and FDI flows on both the Chinese economy and its trading partners warrants the focus of research attention. However, these relationships need to be examined in a different framework from the conventional model, as China's major trading partners and investors are located in the same region and most of the existing theoretical explanations have been put forward from the Western countries' point

Table 7.1 **Total Exports, Imports and Trade/GDP Ratio (100 million Yuan, and %)**

Year	GDP	Exports	Imports	Trade/ GDP ratio[a] (%)
1978	3 624.1	167.6	187.4	9.7
1980	4 517.8	271.2	298.8	12.6
1985	8 989.1	808.9	1 257.8	22.9
1987	11 954.5	1 470.0	1 614.2	21.5
1988	14 922.3	1 766.7	2 055.1	20.7
1989	16 917.8	1 956.0	2 199.9	24.6
1990	18 598.4	1 985.8	2 574.3	29.8
1991	21 662.5	3 827.1	3 398.7	33.4
1992	26 651.9	4 676.3	4 443.3	34.2
1993	34 560.5	5 284.8	5 986.2	32.6
1994	46 670.0	10 421.8	9 960.1	43.6
1995	57 494.9	12 451.8	11 057.1	40.9
1996	67 559.7	12 576.4	11 557.4	35.7

a   (Exports + Imports)/GDP
Source: *China Statistical Yearbook*, 1997

of view. Although there have been some attempts to explain such relationships, the analyses of the recent changes in trade and FDI flows, and the interdependence between them, have received relatively less attention despite their importance in the world economy.

The principal aim of this chapter is to survey recent developments in China's trade and FDI, and analyze their interdependence. A different framework for explanation is suggested, incorporating the unique features of the Chinese economy and also the business systems of its major trading partners and investors. Sections 2 and 3 survey the recent trends in China's international trade and foreign direct investment respectively, including their regional, industry and country distributions. In section 4 a simple econometric model is established to identify major determinants of FDI flows into China, and the results from doing so are discussed. Section 5 analyzes the interdependence between trade and FDI flows in China, suggesting a different framework of analysis. Concluding remarks are presented in section 6.

7.2   Recent trends in China's trade

Since the opening of the economy, exports and imports have increased at a rapid pace. However unlike most other developing economies that suffer from chronic current account deficits and accompanying debt problems, China has, remarkably, managed to turn its trade balance into surplus during the 1990s. Table 7.2 shows the trade balance for China since 1970. Although the size of the surplus is expected to decrease further in the near future, reinforced by the economic crisis in East and Southeast Asia that began in 1997, this trade surplus is regarded as a structural phenomenon, not a temporary upsurge for a short period of time.[2] An important question therefore arises – 'what are the causes of these massive current account surpluses?'

From a macroeconomic point of view, the savings rate of higher than 30 per cent in excess of domestic investment would be the first candidate as an answer. However, China also experienced a net increase of capital inflows, in both portfolio investment and FDI. Therefore, a conventional explanation comparing the savings and investment rates following a simple macroeconomic model may not be sufficient. Some alternative explanations are suggested in section 5.

Table 7.3 shows the regional distribution of exports, imports and trade balance. As shown in the table, there is a high degree of regional disparity in the sense that the coastal region approximately accounts for 85 per cent of the trade and 78 per cent of the trade surplus. In this region Guangdong province is particularly important, accounting for approximately 40 per cent of total exports and imports and 65 per cent

Table 7.2 **Trade Balance of China (US$, billion)**

Year	Exports	Imports	Trade Balance
1970	2.26	2.33	−0.07
1975	7.26	7.49	−0.23
1978	9.75	10.89	−1.14
1980	18.12	20.02	−1.90
1985	27.35	42.25	−14.90
1986	30.94	42.91	−11.97
1987	39.44	43.21	−3.77
1988	47.52	55.27	−7.75
1989	52.54	59.14	−6.60
1990	62.09	53.35	8.74
1991	71.84	63.79	8.05
1992	84.94	80.59	4.35
1993	91.74	103.96	−12.22
1994	121.01	115.61	5.40
1995	148.78	132.08	16.70
1996	151.06	138.84	12.22

Source: *China Statistical Yearbook*, 1997

of the trade surplus. This high degree of concentration suggests several important questions, including 'Apart from its proximity to Hong Kong, are there any structural differences between Guangdong and other coastal provinces?', 'Will other coastal provinces achieve high export growth as industrialization deepens in China?', 'Are there any spill over effects from the fast export growth of Guangdong to other provinces and regions?' and 'Will industries be relocated to other regions and provinces when wage rates in Guangdong increase?' It is beyond the scope of this chapter to answer all these questions.[3] However, a careful analysis of the pattern of FDI in Guangdong province and other coastal provinces and regions enables us to answer some of these questions, and is elaborated upon further in section 5.

Table 7.4 shows exports and imports by commodities. As might be expected, the pattern of China's trade reveals the typical pattern of a fast growing developing country with an abundance of cheap labour. Exports are concentrated in the textile and footwear industries, which are the most important sources of the trade surpluses. On the contrary, deficits are recorded in more capital- and technology-intensive products, mainly from machinery and electric equipment industries. Nevertheless,

***Table 7.3* Exports and Imports by Province in 1996 (US$, billion)**

Province	Exports	Imports	Balance
Major Coastal Provinces			
Guangdong	59.971	52.046	7.925
(Share of Guangdong)	(39.6%)	(37.5%)	(64.8%)
Shanghai	13.135	14.757	−1.622
Jiangsu	11.954	10.324	1.630
Shandong	9.992	8.098	1.894
Fujian	8.451	7.431	1.020
Zhejiang	8.664	5.766	2.898
Liaoning	7.300	6.272	1.028
Beijing	5.067	9.865	−4.798
Tianjin	4.682	5.476	−0.794
(Share of Major Coastal provinces)	(85.5%)	(86.4%)	(77.5%)
Other Provinces			
Hebei	2.338	1.832	0.506
Shanxi	1.736	0.420	1.316
Inner Mongolia	0.491	0.517	−0.026
Jilin	1.081	1.395	−0.314
Heilongjiang	3.026	1.292	1.734
Anhui	1.306	1.085	0.221
Jiangxi	0.776	0.417	0.360
Henan	1.404	1.073	0.332
Hubei	1.414	1.685	−0.271
Hunan	1.330	0.667	0.663
Guangxi	1.387	1.027	0.360
Hainan	0.400	1.553	−1.153
Sichuan	1.798	2.124	−0.326
Guixhou	0.380	0.233	0.147
Yunnan	1.007	1.193	−0.186
Tibet	0.019	0.147	−0.128
Shaanxi	0.985	0.837	0.148
Gansu	0.279	0.332	−0.053
Qinghai	0.110	0.096	0.014
Ningxia	0.163	0.061	0.102
Xinjiang	0.369	0.819	−0.450
National Total	151.066	138.838	12.228

Source: China Statistical Yearbook, 1997

Table 7.4 **Value of Imports and Exports by Category of Commodities (Customs Statistics, US$, billion, 1996)**

Commodities	Exports	Imports	Balance
Live Animals & Animal Products	4.184	0.954	3.230
Animal & Vegetable Oils, Fats	0.382	1.695	−1.313
Food Beverages, Liquor, Tobacco	5.076	2.410	2.666
Minerals	7.372	9.233	−1.861
Chemicals and Related Products	8.427	10.413	−1.986
Plastics, Rubber & Related Products	4.421	10.251	−5.831
Leather and Related products	5.388	2.563	2.825
Wood and Wooden products	2.053	1.571	0.482
Paper, Pulp and Related products	1.025	4.236	−3.211
Textile Materials and products	**34.969**	**16.683**	**18.286**
(Share of Textile industry)	(23.15%)	(12.01%)	
Footwear, Headgear etc.	8.545	0.456	8.089
Gymsum, Cement, Ceramic glass	2.639	1.012	1.627
Pearls, Precious metals and stones	1.278	1.049	0.229
Base Metals and Related Products	10.407	12.671	−2.264
Machinery, Electric equipment	**31.065**	**49.028**	**−17.959**
(share of Machinery & Electric equipment)	(20.56%)	(35.31%)	
Transportation Equipment	4.181	5.350	−1.169
Optical, medical and precision instruments	5.187	4.644	0.543
Others	10.379	1.213	10.266
Total	**151.066**	**138.838**	**12.228**

Source: China Statistical Yearbook, 1997

with the exception of the animal, vegetable oil industry and the footwear industry, the differences between exports and imports at the industry level are not conspicuous. This suggests that the degree of intra-industry trade is quite high apart from the two industries mentioned above. Both horizontal and vertical intra-industry trade co-exists. For example in the electric and electronic industries, horizontal intra-industry trade occurs when China exports low-quality finished products while importing high-quality products. However, there exists a high degree of vertical intra-industry trade in the export processing industry which imports parts and intermediate products and exports the final goods.

Table 7.5 shows China's trade pattern by trading partners. On the surface the pattern is markedly different from the experiences of neighbouring economies such as South Korea and Taiwan, in the sense that the share of the US is rather low at less than 20 per cent. The share of Asia in China's overall trade was over 60 per cent in 1996. During the industrialization process of its neighbouring economies such as Japan, South Korea, Taiwan and Hong Kong, the share of exports to

Table 7.5 **China's Foreign Trade with Major Trading Partners (Customs Statistics, US$ billion, (%), 1996)**

Region (Country)	Exports Value	Share	Imports Value	Share	Balance
Asia	**91.247**	**60.4**	**83.444**	**60.1**	**7.802**
Hong Kong	32.906	21.7	7.828	5.6	25.078
Indonesia	1.428	0.9	2.280	1.6	−0.852
Japan	30.875	20.4	29.184	21.0	1.691
Malaysia	1.371	0.9	2.244	1.6	−0.873
The Philippines	1.015	0.7	0.372	0.3	0.643
Singapore	3.749	2.5	3.601	2.6	0.148
South Korea	7.511	5.0	12.482	9.0	−4.970
Thailand	1.255	0.8	1.890	1.4	−0.635
Taiwan	2.803	1.9	16.182	11.7	−13.380
Africa	**2.567**	**1.7**	**1.464**	**1.1**	**1.103**
Europe	**23.867**	**15.8**	**27.656**	**19.9**	**−3.788**
Belgium	1.043	0.7	1.023	0.7	0.020
UK	3.201	2.1	1.881	1.4	1.319
Germany	5.845	3.9	7.324	5.3	−1.480
France	1.907	1.3	2.240	1.6	−0.333
Italy	1.838	1.2	3.246	2.3	−1.408
Netherlands	3.539	2.3	0.919	0.7	2.620
Russia	1.693	1.1	5.153	3.7	−3.461
Latin America	**3.121**	**2.1**	**3.608**	**2.6**	**−0.487**
North America	**28.302**	**18.7**	**18.725**	**13.5**	**9.577**
Canada	1.616	1.1	2.570	1.9	−0.954
US	26.686	17.7	16.155	11.6	10.530
Oceania	**1.962**	**1.3**	**3.936**	**2.8**	**−1.974**
Australia	1.673	1.1	3.434	2.5	−1.761
New Zealand	0.231	0.2	0.403	0.3	−0.172
Total	**151.066**	**100.00**	**138.838**	**100.00**	**12.228**

Source: *China Statistical Yearbook*, 1997

the US was much higher especially in the initial phase of the export expansion. In this regard, it is important to take into account the role of Hong Kong as an entrepot in China's trade. The ratio of re-exports to total exports with Hong Kong declined since the early 1950s, but increased after 1979 when China opened its economy to foreign trade and investment. Currently more than 20 per cent of China's exports head for Hong Kong, most of which are re-exported to other destinations. Yet, the proportion of imports channeled through Hong Kong is much lower, creating a huge imbalance in trade with Hong Kong. This also partly explains the huge deficits with Taiwan and South Korea. If exports via Hong Kong are included, the share of the US in China's exports would increase further. This massive trade surplus has been a major concern to the US, creating trade conflicts between the two countries. On the other hand the trade balances with the European countries show a more diversified pattern, if Russia is excluded, although Europe's share is rather similar to that of the US.

7.3 Upsurge of FDI in the 1990s

Although FDI inflows to China showed a similar growth rate as the trade volume in the 1980s, they increased much faster in the 1990s.[4] In 1993 China became the second largest host country of FDI flows in the world, and FDI has continued to increase rapidly since then. Table 7.6 summarizes the utilization of foreign capital in China since 1979. A number of observations can be made from the table. Firstly, there exist large discrepancies between the contracted value and the actual flow of foreign capital. With foreign loans most of the differences can be explained by the lags between the times of agreement and the actual flows.[5] For FDI, on average, only one third of the contracted values are transferred in reality. Secondly, in the 1990s, FDI flows have exceeded the flows of foreign loans. Considering that loans are generally channeled through official routes, private flows of funds, however, have become much more important in the 1990s as private firms gained confidence in the Chinese economy. Thirdly, the average size of the contracted FDI has been continually increasing in the 1990s. In the 1980s, small and medium-size investors from Hong Kong and Taiwan, with the culture and language proximity, have been the first group investing in Guangdong and Fujian. As investors from other countries gained confidence in the Chinese economy, FDI inflows from other countries, especially Japan, have increased relatively faster and the average size has increased accordingly.

Table 7.7 shows the distribution of FDI and foreign loans in each province in 1996. As shown in the table, foreign loans showed a rather

Table 7.6 Utilization of Foreign Capital (US$, billion)

Year	Total		Foreign Loans			Foreign Direct Investment		
	Cont[a]	Actual[b] Value	No.[c]	Cont[a]	Actual[b] Value	No.[c]	Cont[a]	Actual[b] Value
1979–83	23.978	14.438	79	15.062	11.755	1 392	7.742	1.802
1984	4.791	2.705	38	1.916	1.286	1 856	2.651	1.258
1985	9.867	4.647	72	3.534	2.688	3 073	5.932	1.661
1986	11.737	7.258	53	8.407	5.014	1 498	2.834	1.874
1987	12.136	8.452	56	7.817	5.805	2 233	3.709	2.314
1988	16.004	10.226	118	9.813	6.487	5 945	5.297	3.194
1989	11.479	10.059	130	5.185	6.286	5 779	5.600	3.392
1990	12.086	10.289	98	5.099	6.534	7 273	6.596	3.487
1991	19.583	11.554	108	7.161	6.888	12 978	11.977	4.366
1992	69.439	19.202	94	10.703	7.911	48 764	58.124	11.007
1993	123.273	38.960	158	11.306	11.189	83 437	111.436	27.515
1994	93.756	43.213	97	10.668	9.267	47 549	82.680	33.767
1995	103.205	48.133	173	11.288	10.327	37 011	91.282	37.521
1996	81.610	54.800	117	7.960	12.670	24 556	73.276	41.880

a Total amount of foreign capital to be utilized through signed agreements
   and contracts
b Total amount of foreign capital actually used
c Number of projects
Source: China Statistical Yearbook, 1997

Table 7.7 Amount of Foreign Capital Actually Used by Province (US$, billion, 1996)

Region	Foreign Loans	Foreign Direct Investment Value	Share of Nat. Total (%)
Major Coastal Provinces			
Guangdong	1.504	11.754	27.9
Shanghai	0.897	3.941	9.6
Jiangsu	0.279	5.210	13.1
Shandong	0.238	2.634	6.3
Fujian	0.051	4.085	9.9
Zhejiang	0.114	1.521	3.7
Liaoning	0.154	1.738	4.2
Beijing	0.168	1.553	3.8
Tianjin	0.084	2.153	5.2
(sub-Total)	(3.489)	(34.589)	(82.1)
Other Provinces			
Hebei	0.087	0.830	2.0
Shanxi	0.061	0.138	0.3
Inner Mongolia	0.158	0.072	0.2
Jilin	0.166	0.452	1.1
Heilongjiang	0.276	0.567	1.4
Anhui	0.230	0.507	1.2
Jiangxi	0.023	0.301	0.7
Henan	0.260	0.524	1.2
Hubei	0.418	0.681	1.6
Hunan	0.012	0.745	1.8
Guangxi	0.118	0.663	1.6
Hainan	0.108	0.789	1.9
Sichuan	0.190	0.441	1.0
Guixhou	0.311	0.031	0.1
Yunnan	0.010	0.065	0.2
Tibet	0.002	–	0.0
Shaanxi	0.041	0.326	0.8
Gansu	0.131	0.090	0.2
Qinghai	0.009	0.001	0.0
Ningxia	0.044	0.006	0.0
Xinjiang	0.219	0.064	0.2
Provincial Total	**6.362**	**41.878**	**99.4**
Ministries and Other Department	6.307	0.256	0.6
National Total	**12.670**	**42.135**	**100.0**

Source: *China Statistical Yearbook*, 1997

even distribution across the provinces. FDI, however, is concentrated in the major coastal provinces and region, with a share of 82.1 per cent of the national total. As was the case with trade flows, Guangdong attracted the largest share of 27.9 per cent. However, each province's ranking in terms of FDI volume does not deviate much from that in terms of trade volume.

The major investors in Guangdong are the small-scale manufacturers from Hong Kong and Taiwan, while the major investors in Fujian are from Taiwan. For example, the firms established by FDI from Hong Kong employ approximately six million workers, which is approximately equivalent to the population of Hong Kong itself. This is easily explained by the geographical and cultural proximity. FDI in other regions show a more diversified pattern in terms of their source countries.

Tables 7.8 and 7.9 show the distribution of FDI in each industry published in the *China Statistical Yearbook* (1997). As might be expected, manufacturing industry and real estate, and public utilities industries attracted most FDI in 1996. As for the source country distribution,

Table 7.8 **Contracted Foreign Direct Investment by Sector in 1996 (US$, billion)**

Sector	No. of Projects	Value
Farming, Forestry, Animal Husbandry, Fishery and Water Conservancy	812	1.139
Industry	18 280	50.486
Construction	387	2.001
Transportation, Postal and Telecommunications Services	196	1.599
Commerce, Catering Services, Material Supply and Marketing	1 655	2.347
Real Estate, Public Utilities and Services	1 961	12.851
Tourist Hotels	81	0.291
Health Care, Sports and Social Welfare	128	0.354
Education, Culture and Arts	63	0.171
Scientific Research and Polytechnic Services	124	0.175
Others	950	2.154
Total	24 556	73.276

Source: China Statistical Yearbook, 1997

Table 7.9 Source of Foreign Capital actually used by China in 1996 (US$, billion)

Region (Country)	Total	Foreign Loans	FDI and Other
Total	**54.804**	**12.669**	**42.135**
Asia			
Hong Kong	20.873	0.021	20.852
Japan	6.097	2.405	3.692
Macao	0.606		0.606
Malaysia	0.460		0.460
Singapore	2.247		2.247
South Korea	1.566	0.062	1.504
Thailand	0.328		0.328
Taiwan	3.482		3.482
Europe			
UK	1.400	0.098	1.302
Germany	1.131	0.612	0.519
France	0.921	0.496	0.425
Italy	0.343	0.173	0.169
Netherlands	0.155	0.029	0.125
Spain	0.430	0.409	0.021
North America			
Canada	0.480	0.142	0.338
US	5.051	1.607	3.444
Oceania			
Australia	0.199	0.004	0.194
New Zealand	0.022	0.022	
International Organisations			
World Bank	1.880	1.880	
Asian Development Bank	1.102	1.102	

Source: *China Statistical Yearbook*, 1997

Hong Kong was the largest single source of FDI. Japan was the second largest investor country in 1996, showing a quantum leap from its relatively low position in the early 1990s. This may be due to the bursting of Japan's bubble economy in the early 1990s, and also the cautious decision-making process in Japanese firms. As the domestic economy stabilized, and confidence in China was established, the globalization efforts of large Japanese enterprises increased, resulting in increased investment in China.

No official statistics of any detailed industry distribution of FDI, including that within the manufacturing sector, are published by the Chinese government. Table 7.10, however, reports a more detailed industry distribution of the stock of FDI in China, compiled in Taiwan from 1992 survey data. The survey results suggest that Japanese FDI stands out in the services and construction industries, accounting for approximately 65 per cent of the total stock of FDI. FDI from other major source countries show that a similar proportion has gone into manufacturing industry. As might be expected, the majority of FDI from Hong Kong and Taiwan flowed into light industry whereas manufacturing FDI from the US and Japan went more into capital-intensive industry.

7.4   Determinants of FDI in China

In a previous section it was noted that exports and imports from Guangdong accounted for nearly 40 per cent of the country's total. Why does Guangdong export so much? Furthermore, the trade surplus in Guangdong amounted to 65 per cent of the country's total in 1996. Why then does Guangdong not import as much? The explanation can be found in its link with FDI. In 1996 Guangdong attracted 30 per cent of the total FDI inflows to China. In fact all the provinces with high trade growth attracted high levels of FDI. Is there then any difference between Guangdong and other provinces?

Before addressing these specific questions, we start with more general questions. What characterizes the relationship between trade and investment in China? What motivates FDI and what are its effects on trade? In this section the determinants of FDI are examined, and the relationship between trade and FDI will be addressed in the following section.

The framework used for the FDI analysis is that of Dunning's OLI paradigm (Dunning 1977, 1981), which outlines three necessary conditions for FDI: ownership advantage; internalization advantage; and location advantage. Of particular interest are the location advantages possessed by China in attracting FDI. In earlier work Suh and Seo (1998) and Sung (1995) argue that two types of FDI flowed into China concurrently: the first to make use of low-cost labour, and the second to explore the huge market in China. Sung (1995, p. 62) confirms this and reports that the first group tended to involve small-scale, labour-intensive manufacturing industry, and the second type larger and more capital- or technology-intensive manufacturing and services

Table 7.10 **Industrial Distribution of the Stock of FDI in China: 1992 Survey Data (%)**

FDI Source	HK	Taiwan	US	Japan	Sing-apore	Others	Total
Industry							
Agriculture and Forestry	1.62	0.80	1.33	2.07	1.53	4.35	1.80
Manufacturing	59.13	76.72	73.71	33.93	61.61	72.34	62.12
Processed Foods	2.72	8.09	7.71	1.43	15.64	7.56	4.13
Beverages & Tobacco	1.18	0.86	5.77	0.07	1.32	1.57	1.33
Textiles	9.59	7.92	3.23	1.15	4.41	4.92	7.95
Wearing Apparel	5.98	5.12	2.24	4.12	2.29	1.82	5.14
Leather Products	2.15	1.78	1.46	0.74	0.46	1.82	1.91
Wood & Bamboo Products	1.25	3.31	1.11	2.84	3.45	3.68	1.85
Paper Products	1.93	1.39	1.74	0.32	0.54	2.41	1.75
Chemicals	1.88	1.72	8.72	0.74	2.13	1.79	2.13
Chemical Products	2.01	3.64	4.75	1.32	7.43	2.60	2.44
Petroleum & Coal	0.15	0.05	0.39	0.00	1.38	0.68	0.20
Rubber Products	0.41	1.43	0.69	0.05	0.05	0.54	0.51
Plastic Products	5.44	9.35	2.23	0.69	4.36	8.40	5.59
Non-metallic Mineral Products	5.22	2.51	5.82	1.36	6.39	5.29	4.68
Basic Metals	1.18	0.85	0.66	1.85	0.45	2.21	1.24
Metal Products	2.83	5.25	6.94	1.07	1.09	2.62	3.13
Machinery	1.10	3.59	3.13	2.34	1.54	2.99	1.75
Electrical Appliances	9.47	9.37	9.42	3.87	6.75	9.23	9.40
Transportation Equipment	1.07	1.86	3.00	3.11	0.21	7.17	1.91
Precision Instruments	0.83	0.81	0.59	0.39	0.63	1.11	0.80
Miscellaneous Products	2.71	7.82	3.57	0.95	1.10	3.93	3.27
Services and Construction	39.25	22.48	25.50	64.01	36.86	23.13	37.09
Total	100	100	100	100	100	100	100

Source: Chung, 1996, p. 10

for the domestic market. Whereas Hong Kong and Taiwan invested in both types of projects, developed countries such as the US and Japan tended to concentrate on the second type.

Given that foreign firms have the ownership and internationalization advantage for FDI, they will then conduct FDI in a country in which sources of location advantage are best for the foreign firms' production. The literature in the field suggests the following functional relationship between inward FDI flows and several variables representing location advantages:[6]

$$\text{FDI} \;=\; f(\text{market size, wage cost, cost of capital, degree of openness, competitiveness, human capital, stability, ...})$$

As FDI is motivated by the size of market, or proximity to a potentially large market, real GDP per capita is used to capture the market opportunity, while alternative measures such as population and GDP of the host country are also considered. Usually the wage bill accounts for a significant proportion of the total production costs in a labour-intensive industry. Hence, foreign firms are also attracted by the availability of cheap labour in China. The real wage index is used in order to see how sensitive FDI is to changes in wage costs. Higher interest rates make capital borrowing more costly, thus included in the model is the Chinese user cost of capital which should be negatively related to FDI inflows. As discussed in section 2, China has achieved a remarkable growth of exports since 1979, and this consequently has increased its openness as measured by the trade/GDP ratio. Not only does the openness of an economy indicate the trade regime operative, but it also represents the dynamic nature of the economy.

The exchange rate affects FDI in various ways. It affects the competitiveness of the host country's exports. Furthermore, there exists a wealth effect of a lower real value of domestic currency arising from informational imperfection in the capital market, which is associated with FDI inflows (Froot and Stein, 1991). Thus, we include the exchange rate of the Chinese Yuan to the US dollar adjusted by relative price levels, to obtain the real exchange rate. Human capital provides some attractiveness to foreign firms, especially when the objective is to improve productivity. The primary school enrolment rate is used as a proxy for the availability of human capital. Finally, the inflation rate is also included to indicate the macroeconomic stability of the host country, which also indicates the competitiveness of China's exports.

Thus, our econometric model is implemented in a log linear form and estimated by using the ordinary least squares method over the period 1980–96.[7] However, in order to avoid simultaneity problems, the regressors are lagged by one period. As the variables are expressed in logarithmic terms, except the SER dummy variables, the estimated coefficients are the partial elasticities of inward FDI with respect to each of the variables.

$$LFDI_t = b_0 + b_2LGDP_t + b_2LWAGE + b_3LOPEN_t + b_4LPS_t + b_5LCPI + b_6LRXCR_t + e_t$$

The expected signs of the coefficients are $b_1 > 0$, $b_2 < 0$, $b_3 > 0$, $b_4 > 0$, $b_5 < 0$, and $b_6 > 0$.

The results obtained from two different models, the full model (Model 1) and the most preferred model (Model 2) are presented in Table 7.11. Several points are worthy of emphasis. Firstly, it seems that inward FDI flows to China during the period was primarily to exploit market opportunities (GDPP), as indicated for both Model 1 and Model 2. Similar results were obtained when alternative measures of market opportunity variables, GDP and population, were used. Secondly, the real wage index (RW) was of the expected negative sign, but not significant in Model 1 and only marginally so, at the 10-per-cent significance level, in Model 2. This lack of significance can be interpreted in two ways, in addition to the fact that the real wage index was based on all firms in China including state-owned firms. Firstly, it implies that China's labour market has a surplus of labour supply so that increases in the real wage are important but, to date, have only had a marginal impact on inward FDI flows. Secondly, what matters to foreign firms is not the mere level of real wages but productivity-cum real wage. Human capital, the primary school enrolment ratio (PS), is not significant, with an unexpected negative sign.[8] Thirdly, the impact of the real exchange rate (RXR) is important to FDI inflows in China. Not only did the coefficient have the expected sign, but it also revealed a very high elasticity. Hence the real exchange rate increased the competitiveness of China's exports, attracting export-oriented foreign firms wishing to take advantage of China as an export platform, through either simple assembly or sophisticated value chains, and fitted in well with the globalization strategies of MNEs. This attractiveness is reinforced by the wealth effect arising from the low value of the Chinese Yuan, making it relatively easy for foreign firms to finance their projects in China.

However, it was not statistically supported that macroeconomic stability (INF) and the interest rate in China have had a negative impact on FDI.[9] Finally, the SER dummy variable is positive and highly significant, implying that a more liberal investment regime, and extensive investment opportunities in China arising from changes in inward FDI policy, are more conducive to inward FDI.

Table 7.11　**Estimation Results**

Variables	Model 1	Model 2
Constant	−16.5934	−23.3499
	(−1.5542)	(−5.4134)
LGDPP(−1)	7.0814	6.4008
	(3.5230*)	(5.242409*)
LRXR(−1)	6.7065	5.6789
	(3.7224*)	(5.247894*)
SER	0.5231	0.7572
	(2.0894)	(5.026262*)
LRWI(−1)	−4.2338	−3.1383
	(−1.8875)	(−1.8629***)
LINFL(−1)	−0.0623	−0.0904
	(−0.8273)	(−1.3937)
LPS(−1)	−1.3570	−0.3363
	(−1.0072)	(−0.6783)
Adjusted R^2	0.9861	0.9870
S.E.	0.1535	0.1485
AIC	−3.4442	−3.5248
F−statistic	143.2636	213.7974
DW stat	2.3541	2.3408
RESEAT	0.6332	0.1894
LM(2)	3.9547***	1.5565
ARCH(2)	3.1206***	0.1989
JB Normality	0.5048	0.5163

Note:　*, ** and *** indicate statistical significance at the 1%, 5% and 10% levels respectively.

The figures in parentheses are t-values.

Sources of data: IMF (1997), *International Financial Statistics Yearbook*, Washington DC.

7.5　The trade effect of FDI

In the previous section two types of FDI were distinguished in order to identify its determinants: market oriented (demand-driven) FDI; and trade oriented (cost-driven) FDI. However within the cost-driven FDI further distinctions can be made according to the structure of business systems and their behaviour, as their trade effects would be different.

When a firm adopts a global strategy as part of its efforts to reduce costs and serve its international customers, its value chain is divided into various sections and the firm looks for the ideal production location for each segment of the value chain.[10] Japanese firms' investments in East and Southeast Asia in the 1990s are a good example. As the most important location advantage in China is low labour cost, the segment of the value chain that will move to China would be heavily labour intensive whether that is final assembly, production of parts, or intermediate products. In this case, vertical integration takes place between the home and host countries.

The effect of this global strategy on the trade pattern will be different, however, depending on the nature of business systems in the home and host countries. This may take the form of intra-firm trade, or intra-industry trade. Although there are many common features in the business systems in East Asia, there exist substantial differences among them. Both Japanese firms and Chinese family businesses (CFB) rely more on outsourcing, whereas Korean firms tend to keep most of the value chain within their system (Whitley, 1994, pp. 64–84). However, the relationship between the parent firm and the subsidiaries producing parts and intermediate products is different in the Japanese and Chinese business systems. The competitive advantage of Japanese firms arises from their long-term stable relationship with the related firms, whereas CFB maintain their competitive advantage by minimizing their long-term commitments and maximizing flexibility. Most of the CFB usually produce only one segment of the value chain, and are interrelated with other firms that produce other parts of the value chain.

Therefore, the trade effect of cost-driven FDI will be different depending on the business strategy in the home country. When a Japanese firm moves part of its value chain overseas, it will tend to increase intra-industry trade between the home and the host countries. As the firm will continue to use the parts or other intermediate products from the firms in the home country, with whom a long-term relationship is maintained. The adoption of a global strategy by a large Korean firm will increase intra-firm and/or intra-industry trade depending on how the subsidiary is established. On the other hand, the relocation of CFB overseas may increase intra-industry trade in the short run, but it will tend to decrease over time. In order to increase their flexibility, and the opportunity of a quick turn-over, the firms may decide to outsource among local firms, and the firms producing parts and intermediate products might decide to move together. In this case, trade between the home and host countries will decrease.

Table 7.12 shows the changes in sourcing behaviour of Taiwanese FDI in China during the 1990s, which confirms this argument. According to the table, the degree of local sourcing by Taiwanese firms

Table 7.12 **Changes in Sourcing Behaviour of Taiwanese FDI in China, 1992–95 (%)**

Study and Sample Size	Yen, Lin & Chung) (1992) (n = 431)	Industrial Federation (1994) (n = 317)	Industrial Federation (1995) (n = 285)
Sourcing Behaviour			
Purchases of raw material, components, and parts (%)			
From Taiwanese (or parent) firm	71.4	47.2	36.2
From local Chinese firms	16.0	29.8	40.2
From local Foreign firms	4.8	11.4	10.0
From a third country	7.2	11.6	13.6
Purchases of machinery and equipment (%)			
From Taiwanese (or parent) firm	85.7	73.0	68.5
From local firms	7.4	17.0	18.3
From a third country	6.2	10.0	13.2

Source: Chin, 1996, p. 16.

in China increased substantially in the 1990s. Sung (1995, p. 63) also reports that some heavy and capital-intensive FDI from Taiwan entered China to support their labour-intensive export industries set up in China. For example, the textile and clothing industry moved to China at an earlier stage, and the chemical and machinery industries followed later to supply raw materials and spinning machines to Taiwanese firms producing such textiles and clothing.

Cost-driven FDI can thus be further divided into two types, according to their effect on trade: Locally Networked FDI (LN-FDI) and Globally Networked FDI (GN-FDI). Table 7.12 indicates that FDI from Taiwan has changed from GN-FDI to LN-FDI. GN-FDI will increase exports of parts and intermediate products to the host country from the home or other third countries. On the other hand, LN-FDI will not increase intra-industry imports for the host country, as far as it outsources from local firms. Despite the decrease of final goods exports from the home country, GN-FDI will not change the overall exports of the home country substantially and might even increase them (Hirsch, 1976). However, LN-FDI will decrease the exports of the home country and increase over time the exports of the host country significantly, especially if it is export-oriented.

In summary, market-driven FDI will decrease the import of the final good but increase the import of parts and intermediate products. Overall, its effect on trade is not clear a priori. If market-driven FDI is attracted by high trade barriers, and a lower degree of protective measures are applied to intermediate products, it may worsen, relatively, the trade balance. GN-FDI not only increases the exports of the host country, but also increases the import of parts and intermediate products as well. Most of Japanese manufacturing FDI in Southeast and East Asia in the 1990s falls into this category. LN-FDI can increase the host country's exports without increasing imports significantly, while deteriorating the trade balance of the home country relatively.

Having discussed the framework relevant to the Chinese economy, we now turn to the effect of FDI on trade in China. Table 7.13 shows the share of imports and exports by foreign-funded firms in total trade. Several important observations can be made. Firstly, the share of FDI-related trade is increasing in almost all of the provinces. Within two years, from 1994 to 1996, the share of FDI-related trade for the whole country increased from 37 per cent to 47.3 per cent. The increase is much more obvious in exports, from 28.7 per cent to 40.7 per cent. Secondly, the share of FDI-related exports showed marked provincial variations between the coastal provinces and the other provinces. Whereas the share of FDI-related imports do not show much variation across the provinces. Thirdly, even within the fast growing coastal provinces, the shares of FDI-related exports in Guangdong, Fujian and Tianjin are much higher than those in other coastal provinces. This is not surprising considering that FDI from Hong Kong and Taiwan is concentrated in Guangdong and Fujian.

Currently, all three types of FDI, market-driven FDI, GN-FDI and LN-FDI, co-exist in China (Chin, 1996, pp. 12–23; Sung, 1995, p. 63). Most of the FDI from the US and Europe belongs to the first category. FDI from Japan and South Korea falls into the first and second categories. FDI from Hong Kong and Taiwan are changing from GN-FDI to LN-FDI. In section 2 we questioned why China has experienced sizeable current account surpluses along with a large inflow of FDI. An analysis of FDI from Hong Kong and Taiwan helps provide an answer.

Most FDI from Hong Kong and Taiwan is now mainly LN-FDI. As previously explained this type of FDI tends to increase the exports of the host country and decrease those of the investing countries. Chung (1996) argues that the massive increases in the trade surplus of China have been, in fact, a transfer of the surpluses from Hong Kong.[11] Therefore, it is not surprising in China that FDI-related exports have been increasing faster than FDI-related imports, and that the share of FDI-related imports are relatively lower in Guangdong than in other

Table 7.13   Imports and Exports of Foreign-Funded Firms by Province (Share of Total Trade, Imports, Exports by Province)

	Total			Exports			Imports		
	1994	1995	1996	1994	1995	1996	1994	1995	1996
Total for all Provinces	37.04	39.10	47.30	28.69	31.51	40.71	45.79	47.65	54.45
Major Coastal Provinces									
Guangdong	44.73	49.02	54.43	37.25	43.63	51.18	53.07	55.46	58.17
Shanghai	37.73	43.31	53.31	26.75	30.59	41.47	48.41	56.39	63.84
Jiangsu	42.05	43.31	54.48	29.70	29.18	42.41	55.71	61.15	68.45
Shandong	36.16	37.18	47.07	24.42	28.10	38.55	51.79	48.03	57.59
Fujian	59.94	54.62	59.97	47.22	43.71	53.26	72.92	67.33	67.60
Zhejiang	25.15	24.06	32.79	15.94	13.41	23.36	43.22	43.86	46.97
Liaoning	35.47	38.03	46.93	31.43	33.42	43.55	39.29	43.42	50.88
Beijing	16.59	15.36	21.62	12.79	11.91	19.50	18.42	17.26	22.71
Tianjin	43.68	55.63	69.10	33.50	44.79	63.03	52.15	66.21	74.29

(continued on next page)

Table 7.13 Imports and Exports of Foreign-Funded Firms by Province (Share of Total Trade, Imports, Exports by Province) (continued)

	Total			Exports			Imports		
	1994	1995	1996	1994	1995	1996	1994	1995	1996
Other Provinces									
Hebei	23.97	22.12	34.09	14.61	13.10	22.70	35.74	33.96	48.93
Shanxi	10.52	7.53	8.29	7.26	6.45	7.25	21.46	11.88	12.61
Inner Mongolia	1.75	11.62	15.23	8.74	10.16	16.18	14.39	12.55	14.32
Jilin	18.99	29.45	35.18	8.45	17.18	24.10	29.87	37.29	43.76
Heilongjiang	9.10	11.48	16.76	3.92	5.43	8.02	19.25	22.48	37.22
Jiangxi	22.95	13.46	13.45	6.58	5.29	7.62	38.28	24.51	24.30
Henan	18.28	17.32	25.03	8.80	7.88	15.53	27.38	27.75	37.47
Hubei	21.24	24.41	36.40	10.32	10.30	20.17	31.69	37.73	50.01
Hunan	14.72	12.17	18.13	5.07	5.06	8.10	31.67	21.89	38.13
Guangxi	26.98	24.36	28.94	10.85	13.36	19.04	38.27	34.72	42.30
Hainan	29.37	30.11	32.64	12.17	12.00	17.06	33.54	36.31	36.65
Sichuan	13.99	13.05	29.10	6.27	4.47	7.30	19.22	22.19	47.55
Guizhou	14.58	11.99	11.06	7.24	7.29	10.96	23.89	17.46	11.20
Yunnan	11.12	8.75	11.62	2.90	2.92	4.23	20.22	14.82	17.86
Tibet	3.27	13.10	38.09	6.46	2.36	12.24	3.05	13.87	41.47
Shaanxi	19.42	10.35	19.68	5.25	4.03	8.56	19.42	17.31	32.76
Gansu	10.51	6.92	10.83	4.76	5.69	8.65	17.92	7.91	12.67
Qinghai	5.35	3.92	4.44	3.69	5.10	7.53	10.27	0.49	0.90
Ningxia	14.66	6.19	16.75	6.27	5.90	12.81	27.09	6.85	27.34
Xinjiang	6.02	7.10	8.17	7.57	5.97	11.23	5.34	7.72	6.79

Source: Calculated from *China Statistical Yearbook*, 1997

coastal provinces as shown in Table 7.13. Therefore, the differences in the trade performances in Guangdong and Fujian provinces, and those of other provinces where FDI from other countries show a strong presence, need to be explained not only in terms of the magnitudes but also in terms of structural differences.

Considering that FDI-related imports are widespread across all provinces, it is likely to be caused by both market-driven FDI and GN-FDI in coastal provinces and by market-driven FDI in other provinces. As there is no break down of FDI-related imports into the first and second type, in the published statistics, it is not easy to identify exactly how each type of FDI affects the trade performance of China. Further research is warranted in this area.

7.6   Concluding remarks

As China continues to liberalize its trade and investment regime in the new decade, its share in world trade and investment flows will continue to increase as well. What will be the trends in FDI and trade?

Hong Kong has already completed its economic restructuring and its main role has changed into the old role of entrepot, linking China with the rest of the world. Therefore, new manufacturing FDI is now likely to flow further from Hong Kong on a massive scale. Taiwan has been undergoing massive restructuring as well. The share of manufacturing in GDP has decreased from 43.6 per cent to 29 per cent. As part of its restructuring efforts further relocation of business is expected to occur, although the speed might taper off the scale might become larger. Considering that CFB rely mainly on maximum flexibility and minimum long-term commitments, FDI from Taiwan and Hong Kong are not likely to expand its vertical integration either on a global scale nor across wide regions of China. Instead, the CFB in Guangdong and Fujian will form their own clusters integrating themselves within the region. Firms in Hong Kong and Taiwan will serve as their financial, R & D and marketing centres.

Even if wage rates increase existing firms in Guangdong and Fujian are not expected to be relocated to other regions, since the most important location advantages are cultural, geographical and language proximity. Also, the trade surpluses created by cost-driven FDI in other provinces and regions may not be as high as those in Guangdong.

On the other hand, firms pursuing a global strategy will continue to expand in the region. With a globalized market a higher proportion of the value chain is divided and distributed to the relevant production centres with appropriate location advantages. Market-driven FDI will continue to increase as liberalization continues. However, already some

inefficiency has been identified in this area.[12] As liberalization contin
the efficiency of the firms established by FDI will improve, while there
will be a gradual transition in the new FDI from the market-driven FDI
to GN-FDI.

Notes

1   However, this trade/GDP ratio in China would be an overestimation,
    as the value added of non-tradables is underestimated and a
    substantial part of its informal economy is not reported in the formal
    statistics.
2   Due to massive depreciation of most currencies in East and Southeast
    Asia, the competitiveness of Chinese exports has declined to some
    extent.
3   See Chapter 10 for a discussion of the impact on regional income
    disparities arising from the success of the coastal region in general in
    terms of trade and FDI, against that of the central and western region.
4   Since the adoption of 'socialist capitalism' as a national goal, China
    gradually opened its domestic market to foreign investment, especially
    in the services sector including retail and real estate and social infra-
    structure development. This trend accelerated dramatically after 1992.
5   The differences between the two arise also from an institutional lag,
    an implementation lag and cancellation of projects.
6   See Agarwal (1980) for a survey of determinants of FDI.
7   In order to avoid a potential simultaneity problem, we used lagged
    regressors, except the SER dummy which is intended to reflect changes
    in Chinese FDI policy since 1992.
8   The negative sign of this variable is also reported in other related
    studies. For example, see Cheng and Kwan (1998).
9   The openness variable is not included in the regression due to its high
    partial correlation with some of the other variables. Since this variable
    captures the dynamic nature of the economy, this variable may become
    more important over time as China's economy matures.
10 Hill (1998) identifies four different international strategies: an
    international strategy, a multi-domestic strategy, a global strategy and
    a transnational strategy. See Chapters 13–14.
11 He compares the total trade surpluses of the three economies, China,
    Hong Kong and Taiwan. The total surplus has not changed drastically.
    See Chung (1996), Table 8, p. 22.
12 For example, in the automobile industry a high import barrier is one
    of the major reasons for such investment. Yet, the auto industry is
    found to be inefficient and has many problems (World Bank, 1997,
    pp. 11–17).

References

Agarwal, J.P. (1980), 'Determinants of Foreign Direct Investment: a Survey,' *Weltwirtschaftliches Archiv*, Vol. 116, pp. 739–73.

Cheng, L.K., and Y.K. Kwan (1998), 'What are the Determinants of the Location of Foreign Direct Investment? The Chinese Experience', Discussion Paper No. 242, School of Economics and Finance, The University of Hong Kong.

Chung, C. (1996), 'Double-edged Trade Effect of Foreign Direct Investment and Firm-Specific Assets: Evidence from the Chinese Trio', Discussion Paper Series No. 9609, Chung-Hua Institution for Economic Research, Taipei.

Dunning, J. (1977), 'Trade, Location of Economic Activity and the MNE: A Search for an Eclectic Approach', In B.O. Hesselborn and P.M. Wijkman (eds), *The International Allocation of Economic Activity*, Holmes and Meier Publishers, New York.

―― (1981), *International Production and the Multinational Enterprise*, Allen and Unwin, London.

Froot, K., and J. Stein (1991), 'Exchange Rates and Foreign Direct Investments: An Imperfect Capital Market Approach,' *Quarterly Journal of Economics*, November, pp. 1191–217.

Hatch, W. and K. Yamamura (1996), *Asia in Japan's Embrace: Building a Regional Production Alliance*, Cambridge University Press, Cambridge.

Hill, C. (1997), *International Business: Competing in the Global Marketplace*, Irwin, Chicago.

Hirsch, S. (1976), 'An International Trade and Investment Theory of the Firm,' *Oxford Economic Papers*, Vol. 28, pp. 258–70.

Japan External Trade Organization [JETRO] (1996), JETRO White Paper on Foreign Direct Investment: Increasing Foreign Investment in APEC and Japan's Response, Tokyo.

Jung, K.H., and R.W. Moxon, (1996), 'Foreign Direct Investment in Developing East Asia: New Players, Pressures and Strategies', in Ku-Hyun Jung and Jang-Hee Yoo (eds), *Asia-Pacific Economic Cooperation: Current Issues and Agenda for the Future*, Korea Institute for International Economic Policy, Seoul, pp. 153–74.

Kawai, M., and S. Urata (1996), 'Trade Imbalances and Japanese Foreign Direct Investment: Bilateral and Triangular Issues', in Ku-Hyun Jung and Jang-Hee Yoo (eds), *Asia-Pacific Economic Cooperation: Current Issues and Agenda for the Future*, Korea Institute for International Economic Policy, Seoul, pp. 61–88.

Kojima, K. (1978), *Direct Foreign Investment: A Japanese Model Multinational Business Operations*, Croom Helm, London.

Markusen, J.R. (1991), 'The Theory of the Multinational Enterprise: A Common Analytical Framework', in E.D. Ramstetter (ed.), *Direct Foreign Investment in Asia's Developing Economies and Structural Change in the Asia-Pacific Region*, Westview Press, Boulder, pp. 11–34.

Petri, P.A. (1995), 'The Interdependence of Trade and Investment in the Pacific', in Edward K.Y. Chen and Peter Drysdale (eds), *Corporate Links and Foreign Direct Investment in Asia and the Pacific*, HarperEducational, Sydney, pp. 29–54.

Seo, J.S. (1997), Dynamics of Comparative Advantage and Foreign Direct Investment in Republic of Korea and Taiwan: an Analysis of the Relationship between FDI and Trade, unpublished PhD thesis, School of Economics, the University of New South Wales, Sydney.

Simon, D.F., and Y.W. Jun (1995), 'Technological Change, Foreign Investment and the New Strategic Thrust of Japanese Firms in the Asia Pacific', in Edward K.Y. Chen and P. Drysdale (eds), *Corporate Links and Foreign Direct Investment in Asia and the Pacific*, HarperEducational, Sydney, pp. 203–26.

Suh, C.S., and J.S. Seo (1998), 'Trends in Foreign Direct Investment: The Case of the Asia-Pacific Region', in A. Levy (ed.), *Handbook on the Globalization of the World Economy*, Edward Elgar, Aldershot UK.

Sung, Y.W. (1995), 'Subregional Economic Integration: Hong Kong, Taiwan, South China and Beyond', in Edward K.Y. Chen and P. Drysdale (eds), *Corporate Links and Foreign Direct Investment in Asia and the Pacific*, Harper Educational, Sydney, pp. 56–86.

Whitley, R. (1994), *Business Systems in East Asia: Firms, Markets and Societies*, SAGE Publications, London.

World Bank (1997), *China Engaged: Integration with the Global Economy*, World Bank, Washington DC.

Part 2

Key Issues

8

Balanced Development: The Challenge for Science, Technology and Innovation Policy

Tim Turpin
Xielin Liu

This chapter focuses upon science, technology and innovation policy in China. It argues that production in China is predominantly concentrated along the eastern seaboard but innovation appears unevenly spread within this region. An analysis of indicators of innovation by province shows a pattern of development toward two different types of innovation system: a strong science based system predominantly linked to public institutions and state enterprises, and a commercial system, more responsive to market forces, less science-intensive but more closely linked to the business sector and non-state enterprises. An implication is that unless the two systems become better aligned, market-driven firms will have little choice but to forge alternative innovation alliances with foreign firms.

8.1   Introduction

Since the late 1970s, science and technology (S&T) and policies for increasing innovation have become major features of China's strategies for economic development. Through the 1980s China progressively introduced a series of S&T reform initiatives to encourage the formation of high technology non-state-owned enterprises, and develop an environment favourable to the commercialization of science and technology achievements.

In essence, the general thrust of reforms has been to shift a vertical, hierarchical relationship between a largely public sector research-and-development (R&D) system and production enterprises toward a system based on horizontal linkages. The strategy has been to reform the previous centrally dominated innovation system and transform it into one that is steered by both market and government policies. The S&T policies and reforms introduced over the past two decades have carried significant implications for major institutions in China. Reforms have redirected large research institutes toward market-based funding. They have created imperatives for new forms of organizational structure and management. But in particular, they have changed the ways that public research institutes, universities and industrial enterprises interact with each other.[1]

Through this period of reform two important observations emerge. Firstly, while research and development and innovation activity is predominantly concentrated in the strong economic provinces along the eastern seaboard, it is unevenly spread within these provinces.[2] The provinces where R&D activity is most concentrated are not those that are most productive. Some provinces have comparatively very high levels of scientific activity but contribute far less significantly to the nation's GDP. Conversely, other provinces are major contributors to national GDP but far less significant in terms of scientific production or R&D investments.

To some extent this can largely be explained by regional history, geography, availability of human and natural resources and the industrial structure that has emerged in particular provinces. However, whatever the reason, this variation raises an important challenge for achieving a productive national innovation system. The extent to which a national innovation system contributes to a nation's economic performance depends on the capacity of its institutions, agencies and actors to inter-link and create a collective system of knowledge creation and use (Freeman, 1987; Porter, 1990; Nelson, 1993).

In China, structural variation in innovation can be observed across the highly productive eastern provinces. Enterprises and institutions should, according to prevailing innovation theory (and current policy expectations), be inter-linked to create a national system of innovation. To some extent this may already be occurring. However, it is possible that two alternative directions may ensue. One possibility is that the sheer size and diversity across China may lead to quite different *provincial/regional* systems of innovation. A second, and associated, possibility is that some of these provinces may develop as part of quite separate *transnational* innovation systems.

A second observation that can be drawn from the S&T policy reforms over the past two decades is that the shift toward market imperatives in driving innovation is leading to greater bifurcation between state-owned enterprises (SOEs) and the emerging non-state sector. Reforms in the SOE sector have progressed more slowly than in other areas. This has meant that in many cases those enterprises most subject to market pressures, most creative in building horizontal linkages and most dynamic and innovative, have reached a 'glass-ceiling'. Unless SOEs become more innovative and more horizontally integrated with the more dynamic non-state sector these emerging market-driven firms will be driven to forge alternative alliances with large international firms. Thus the SOE sector itself can be seen to stand as a critical barrier against building a *national* or *regional* system of innovation.

The remainder of this chapter proceeds as follows. In section 2 the evolution and impact of China's science and technology and innovation policies are discussed. Section 3 identifies the impact of overall economic reform upon science and technology policy. Section 4 conducts an appraisal of innovation activity and regional development. The impact of the Asian economic crisis and policy implications for science and technology and innovation policy is identified in section 5. Section 6 presents a brief summary of the major issues arising from this chapter.

8.2   Evolution and impact of China's S&T and innovation policies

China's scientific and technological system has been dominated by three types of institutions: the Chinese Academy of Science Institutes; the R&D institutions attached to universities; and R&D institutions within the industrial sector. The first group was traditionally responsible for carrying out basic research and supporting major mission-oriented projects. The second group has been responsible for a combination of research and education, and the third group was responsible for solving problems within specific industry sectors. The role of government was to coordinate these activities.

In some cases, where major government projects were concerned, coordination was effective and major outcomes were achieved. For example, as Liu (1998) has pointed out, it was centralized coordination that enabled many breakthroughs to be achieved through the 1960s and 1970s. In the case of the pharmaceutical industry, for example, China initiated a major program on drug research as part of the effort to support the Vietnamese government during the Vietnam war. A national task force was established involving R&D organizations, manufacturing firms, hospitals, and medical experts. More than 100 institutions were involved in the project. The task force had absolute power to allocate financial, technical and human resources and to transfer ideas or results from one institution to the other for further development. As Liu notes, two bomb projects and one satellite project worked in the same way (Liu, 1998).

The point is, however, that while this kind of centralized innovation system worked well for mission-oriented activities it was totally dependent on centralized decisions. As a means for linking science to commercial activities it was neither efficient nor innovative. For commercial production and upgrading technology, firms were driven to rely heavily on foreign imports. There were few incentives in place to stimulate innovation or adaptation around these technologies. The Liberation Truck, for example, designed and manufactured on former Soviet technologies, remained virtually unchanged for forty years (Liu, 1998, p.8).

The barriers confronting China's innovative capacity as it approached the 1980s have now been well articulated. They have been summarized recently by Xu and Fang (1998) as being characterized by:

- a self-contained system located within a rigid vertical structure;

- R&D institutions responsible to a higher authority rather than customers;

- weak links between R&D, education and production; and

- excessive management leading to lack of incentives for innovation and production.

Policy initiatives introduced progressively from 1979 were designed to remove this rigidity in the system and pave the way for market reforms within the economy more generally. China's first national conference on science and technology, held in 1978, laid the foundations for much of the reform that followed. This conference set down a set of guidelines to reform the entire national R&D system. From 1979 on, a range of policy instruments were progressively put in place with the intention of reducing centralized control for a 'science push' and increasing the role of the market in order to stimulate innovation at local levels.

Legislative changes to the contract responsibility system in 1982 paved the way for establishing a technology market (Xu and Fang, 1997). In 1984 China joined the international community in enacting intellectual property legislation. This was the start of the country's efforts to systematically install a modern legal system for the protection of intellectual property rights (see Innes and Turpin, forthcoming, for a review of China's intellectual property rights system). These changes served to both encourage foreign direct investment in local innovative activities, as well as provide incentive for local firms to engage in commercially oriented science-based activities.

The S&T institution reform has also had dramatic influence on outputs of S&T activity. Transition-era policies have had two fundamental objectives regarding R&D activities. The first has been to make R&D institutes more responsive to applied, downstream problems. The most basic research institutes have been less subject to this shift, while the industrial research institutes have been the primary target of these policies. The government has done this by allowing research institutes more freedom to choose and pursue research projects or even other functional activities, like manufacturing, but at the same time reducing government support to force the institutes to find outside support. Research institutes are now able to sell or license the technology they develop to other organizations or, if they so decide, implement the technology themselves by setting up manufacturing operations on-site or creating science-based spin-offs. They may also increase their revenues by conducting contract research or consulting for other organizations.

The government has also made it possible for the research institutes to recover some of the shortfall in government subsidies by creating competitively awarded project grants. The second fundamental objective of transition-era policies regarding R&D has been to promote active and formally organized R&D activities within manufacturing enterprises. Indeed, this explains the dramatic increase in the number of R&D units within state-owned firms and for township and village enterprises (TVEs).

Throughout the 1980s the government progressively implemented a series of science and technology development programs with quite specific objectives.

1. The *863 High-tech Research and Development Program*, started in 1996, targeted applied research for priority areas including: biotechnology; space technology, information, laser technology, automation, energy and advanced materials. This reflected a major shift from large-scale mission focused science investment to areas identified as priority for commercially oriented industrial production.

2. The *Torch Program* was established in 1988 to commercialize discoveries from institutes and universities and to create new technology enterprises. The Torch program was a key initiative in providing technological links for the establishment of the 53 New High Technology Zones (NHTZ) across China. The success of the Legend and Stone computer companies are well-known

examples of commercial success resulting from this program. These initiatives typically do not include state-owned enterprises, but they have served to encourage links between researchers from within institutes and universities.

3. The *Spark Program* was conceived in 1986 to provide new vitality for the rural economy. The intention of Spark is to diffuse technology appropriate for TVEs. The growth of TVEs and their contribution to China's economic production have been considerable.[3] While the Spark and Torch programs were designed to generate reforms in separate sectors, they both contributed to the somewhat unexpected scale of technology development in TVEs and the private sector.

8.3   Impact of policy reforms

National R&D expenditure has increased dramatically. From 1987 to 1995 it more than doubled. Government funding for R&D has increased, but firm expenditure increased even more rapidly. Further, there has been a shift from investments in research institutions and universities toward industry based investment. In 1995 firms accounted for 37 per cent of all R&D, institutes for 41 per cent, and universities for 13 per cent (Liu, 1998, p. 11). Increasingly, R&D investments have been made by the emerging private sector and the TVE sector.

China's TVEs have achieved remarkable levels of growth and production. Their output increased by 25 per cent a year during the decade from the mid-1980s. This resulted in their share of GDP increasing from 13 per cent in 1985 to 31 per cent in 1994. Figure 8.1 shows the growth in the formation of TVEs through the late 1980s and early 1990s. The growth has tailed off after a peak in 1994. The majority of this TVE growth has been concentrated in advanced periphery-urban regions. For example, in 1988, TVEs in three provinces, Jiangsu, Zhejiang and Shandong, produced half of all TVE output. For innovation and economic growth generally, linkages with urban firms and research institutes and with firms located in NHTZs were central to such growth. However, rapid growth has brought with it increased levels of competition. Recent evidence (Xue and Wang, 1998) suggests a decline in R&D activities in NHTZs, identified by reduced average firm expenditure on R&D and reduced R&D intensity. Obviously the market opportunities for new enterprises is finite, and the peak in 1994 corresponds with a 'shake-out', in particular, in the NHTZs.

In 1996, the former State Science and Technology Commission and the State Statistical Bureau carried out an innovation survey covering

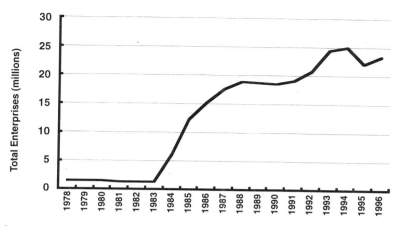

Source: *China Statistical Year Book*, 1997

Figure 8.1   Township and Village Enterprises in China, 1978–96

5 000 enterprises covering six separate provinces. An interesting feature of the innovation survey, for the issues covered in this chapter, is that it investigated the status and nature of links between enterprises, universities and research institutes. The results of this survey showed a strong relationship between innovation and collaboration with research institutes or universities. In other words there was a strong connection between business innovation and research links outside the firm. The survey also showed that SOEs were less likely to collaborate with outside institutions than newly formed 'science-based' enterprises. A third observation is that the most common type of link was R&D collaboration. However, 'science-based' enterprises were also very involved in such links for the purpose of recruiting 'expert' staff. The SOEs on the other hand, were far less likely to have links for this purpose. This is not surprising given that most of this type of enterprise emerged as 'spin-offs' from institutions in the first place. However, it does illustrate the emergence of a more alliance-oriented structure compared to the more self-sufficient, but isolated, structure evident in the SOE pattern of relationship.

The impact and developments following in the wake of the S&T policy reforms suggest that two important events are occurring. Firstly, the non-SOE sector, particularly TVEs, has grown rapidly in the new market-oriented environment. Secondly, this sector appears to be more reliant on links with research institutes and universities, both for research and development as well as for recruiting expert personnel.

Important issues now emerge for the development of national innovation policies. Can China manage to develop and maintain an internationally competitive national innovation system? If so, how can the state and non-state sectors become mutually supportive? Can the various provinces and sub-provinces (NHTZs) contribute to a national knowledge production and use system? This requires a regional rather than national perspective. The next section provides an overview of the relationship between some selected policy initiatives and science and technology activity on a provincial basis. It can be observed from these data that key productive provinces are developing quite different innovation structures. An immediate and critical issue for national innovation that follows is the need to improve links between these provinces and between state and non-state enterprises within and beyond these provinces.

8.4   Innovation activity and regional development

Regional GDP and R&D investment

Levels of regional development and GDP are discussed in more detail in Chapter 10. In this chapter, however, we are concerned with the relationships between patterns of GDP, S&T and innovation policies and innovative activity. Gross expenditure on R&D has been rising steadily through the past decade, although as a proportion of GDP it has not increased. In the data presented below we seek to explain why this is so. In Table 8.1 we present a comparison between R&D expenditure for 1995 and GDP for 1997 across provinces. We have chosen these different years to make some allowance for the delayed impact of R&D. Some interesting points can be observed in this comparison.

As pointed out elsewhere, GDP is highly concentrated in the eastern provinces, three of which in particular stand out. Guangdong, Jiangsu and Shandong alone account for almost 30 per cent of total GDP. One would expect to find correspondingly high levels of R&D expenditure associated with these high levels of production. However, R&D expenditure is most highly concentrated in *different* provinces. Three provinces, Beijing, Shanghai and Sichuan alone account for nearly 40 per cent of all R&D expenditure. In other words the major concentrations of R&D expenditure on the one hand, and production on the other, are in different regions. To some extent this reflects the historical concentration of research institutions and universities in Beijing and Shanghai, but the relationship is more interesting than that. Jiangsu is home to a comparatively small number of institutes

Table 8.1   GDP and R&D Investment by Province

Province	GDP –1997 Yuan 100 million	% China	R&D Exp. 1995 Yuan 100 million	% China
Beijing	1 810	2.4	145	15.8
Tianjin	1 240	1.6	25	2.7
Hebei	3 954	5.1	25	2.7
Shanxi	1 480	1.9	11	1.2
Inner Mongolia	1,095	1.4	6	0.7
Liaoning	3 490	4.5	50	5.4
Jilin	1 447	1.9	19	2.1
Heilongjiang	2 708	3.5	19	2.1
Shanghai	3 360	4.4	120	13.1
Jiangsu	6 680	8.7	79	8.6
Zhejiang	4 638	6.0	28	3.1
Anhui	2 670	3.5	15	1.6
Fujian	3 000	3.9	8	0.9
Jiangxi	1 715	2.2	11	1.2
Shandong	6 650	8.6	44	4.8
Henan	4 079	5.3	35	3.8
Hubei	3 450	4.5	31	3.4
Hunan	2 993	3.9	24	2.6
Guangdong	7 316	9.5	47	5.1
Guangxi	2 015	2.6	14	1.5
Hainan	410	0.5	1	0.1
Changqing	1 350	1.8	0	0.0
Sichuan	3 320	4.3	79	8.6
Guizhou	793	1.0	5	0.5
Yunnan	1 644	2.1	10	1.1
Tibet	77	0.1	*	*
Shaanxi	1 326	1.7	42	4.6
Gansu	781	1.0	14	1.5
Qinghai	202	0.3	2	0.2
Ningxia	211	0.3	2	0.2
Xinjiang	1 050	1.4	7	0.8
Total	76 954	100.0	918	100.0

Source: *China Statistical Yearbook* 1998 and *China S&T Indicators* 1996

* data not available

and universities, yet is the next highest spender on R&D after Sichuan. So this bifurcation cannot simply be explained by an historical concentration of research institutes in particular provinces.

Scientists and engineers engaged in R&D activities

Apart from financial investments the capacity for provincial/regional and national innovation depends on the availability of knowledge and skills. Scientists and engineers are a key component of this human resource requirement. In Table 8.2 we show the numbers of scientists and engineers engaged in S&T activities according to different types of institutions: state and provincial R&D institutions; institutions attached to universities; and institutions attached to industrial enterprises. These data help to explain some of the differences between R&D expenditure and GDP at the provincial level.

The three top R&D spending provinces, Beijing, Shanghai and Sichuan, have the highest proportion of the scientists and engineers engaged in research institutes and universities. Other regions have higher proportions of these human resources working in industrial R&D institutions. In Beijing, for example, only 13 per cent of scientists and engineers are employed in industrial research institutes. Shandong, on the other hand, has 45 per cent employed in industrial enterprises. In short, the major investments in R&D activity, financially and in terms of human resources, is to a large extent concentrated in state-owned research institutions and universities. In the provinces with higher GDP the levels of R&D activity are comparatively less, but their human resources are more closely linked to industrial enterprises.

S&T policy program investments

Earlier in this chapter we discussed two major policy programs designed to reform the production and diffusion of new scientific knowledge. The Torch Program had the objective of supporting basic research in areas with the potential for commercial returns from developing Chinese industry. The Spark Program was established with the objective of diffusing appropriate technologies at the township and village level. A considerable amount of resources have been directed to these two programs. In the context of the present discussion it is interesting to examine the provincial distribution of these funds.

Table 8.3 shows the distribution of funds through these two programs for 1995. The high levels of investment in some provinces here reflect the pattern of high GDP production across provinces. The three top provinces in terms of GDP, for example, are among the top four regional recipients of Torch and Spark funding.

Table 8.2 **Scientists and Engineers at Research Institutes Engaged in S&T Activities, by type of Research Institute and Province**

Province	R&D Institutions		Higher Education Institutions		Industrial Enterprises	
	Persons	%	Persons	%	Persons	%
Beijing	66 885	20.4	47 754	9.2	18 028	4.0
Tianjin	11 883	3.6	14 681	2.8	12 630	2.8
Hebei	7 337	2.2	20 806	4.0	16 371	3.6
Shanxi	6 427	2.0	9 879	1.9	10 654	2.4
Inner Mongolia	4 590	1.4	7 556	1.4	7 165	1.6
Liaoning	20 268	6.2	31 570	6.1	41 044	9.1
Jilin	12 211	3.7	20 193	3.9	10 696	2.4
Heilongjiang	9 741	3.0	24 042	4.6	18 795	4.2
Shanghai	26 586	8.1	37 325	7.2	33 340	7.4
Jiangsu	17 060	5.2	40 397	7.7	36 702	8.1
Zhejiang	6 698	2.0	13 220	2.5	11 807	2.6
Anhui	6 164	1.9	14 619	2.8	10 252	2.3
Fujian	4 295	1.3	8 770	1.7	4 239	0.9
Jiangxi	3 973	1.2	10 844	2.1	9 190	2.0
Shandong	13 920	4.3	24 549	4.7	31 409	7.0
Henan	10 433	3.2	16 146	3.1	23 083	5.1
Hubei	13 583	4.2	31 667	6.1	25 602	5.7
Hunan	8 847	2.7	19 856	3.8	14 998	3.3
Guangdong	11 675	3.6	23 096	4.4	15 224	3.4
Guangxi	6 365	1.9	8 985	1.7	6 249	1.4
Hainan	651	0.2	1 613	0.3	480	0.1
Sichuan	20 333	6.2	34 583	6.6	42 979	9.5
Guizhou	3 655	1.1	7 429	1.4	7 368	1.6
Yunnan	5 877	1.8	9 880	1.9	4 701	1.0
Tibet	244	0.1	*	*	*	*
Shaanxi	11 469	3.5	24 328	4.7	20 888	4.6
Gansu	8 056	2.5	5 608	1.1	10 349	2.3
Qinghai	1 681	0.5	1 834	0.4	1 990	0.4
Ningxia	1 843	0.6	2 396	0.5	1 679	0.4
Xinjiang	4 458	1.4	8 118	1.6	3 999	0.9
Total	**327 208**	**100.0**	**521 744**	**100.0**	**451 911**	**100.0**

Source: State Science & Technology Commission of the People's Republic of China, *China Science and Technology Indicators*, 1996

Table 8.3   S&T Program Investments, Patent Inventions and Scientific Publications by Province

Province	Torch Program 1995 ¥ 000	% total	Spark Program 1995 ¥ 000	% total	Invention Patents 1985–97 Patents	% total	Domestic Publications 1996 Publics.	% total
Beijing	196 310	5.4	26 220	0.6	3 065	21.6	13 436	21.0
Tianjin	85 860	2.3	45 900	1.0	613	4.3	2 175	3.4
Hebei	49 450	1.3	93 600	2.1	473	3.3	909	1.4
Shanxi	48 400	1.3	38 300	0.9	334	2.4	790	1.2
Inner Mongolia	2 800	0.1	27 410	0.6	*	*	*	*
Liaoning	337 980	9.2	223 600	5.0	1 148	8.1	2 381	3.7
Jilin	50 000	1.4	70 000	1.6	410	2.9	2 331	3.6
Heilongjiang	34 100	0.9	100 920	2.3	422	3.0	1 750	2.7
Shanghai	532 050	14.5	429 000	9.6	949	6.7	6 288	9.8
Jiangsu	379 440	10.3	393 368	8.8	780	5.5	4 981	7.8
Zhejiang	192 290	5.2	250 650	5.6	599	4.2	2 072	3.2
Anhui	76 830	2.1	141 008	3.1	182	1.3	1 534	2.4
Fujian	75 430	2.1	90 060	2.0	214	1.5	1 494	2.3
Jiangxi	35 500	1.0	17 600	0.4	196	1.4	402	0.6
Shandong	545 860	14.9	864 000	19.3	836	5.9	2 726	4.3
Henan	113 140	3.1	154 810	3.5	381	2.7	872	1.4
Hubei	40 000	1.1	154 900	3.5	591	4.2	3 736	5.8

(continued on next page)

Table 8.3   S&T Program Investments, Patent Inventions and Scientific Publications by Province (cont.)

Province	Torch Program 1995 ¥000	% total	Spark Program 1995 ¥000	% total	Invention Patents 1985–97 Patents	% total	Domestic Publications 1996 Publics.	% total
Hunan	80 150	2.2	127 995	2.9	517	3.6	1 946	3.0
Guangdong	347 870	9.5	414 275	9.3	489	3.4	3 693	5.8
Guangxi	104 400	2.8	88 000	2.0	176	1.2	405	0.6
Hainan	4 000	0.1	4 000	0.1	21	0.1	91	0.1
Sichuan	145 080	4.0	327 678	7.3	650	4.6	4 021	6.3
Guizhou	2 420	0.1	10 690	0.2	106	0.7	328	0.5
Yunnan	43 610	1.2	141 080	3.2	253	1.8	638	1.0
Tibet	*	*	*	*	*	*	19	0.0
Shaanxi	57 800	1.6	190 620	4.3	473	3.3	3 366	5.3
Gansu	22 000	0.6	11 700	0.3	177	1.2	1 158	1.8
Qinghai	1 500	0.0	4 000	0.1	39	0.3	127	0.2
Ningxia	12 340	0.3	15 250	0.3	28	0.2	64	0.1
Xinjiang	49 950	1.4	22 000	0.5	75	0.5	346	0.5
Total	**3 666 560**	**100.0**	**4 478 634**	**100.0**	**14 197**	**100.0**	**64 079**	**100.0**

Source: *Annual Patent Statistical Report, 1987–97* (selected years)
China State Science and technology Commission, China Science and Technology Indicators, 1996
Documentation and Information Centre, China Academy of Science, 1998

* data not available

Scientific and technological output

Investments in R&D can contribute to two forms of output. They can produce tacit knowledge, or know-how, embedded in people who have learned through R&D and innovation processes. This form of knowledge is primarily transferred through people. It can be produced and acquired through training, learning, and the movement of people across enterprises and regions. To some extent the data presented above showing numbers of scientists and engineers shows the potential to capture and make use of tacit knowledge.

A second type of output is knowledge that is codified in technologies, designs and publications. This type of knowledge can be transferred through a variety of means. It can be bought, sold, or otherwise acquired through the public domain.

Table 8.3 shows two indicators of codified knowledge output: patented inventions, and scientific publications. The data on patents show the accumulated number of *invention* patents approved since China's patent law was established in the mid-1980s. The publications data show the total number of scientific publications for the one year: 1996. The data have been disaggregated by province.

Again, these indicators show the significance of two provinces, Beijing and Shanghai, in contributing to the national scientific and technological output. However, they also show the extent to which other provinces are also contributing to this output. Liaoning, for example, records the second highest level of invention patent activity. It is interesting to note that this region also received a high proportion of Torch Program funding.

Enterprise structure

In the earlier part of this chapter we discussed the emergence of TVEs as major engines of production in China. We conclude this section by returning to the TVEs and making some observations about their relationship with SOEs. For this regional overview of innovation, science and technology policy and production, it is important to take into account the comparative relationship between TVEs and SOEs in each province. This carries important implications for innovation, because TVEs are driven largely by market forces while the SOEs remain somewhat protected and driven by government agencies.

Table 8.4 presents data on the number of enterprises in each of the two sectors and the average numbers of employees for the year (in this case 1996). Again, the data is presented by province. The last column in this table illustrates the comparative significance of the SOE sector

Table 8.4 State-Owned and Township and Village Enterprises and Personnel by Province (1996)

	State-Owned Enterprises				Township and Village Enterprises				% Emp. in SOEs
	Enterprises		Employees '000s		Enterprises		Employees '000s		
Province	No.	%	(avg. of year)	%	No.	%	(avg. of year)	%	
Beijing	4 025	4.6	977	2.3	77 000	0.3	1 012	0.7	49.1
Tianjin	1 918	2.2	831	2.0	97 000	0.4	1 137	0.8	42.2
Hebei	4 053	4.7	2 164	5.1	1 813 000	7.8	9 115	6.7	19.2
Shanxi	2 751	3.2	1 727	4.1	829 000	3.5	4 382	3.2	28.3
Inner Mongolia	2 449	2.8	1 050	2.5	716 000	3.1	2 755	2.0	27.6
Liaoning	4 374	5.0	3 295	7.8	802 000	3.4	4 450	3.3	42.5
Jilin	2 673	3.1	1 591	3.8	703 000	3.0	2 251	1.7	41.4
Heilongjiang	3 807	4.4	2 406	5.7	768 000	3.3	2 596	1.9	48.1
Shanghai	3 236	3.7	1 408	3.3	16 000	0.1	1 362	1.0	50.8
Jiangsu	3 853	4.4	2 404	5.7	914 000	3.9	8 795	6.5	21.5
Zhejiang	3 118	3.6	1 033	2.4	929 000	4.0	7 864	5.8	11.6
Anhui	2 529	2.9	1 516	3.6	701 000	3.0	7 955	5.9	16.0
Fujian	2 415	2.8	604	1.4	727 000	3.1	4 932	3.7	10.9
Jiangxi	4 436	5.1	1 391	3.3	820 000	3.5	3 088	2.3	31.1
Shandong	4 855	5.6	2 914	6.9	1 783 000	7.6	13 696	10.1	17.5
Henan	4 243	4.9	2 610	6.2	1 315 000	5.6	9 410	7.0	21.7

(continued on next page)

Table 8.4 State-Owned and Township and Village Enterprises and Personnel by Province (1996) (cont.)

| | State-Owned Enterprises | | | | Township and Village Enterprises | | | | |
| | Enterprises | | Employees '000s | | Enterprises | | Employees '000s | | % Emp. |
Province	No.	%	(avg. of year)	%	No.	%	(avg. of year)	%	in SOEs
Hubei	3 997	4.6	1 925	4.6	1 598 000	6.8	7 479	5.5	20.5
Hunan	3 770	4.3	1 822	4.3	2 004 000	8.6	8 285	6.1	18.0
Guangdong	5 228	6.0	1 375	3.3	1 450 000	6.2	11 186	8.3	10.9
Guangxi	2 565	2.9	835	2.0	878 000	3.8	3 821	2.8	17.9
Hainan	560	0.6	110	0.3	130 000	0.6	484	0.4	18.5
Sichuan	5 117	5.9	3 104	7.4	1 489 000	6.4	7 669	5.7	28.8
Guizhou	1 941	2.2	730	1.7	251 000	1.1	940	0.7	43.7
Yunnan	2 008	2.3	767	1.8	965 000	4.1	3 241	2.4	19.1
Tibet	176	0.2	140	0.3	1 000	0.0	19	0.0	88.1
Shaanxi	2 677	3.1	1 459	3.5	820 000	3.5	3 680	2.7	28.4
Gansu	1 544	1.8	878	2.1	358 000	1.5	2 171	1.6	28.8
Qinghai	562	0.6	205	0.5	9 000	0.0	91	0.1	69.3
Ningxia	427	0.5	227	0.5	119 000	0.5	433	0.3	34.4
Xinjiang	1 675	1.9	667	1.6	283 000	1.2	782	0.6	46.0
Total	86 982	100.0	42 165	100.0	23 365 000	100.0	135 081	100.0	23.8

Source: *China Statistical Yearbook,* 1997

in each province. This is shown by calculating the proportion of SOE employees of the total of employees in both SOEs and TVEs in each region.

The proportion of SOE employees for all provinces is 23.8 per cent. But there is significant variation across the provinces. The top GDP producers all have SOE components below the national average. The top R&D spenders, on the other hand, tend to be well over the national average. Beijing has a 49 per cent SOE component and Shanghai over 50 per cent.

Comparisons across selected indicators and provinces

The indicators discussed above can be drawn together to show a picture of regional development that takes into account the role of science and technology policies and outputs. Table 8.5 shows the above indicators for seven selected provinces: the top 5 in terms of GDP and the top 3 in terms of R&D investments.

These data suggest a number of important issues for innovation and development in the future. Together they illustrate three different pictures of innovation activity.

Group 1 Innovation provinces:

Firstly there is a group of high performing provinces in terms of GDP, but not particularly strong in terms of R&D investments. Two examples are provided here by Guangdong and Zhejiang. This group also has comparatively low proportions of S&T personnel, is less dominant in scientific output, but has low proportions of employees in SOEs compared to TVEs. However, they have received considerable investments through the Torch and Spark Programs. They can be considered as the economic or commercial dynamos in the national system of innovation.

Group 2 Innovation regions:

A second category comprises those provinces that are high on R&D performance but less significant in terms of GDP. Beijing and Shanghai are typical examples here. They are the top performers in terms of S&T indicators, representing nearly a third of all national R&D investment, inventions and scientific publications. They also have the highest proportions of the country's R&D personnel in R&D institutions. However, they have much higher proportions of SOE employees compared to group 1. Because of their strong science base they can be considered as scientific engines for driving the national system of innovation.

Group 3 Innovation provinces:

The third group comprises provinces that are also high performers in terms of GDP, but have higher levels of investment in R&D compared to group one provinces. Examples here are Jiangsu and Shandong. This group of provinces has large numbers of scientists and engineers in R&D institutions and industry. They have high levels of Torch and Spark investment and are strongly represented in scientific output. Like group one, they too have high proportions of employees located in TVEs. In short, this group is high performing in terms of GDP and most S&T indicators. Sichuan, although not as strong in terms of GDP, would also seem to fit this provincial category. This group of provinces is equally strong in both scientific and commercial activity. In terms of a national innovation system they appear more independent than either of the other groups of provinces.

What these three groups appear to represent is two different production systems: a strong science-based system predominantly linked to public institutions and state enterprises; and a commercial system, more responsive to market forces, less science-intensive but more closely linked to the business sector and non-state enterprises. Group 3 in the above classification would appear to transcend the two systems.

8.5   Impact of the Asian economic crisis and policy implications

The regional differences described above raises some interesting issues for the future. Much has been written about economic differences between the eastern, central and western regions of China. That distinction is clearly observable in terms of general economic development. However, an analysis of S&T investments and outputs expose major differences within the highly productive eastern region. These differences reflect varying levels of human and scientific resources, but they also reflect different patterns of production and reform in different sectors.

In the current context China's private sector is struggling in the face of a credit squeeze and high interest rates. The government's determination to reform the state sector remains a high priority. The economy so far appears to be withstanding the crisis afflicting many of its regional neighbours, although ongoing closure and restructuring of failing state-owned enterprises (SOEs) remains an explosive issue with high unemployment levels.[4]

There appear to be two difficult areas confronting China's system,

Table 8.5   **Comparative Selected Innovation Indicators by Selected Provinces**

Selected Provinces	% GDP & Rank 1997		% R&D Exp. & Rank 1995		% of all R&D in province spent in Firms	%S&E R&D Instit. & Rank 1995		% S&E in Industry & Rank 1995	
Guangdong	9.5	(1)	5.1	(6)	49.7	3.6	(10)	3.4	(12)
Jiangsu	8.7	(2)	8.6	(4)	57.9	5.2	(5)	8.1	(3)
Shandong	8.6	(3)	4.8	(7)	64.5	4.3	(6)	7.0	(5)
Zhejiang	6.0	(4)	3.1	(11)	65.5	2.0	(18)	2.6	(15)
Henan	5.3	(5)	3.8	(9)	58.3	3.2	(12)	5.1	(7)
Beijing	2.4	(16)	15.8	(1)	8.7	20.4	(1)	4.0	(10)
Shanghai	4.4	(9)	13.1	(2)	52.0	8.1	(2)	7.4	(4)
Sichuan	4.3	(10)	8.6	(3)	44.8	6.2	(4)	9.5	(1)

Selected Provinces	% Torch Invest. & Rank 1996		% Spark Invest. & Rank 1996		% Patents & Rank 1985–7		% Science Pubs. 1996		% SOE Ent. & Rank 1996		% SO Staff total TVE SOE
Guangdong	9.5	(4)	9.3	(3)	3.4	(11)	5.8	(6)	6.0	(1)	10.9
Jiangsu	10.3	(3)	8.8	(4)	5.5	(5)	7.8	(3)	4.4	(11)	21.5
Shandong	14.9	(1)	19.3	(1)	5.9	(4)	4.3	(8)	5.6	(3)	17.5
Zhejiang	5.2	(7)	5.6	(6)	4.2	(8)	3.2	(12)	3.6	(14)	11.6
Henan	3.1	(9)	3.5	(9)	2.7	(16)	1.4	(19)	4.3	(6)	21.7
Beijing	5.4	(6)	0.6	(21)	21.6	(1)	21.0	(1)	4.6	(8)	49.1
Shanghai	14.5	(2)	9.6	(2)	6.7	(3)	9.8	(2)	3.7	(13)	50.8
Sichuan	4.0	(8)	7.3	(5)	4.6	(6)	6.3	(4)	5.9	(2)	28.8

Source: GDP: *China Statistical Yearbook*, 1998

R&D Expenditure: *China Statistical Yearbook*, 1996

Scientists and Engineers, and Torch and Spark Program: *SSTC, China Science and Technology Indicators*, 1996

Patents: *Annual Patent Statistical Report*, 1987–97, China Patent Office

Publications: Documentation and Information Centre, Chinese Academy of Sciences, 1998

Staff employed in SOEs and TVEs: *China Statistical Yearbook*, 1997.

or systems, of innovation. The first is to complete the transformation of the large state enterprises into independent business enterprises. The second is to transform government functions so that they complement the reforms in the industrial sector (Xu and Fang, 1998).

Significant investments in infrastructure and industrial development have led to rapid growth of science and technology-based enterprises, particularly in the NHTZs. As growth slows and the impact of the economic crisis becomes more overt, there is likely to be increased competition for technological as well as financial resources.

The longer-term challenge appears to be to continue to build an innovative private sector and to transform government from agencies for managing programs to agencies for formulating policies. The major difficulty is likely to be concerned with removing the market shelter that the large state enterprises still enjoy, in order to enable the growing number of smaller and market-driven firms to compete in an innovative environment.

Expectations are that the government will increase S&T budgets through to 1999. The government has recently upgraded the status of the science and technology ministry and placed a higher emphasis on the education of future scientists and engineers. The current economic pressures are, if anything, likely to reinforce the current market-oriented policy approach. It will also give further impetus for the shift away from the government running programs and toward policy instruments in their place. The small and medium-size enterprises (SME) sector continues to be a prime target for such policies.

8.6   Summary and conclusions

The question for the future is perhaps not so much how S&T investment should be steered, but rather where it should be steered. The data presented here, although only sketchy, suggests that quite different patterns of innovation are emerging in different provinces and regions. Perhaps this is all part of the process toward the formation of an inter-related national system of innovation. On the other hand, it may suggest moves toward two different systems. While the notion of two systems is not new to China's policy makers, it has interesting implications in terms of innovation. The level of variation is both a challenge and an opportunity.

The issue of building strategic innovation alliances between provinces within the eastern group of regions remains an important issue for China's contemporary development. Such alliances are necessary for creating an independent Chinese national innovation system that can draw strength from the quite different regional experiences. If reforms in the more state-dominated provinces are not forthcoming, then transnational innovation links through large transnational firms may become more important for the commercial provinces than those with other domestic science provinces.

Notes

The authors gratefully acknowledge the assistance provided by Zhang Jing in China and Paola Crinnion in Australia in compiling and preparing much of the data for the tables in this chapter.

1   See also Chapter 4.
2   See the map on page xxiv of this volume.
3   See Chapter 4 for more discussion on this.
4   See also Chapters 3 and 4.

References

Freeman, C. (1987), *Technology, Policy and Economic Performance: Lessons from Japan*, Pinter, London.

Innes, J., and T. Turpin (forthcoming), *Intellectual Property Legislation and Innovation in the Asia-Pacific Region*, Hybrid Press, Melbourne.

Liu, X. (1998), China System of Innovation in Transition, paper presented to the Centre for Research Policy, *Workshop on Innovation*, Wollongong, May.

Nelson, R. (ed.) (1993), *National Systems of Innovation: A Comparative Study*, Oxford University Press, Oxford.

Porter, M. (1990), *The Competitive Advantage of Nations*, The Free Press, New York.

Xu, W., and F. Xin (1998), Review and Prospect of China's S&T System Reform, paper presented to the Centre for Research Policy, *Workshop on Innovation*, Wollongong, May.

Xue, L., and X. Wang (1998), The Development of Science Parks in China: An Empirical Analysis, draft paper presented to Tsinghua University *Workshop on National Systems of Science Funding*, Beijing, 20 October.

9

China's Labour Migration Since 1978

Robyn Iredale

The scale of internal migration in China has escalated rapidly since the introduction of economic reform. Much of this movement is labour migration, as millions of people move permanently or temporarily to find work or a better standard of living elsewhere. As the regulations controlling movement have gradually weakened, more people have decided to look for work elsewhere. This chapter discusses the trends in labour migration, including the size, spatial pattern and time frame of movements, and provides possible explanations for these trends. All population movements are now seen as part of a total system, not just a response to push-and-pull factors. The chapter also focuses on research findings on the characteristics of labour migrants and the impact on sending and receiving areas.

9.1   Introduction

The Beijing 1 November 1997 migrant census reported 2.86 million transient workers (China Daily, 1998, p. 3). This is the most recent attempt to try to assess one aspect of the labour migration phenomena, a phenomena that has become one of the most crucial issues facing Chinese policy makers. Should they try to continue to control it by means of various administrative tools, or should they encourage or promote it as a means of alleviating unemployment and poverty in rural and other areas? At the very least, should they turn a blind eye and accept that it is an inevitable and perhaps positive part of modernization and economic development?

As the scale of labour migration escalates, sources and destinations are brought into close connection with each other. Migrants settling in urban areas often concentrate in particular sectors and jobs, as well as in particular geographic locations. While the occupational concentration may be welcomed, the residential concentration frequently leads to claims of an escalation in unemployment, crime, disease and other rates. For the migrants themselves, the working and living conditions that they experience may be far from satisfactory. Nevertheless, they may far surpass the conditions at home. They often send money and new ideas back to their source region. Moreover, returning migrants frequently bring back money, skills and knowledge that change the nature of their source regions.

The relationship between labour migration and changes in the economic and social fabric of the society will be dealt with in this chapter. Section 2 attempts to quantify the scale of labour movement. Section 3 identifies the geographic and temporal patterns of such labour migration. The impact of the reform process on labour migration is discussed in section 4. The characteristics of the migrants are identified in section 5, while the environment in which they find themselves after their move is discussed in section 6. Section 7 attempts to provide a clearer explanation of China's labour migration. The consequences of labour migration for sending and receiving areas are discussed in sections 8 and 9 respectively. The explanations for labour migration will link this chapter with the chapter on regional income disparities, Chapter 10, and the changing nature of the Chinese labour market. Finally, section 10 will briefly discuss the outlook for future labour migration, and the major conclusions from this chapter.

9.2   Scale of labour migration

The movement of people to find work has long been part of the Chinese landscape. In the past it incorporated internal and international migration as people sought out opportunities to earn a better income, experience a new environment, or simply expand their horizons. Many people left China for the United States, Canada, Australia, and elsewhere during the gold rushes of the 1840s and onwards. They were preceded by generations of Chinese who went abroad as traders, merchants, businesspeople, shipworkers, performers and in many other areas. Many who went offshore for work never returned home, but established communities in countries throughout the world.

Within China, movement to find better agricultural land, escape catastrophes or as part of government policy to relocate people to less populated areas has been significant. Much of this movement has been a form of labour migration as people sought another livelihood or to escape rural poverty.

For example, Inner Mongolia experienced a high rate of population growth from 1911, largely due to the influx of Han Chinese. In 1912 there were one-and-a-half-million Han Chinese in Inner Mongolia, but the figure increased to 3.7 million in 1937, an increase of 140 per cent or 5.6 per cent per year, and to 4.7 million in 1947 representing an increase of 26 per cent or 2.6 per cent per year. Civil war and agricultural disruption in central China led to the movement of impoverished, landless peasants from north eastern provinces and the coastal regions of China south of Beijing, to the region. Initially the movement was mostly of single men, to build railways, work on Russian cattle farms and to trade. By the 1940s, many Han farming families had arrived and converted most of the eastern pasture to farmland, from pastoralism.

Similar movements are still occurring to Xinjiang Urgur Autonomous Region and other parts of China. The 1998 floods that impacted on over 230 million people can be expected to prompt some emigration from the overcrowded, artificially embanked regions which are prone to flooding.

As well as these types of movement, however, movements of labour in China are on the increase. The exact scale of these movements is extremely difficult to quantify for both definitional and statistical reasons. Firstly, the definitions of what constitutes a 'migrant' and 'labour migrant' vary according to whether the data are collected in a government census or survey or in another form of survey. The census defines as an 'official' migrant a person who has registered with the authorities and, therefore, changed their place of official registration. A person who has been in the current destination for more than twelve months but who has not changed their place of official registration, is captured in the census as a non-official migrant. Once people have been in the destination for five years they cease being classed as 'migrants', and become 'natives'. All other movers, seasonal and circulatory, are not captured in the census. All but official migrants are classed as the 'floating' population.

Definitions are complicated in China by administrative controls over movement. The *hukou* system of household-based registration, and other government policies, identify people according to where they are registered. Permanent urban *hukou* holders enjoy all government subsidies to urban residents – in housing, medical care, education and transportation. Temporary or floating labour migrants, and their families, may be given temporary *hukou* status, without access to subsidies. The *hukou* system still effectively controls the legal change of residential status, but it does little to control movement.

These problems partly explain variations in the estimates of internal migration. The second major factor that explains the variation is the magnitude of the population and the difficulties of conducting censuses, surveys and sample studies. Wu and Li (1996) review the literature on one form of labour migration, the magnitude of permanent rural–urban labour movement. They report wide variation in the findings, but there is a consistent finding of increasing permanent flows. The 1987 one-per-cent sample survey and the 1990 census estimated a flow of 3.9 million per annum in 1982–87 and 4.2 million per annum in 1985–90, respectively. As Wu and Li (1996) point out, however, these migration data still underestimate the total migration rate of China because they do not take account of multiple moves and return migration, migrants less than five years old, and people who died in the intercensal period.

Wu (1994) and Chan (1994) have used another technique, the residual method, to estimate permanent rural-to-urban migration. This technique is based on the total and natural growth of an urban population, with the difference between the two being attributed to rural–urban migration. Using this method, Wu's average annual rate of net rural-to-urban migration was 4.7 million for 1978–83 and 8.7 million for 1984–90. Chan's annual estimates were 7.3 million and 8.4 million for the same periods.

On top of these figures, data for the 'floating' population or temporary migrants, mostly farmers, are patchy and often guesstimates. Goldstein (1990) estimated China's total floating population to be 50 million in 1990, but by 1996–98 it had reached 80 to 100 million (Karmel, 1996; Bu Zhang, 1998). Shanghai had a floating population of 1.6 million in 1986, representing a tripling of the 1984 figure. By 1996, Shanghai's figure had climbed to 2.3 million. Beijing, a city of six million, in 1985 had 700 000 temporary migrants, but by 1997 this figure had climbed to 2.86 million.

9.3 Geographic and temporal patterns

Current movements are rural–rural, rural–urban, urban–rural and urban–urban, across local, county and provincial borders. Some moves are seasonal and temporary, while others are semi-permanent or permanent. As elsewhere there is a degree of crossover between temporary and permanent movement, as peoples' experiences vary from their expectations. There is an increasing tendency to stay longer; 53 per cent stay for more than one year, and the length of stay tends to be associated with the distance between the destination and source (MoA 1995, p. 43). The further the distance travelled the longer the person stays. In 1996, Wu and Li argued, along with many others, that most temporary migrants would end up returning home due to the lack of social services in urban areas.

As in most developing countries, the general direction of labour migration is to the urban areas. The rate of urbanization began to increase in 1982 as social and economic development picked up. Table 9.1 shows the rate of urbanization in China from 1953 to 1990. Data from the 1990 Census were analyzed under both a restricted as well as a more-extended urban definition. The urban proportion of the population increased markedly from 1982 to 1990.

Movement to middle sized towns was never as tightly monitored as movement to large cities, and after 1984 it became even more common. The period after 1984 is described as one of 'half open migration' as a result of legislation introduced in that year to allow peasants and their families to move to urban areas, below the county level. This created a precedent for the migration of couples and families.

Table 9.1 **Rate of Urbanization in China, 1953, 1964, 1982 and 1990**

Population	1st Census (July 1, 1953)	2nd Census (July 1, 1964)	3rd Census (July 1, 1982)	4th Census (July 1, 1990)	
				Previous urban definition	Most extended urban definition
Total (million)	594.3	697.9	1 008.2	1 133.7	1 133.7
Urban (million)	77.3	130.5	206.6	296.5	601.3
% urban	13	19	20	26	53

Source: Day and Ma, 1994.

Notes: The restricted definition covers only that part of (1) the city population residing in districts of cities and in neighbourhood committees of cities without districts; and (2) the town population in neighbourhood committees of towns under city or county administration. The extended definition includes all persons residing in places administratively defined as cities and towns: 'extra large' cities (over 1 million), 'large' cities (500 000 to 1 million), 'medium-sized' cities (200 000 to 500 000), 'small' cities (less than 200 000) and towns.

By the 1990s, the Rural Development Research Institute Project (1993–94) found that 78 per cent of rural emigrants went to cities and towns. Another survey conducted in 1995, the Rural Surplus Labour and Labour Market Project, found a similar percent, with large and small urban areas being more attractive than medium sized ones. This Project also found that 19.1 per cent of rural emigrants moved to other rural areas (Wu and Li, 1996, p. 12). The 1995 1-per-cent census shows a much higher proportion of inter-provincial rural-to-rural migration: 59 per cent for the west, 47 per cent for the central and 40 per cent for the east (Cai, 1998). The differences are due to census versus sample data and different definitions of what constitutes a migrant. The important fact, however, is that there is significant rural-to-rural migration. Increasing inequality in rural growth and in farmer's incomes among regions provide the explanation. Cai hypothesized that people often move from backward areas to more advanced rural areas and then from more advanced rural areas to urban areas, as part of a stepped process. Analysis of the 1995 1-per-cent census confirms this trend (Cai, 1998).

In terms of migration patterns across regions, the general direction of flows is from the inland, central and western, regions to the provinces in the eastern (coastal) region. In the coastal region, inter-provincial migration tends to be within the coastal zone. The boundaries of three broad regions, western, central and eastern, are shown on Figure 9.1. Figure 9.1 also shows the net migration rate for all provinces/ autonomous regions/municipalities between 1985 and 1990, from the 1990 census. Beijing and Shanghai experienced the highest net immigration rate, followed by Guangdong and Tianjin. As the figure shows, many areas experienced net out migration.

Figure 9.2 illustrates the scale of interregional movement from 1985 to 1990 from the 1990 census. While the prevailing trend is towards the east, there is considerable migration in the reverse direction, and within the three broad regions. The 1995 1-per-cent census data show that this pattern continued, with 54 per cent of inter-provincial migrant labourers from the western region moving to the eastern region between 1990 and 1995 and 71 per cent moving from the central region to the eastern region (Cai, 1998). These figures are much higher than those of 15 per cent and 39 per cent, respectively, cited in Wu and Li (1996, p. 13). Distance from the coast, in terms of cost of travelling, less information and isolation from home, account for this pattern.

Figure 9.1   **Interprovincial Migration by Province/Autonomous Region/Municipality, 1985–90**

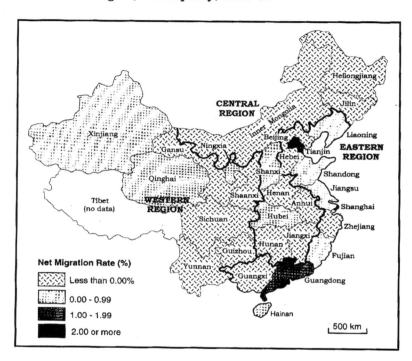

Source: Fan, 1996

9.4   Reform process and labour migration

The proportion of the Chinese population that is classified as part of the agricultural workforce is high, 50.5 per cent in 1996, as shown in Table 9.2. It is estimated that out of the total number of 490 million rural labour force, 150 million are engaged in farming, 135 million are employed by rural enterprises, about 50 million are working in cities, and there is a surplus of 150 to 200 million (either unemployed or underemployed) (Karmel, 1996; Wu and Li, 1996; Zhang, 1998).

Another factor on the supply side of potential labour migrants is the rate of population increase. Due to higher rates of population increase in the countryside, the number of additional new farm workers has been growing rapidly, while the demand for labour has been falling.

Figure 9.2   **Interprovincial Migration by Region, 1985–90**

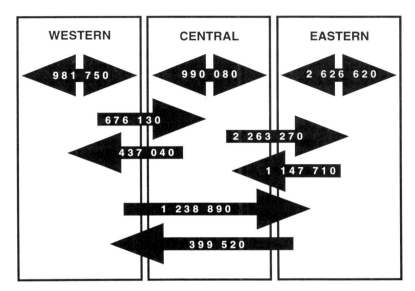

Source: Fan, 1996

According to Song's (1995) estimates, 7 million people reach working age in the rural areas every year at the moment and this will continue until the year 2000. These workers have low educational levels and limited skills, compared with their city counterparts.

Modernization of the agricultural sector has led to the displacement of workers. Firstly, there was the shift from a collective to a household-based farming system, the household responsibility system (HRS). The introduction of the rural responsibility system of family-based units controlling production on land assigned to their care enabled the 'transformation of agriculture into a productive and wealth-producing activity [which] involved a rapid increase in labour productivity and the need to export labour surpluses' (Hoy, 1996, p. 18).

Some of the excess labourers, 10 per cent by the end of 1985, gained employment in non-agricultural activities, primarily TVEs. At the same time the gradual reduction in control over movement to smaller urban areas enabled rural residents to move to urban areas. *Hukou*, or residential status, was retained, but rural labourers could leave their homes and go to work in cities. According to Kwan (1997, p. 333):

Robyn Iredale

Table 9.2 **Employment in China, 1978 to 1996 (10 000)**

Item	1978	1986	1991	1996
Total employees	40 152	51 282	58 360	68 850
Primary Industry				
(number)	28 313	31 212	34 876	34 769
(per cent)	70.5	60.9	59.7	50.5
Secondary Industry				
(number)	6 970	11 251	12 469	16 180
(per cent)	17.4	21.9	21.4	23.5
Tertiary Industry				
(number)	4 869	8 819	11 015	17 901
(per cent)	12.1	17.2	18.9	26.0
Employees by Urban and Rural				
Urban Employees	9 514	13 293	15 260	19 815
State-owned Units	7 451	9 333	10 664	11 244
Urban Collective-owned				
Units	2 048	3 421	3 628	3 016
Joint-owned Units		43	49	49
Share Holding Units				363
Foreign-funded Units			96	275
Overseas Chinese-funded				
Units			69	265
Units of Other Ownership				
Types			2	9
Private Enterprises			68	620
Individuals			692	1709
Rural Employees	30 638	37 990	43 093	49 035
Township & Village				
Enterprises	2 827	7 937	9 609	13 508
Urban areas				
Number of Newly Employed	544	810	765	705
Number of Registered				
Unemployed			352	553
Registered Unemployment				
Rate (%)			2.3	3.0

Sources: *China Statistical Yearbooks*, 1996 and 1997

Note: Since 1990 the data on economically active population, employed persons and urban/rural numbers, have been adjusted in accordance with sample survey data. As a result, the sum of the data by region, by ownership, or by sector, are not equal to the total.

... the greatest change in China's countryside, since the economic reform, has been the rapid expansion of rural township–village industries, TVIs. Its output share to the rural output has increased from 19 per cent in 1978 to 58 per cent in 1994. It accounted for 5.5 per cent and 15.3 per cent of rural employment in 1978 and 1994 respectively.

The growth in the labour force employed in TVEs is shown in Table 9.3. From 1978 to 1993 the growth rate was 10.95 per cent per annum compared with 2.55 per cent per annum for the national labour force (Kwan, 1997, p. 336). In the 1980s, the policy was one of transferring surplus rural labour to rural enterprises. People did not change their place of residence, only their place of work. TVEs grew up around China,

Table 9.3   **Growth of Township and Village Enterprises, 1978–96**

Year	Number of TVEs (million)	Workers employed (million)
1978	1.52	28.3
1979	1.48	29.1
1980	1.43	30.0
1981	1.33	29.7
1982	1.36	31.1
1983	1.35	32.3
1984	6.07	52.1
1985	12.22	69.8
1986	15.15	79.4
1987	17.50	88.1
1988	18.88	95.5
1989	18.69	93.7
1990	18.50	92.6
1991	19.09	96.1
1992	20.79	105.8
1993	24.52	123.5
1994	24.94	120.2
1995(a)	22.03	128.6
1996	23.36	135.1

Sources: Kwong, 1997, *China Statistical Yearbook*, 1997.
Notes: (a) Since 1994, small township and village enterprises not up to standard are not required to fill in and report statistical questionnaires.

predominantly in the wealthier coastal areas. From 1978 to 1984, the initial phase of economic reform, the amount of arable land decreased, and with limited land peasants sought out alternative means of earning a living. The commune system had been abolished and other policy changes enabled them to seek employment in TVEs. The TVEs that emerged in this phase were those with less technology-oriented production and with hard-working rural entrepreneurs. They absorbed large amounts of the labour surplus.

The period from 1985 to 1988 was marked by a decline in labour absorption, as many TVEs became more capital-intensive. The cost of TVE labour became more expensive and many farmers moved back to agricultural production, where the prices gained for their products had risen. From the unstable period of 1989 to 1990, there was concern about too many people moving from agricultural to non-agricultural occupations and into private and individual economic activities, and movement was slowed (Kwan, 1997). The absorption of labour by TVEs declined in 1994. Since 1994 the number of TVEs appears to have declined, even though the number of workers continued to grow. The decline may not be real due to requirements from 1994 that proper reporting mechanisms be followed before an enterprise can be included in the official statistics.

TVEs have become capital-intensive, as they have realigned themselves for operating in a more competitive, global environment. Most products are now produced for export, and high technology products earn more foreign exchange. Technological upgrading and increasing capital intensity in TVEs, therefore, means that they have not been able to continue to absorb all the surplus agricultural labour. Some enterprises, such as paper making, leather and furniture enterprises, have been forced to close because of stricter environmental monitoring by local officials (Huang, 1997). Further, some enterprises have gone out of production due to inefficiency, environmental degradation, ownership disputes or bankruptcy. In the past the bankruptcy rate was less than 7 per cent, but the rate is now 20 per cent (Bai, 1998).

Another major problem has become that of asset rights. When a township-run enterprise (TREs) or a village-run enterprise (VREs) is owned by local government, and worked by local farmers, there is little dispute over ownership. According to Bai (1998), ownership problems have occurred since rural labour began to move to work in TVEs in other regions. Moreover, an increased number of rural enterprises are owned and run by groups of households who pool their resources together for production, called joint household enterprises (JHEs), as well as by private individuals (POEs). JHEs are a fertile ground for disputes over ownership. Table 9.4 gives the ownership breakdown of TVEs from 1984 to 1994. TREs and VREs have decreased from accounting for 85.7 per cent of ownership in 1984 to 67.7 per cent in 1994, with much of the decline in local government ownership occurring in 1985 and 1986.

TVEs also developed in urban areas but somewhat later. They often emerged as rural entrepreneurs saw an opportunity for an enterprise, such as a garbage collection service or a retail or export distribution outlet for products produced in the countryside. In urban areas it is more expensive to set up, as the TVE may have to provide welfare services.

Over 70 per cent of TVEs have debts. In the past they relied primarily on labour, and the goal of TVEs was to maximize employment. Now, under the market system and as TVEs privatize,[1] the goal has changed to one of making profits. Many TVEs are supported by local governments to protect them and to keep them going for employment purposes. Thus, changes in farming activities and the nature of TVEs are due to privatization.

In 1996, TVEs employed some 135 million people. This is a very significant number, and suggests that the problem of rural unemployment would be much greater without them. However, there is still a rural surplus, and from the late 1980s rural labourers began to move to other areas in search of jobs. Many of the jobs they sought were created by the official endorsement in 1983 of private enterprises. Village and township committees became involved in the 1980s in

Table 9.4   **Ownership of Rural Enterprises, 1984–94 (%)**

Year	TREs & VREs	JHEs & POEs
1984	85.7	14.3
1985	75.1	24.9
1986	71.1	28.9
1987	67.9	32.1
1988	67.2	32.8
1989	64.7	35.3
1990	64.2	35.8
1991	66.4	33.5
1992	67.3	32.7
1993	64.5	35.4
1994	67.7	32.3

Source: Kwong, 1997.

exporting surplus rural labourers on a temporary basis to other places in China or overseas.[2] Migration came to be used as a development strategy to improve the local economy and help alleviate poverty.

Another factor on the supply side of potential labour migrants is the instability in the state-owned enterprises (SOEs). SOEs in urban areas of China have been, and still remain, a significant employer of labour.[3] Many of the enterprises are non-competitive, and the reform of enterprise management has to 'some extent forced the state-owned enterprises to face market competition, making some SOEs turn to low-pay, hard-working and obedient migrant workers' (Wu and Li, 1996, p. 23). Others have closed down and sold off or rented out their plant to private operators. Nevertheless, 25 per cent to 33 per cent of the people in this work force are estimated to be 'surplus', and full reform of the sector was announced in early 1997 (Karmel, 1996, p. 114). The problem is most severe in central and western China and in small and medium-sized cities. As these enterprises restructure, or go out of operation, the shedding of labour will add to the unemployed and the potential number of labour migrants. By August 1998, however, Premier Zhu Rongji appeared to have slowed down the rate of reform of this sector in response to fears of rapidly increasing unemployment in urban areas.

On the demand side, Joint Ventures introduced from 1979 do not require permanent *hukou*, only temporary registration which is the same as for TVEs. The increased demand for migrant labourers has also been associated with other important reforms that have led to the growth of labour-intensive, light manufacturing and service industries. Firstly, there has been a shift away from the emphasis on an industry, especially heavy industry-oriented development policy. Secondly, the reform of the investment system has enabled the growth of collectives and private and foreign investors, most of whom are engaged in labour-intensive manufacturing and service provision.

Therefore, there have been institutional changes on both the supply and demand sides that provided the climate for dramatically increased labour migration after 1978. At the individual level the traditional explanation for labour migration has largely been based on the Todaro model, in which people move to earn higher incomes (Todaro, 1969). On this basis one would expect the highest emigration to be from low-income areas. Cai (1998) and others argue that China fits the Todaro model, and that income disparity is a major factor in explaining labour migration. According to Cai, micro-reform is outstripping macro-reform and, in the absence of mobility of capital and due to the decentralization of power and return of profits at the micro-level, the movement of labour has become the major mechanism for reducing the income gap.

Income differences among rural areas, between rural and urban, and between the east, central and western regions are marked. Studies have shown that rural–urban wage differentials have widened since the reform and the urban–rural income ratio reached 2.45 in 1992. Migrant workers in Beijing and Tianjin could earn 3 600 yuan a year in 1994 compared to 660 yuan in rural areas (Wu and Li, 1996, p. 23). Regional income differentials have also increased since the reform. One study found that since 1980 the gap in rural per capita income between eastern and western provinces had increased from 47 to 395 yuan, and between the top and the bottom provinces from 200 to 1 700 yuan (PRURS, 1994, p. 4). More recent evidence (see Chapter 10) supports this continuing widening of the income gap between regions.

Income differentials are an important element in explaining Chinese labour migration but other factors are also at work. Individuals may be motivated by a desire to acquire more skills, experience a different lifestyle or break away from family and other constraints. Networks, investment patterns, local government policies, and former educational involvement all influence patterns of movement.

9.5   Characteristics of labour migrants

On the whole migrant labourers in China tend to be young, mostly less than 35, better educated than rural non-migrant labourers, and more often male. However, both of the latter points are not always the case. For example, a survey by Wenbao (1996) of five villages in Anhui and Zhejiang Provinces in 1992, linked to the Rural Surplus Labour and Its Employment Exploration project mentioned earlier, concluded that there was no positive relationship between level of education and migration. Both people with and without education migrated out. Wenbao (1996, p. 121) concluded that 'the main demand for rural migrants exists in the informal labour market, where no qualifications are required. ... So it would make no difference whether or not workers were educated.'

Most of the discussion in this chapter, and elsewhere, is about the massive migration out of rural areas. At the same time, though, there is a complementary movement of better educated people out of towns and small cities to larger urban areas. This has not been well documented, but it is evident that many tertiary educated people are choosing to remain in the cities where they gain their degrees. When they obtain a job they can usually change their place of registration quite easily. Even those who cannot find a government job are now able to seek employment in the many private and foreign ventures that have been established since the reforms.

Others who have obtained their education in more isolated regions, such as Xinjiang and Inner Mongolia, are also beginning to search out more highly paid jobs on the eastern seaboard. Shanghai's 'blue seal' program, which grants permanent registration to tertiary educated people who obtain a job, is designed to attract the best migrants to Shanghai. According to Lee and Hook (1996, p. 106), Guangdong, Beijing and Shanghai benefit most from the internal movement of qualified human resources, but other urban areas in open economic zones also acquire skilled personnel in this way.

The sex ratio of migrants varies by region, with heavy industrial areas such as Beijing, Tianjin, Shanghai and Liaoning attracting relatively more males, while areas dominated by labour-intensive manufacturing industries such as Guangdong, Fujian and Jiangsu attract a higher proportion of females. A survey carried out in Guangdong found a sex ratio among migrants of 91 males to 100 females (Liu, 1995, p. 68). This can be explained by the presence of many apparel and electronic-assembling plants in the Pearl River Delta, the fastest-growing area in China, and their preference for women workers. An extremely low ratio of 57 males to 100 females was found in a 1990 survey of four provinces – Guangdong, Jiangsu, Zhejiang and Hebei (Wu and Li, 1996). Such a high proportion of females is not just a function of sex-preference by employers. Many rural areas of China deliberately recruit or send women, rather than men, because women are more reliable in terms of sending back remittances. Zhou (1998), in a study of sending and receiving regions, found that men spend most of the money that they earn on consumption, while women send most home. Zhou also found that many women go out to work not so much for money, but for extra experiences and to improve their social status. He found that many labour migrants are relatively rich and are satisfied with their move, even though they do not get well paid. On the other hand Tan's work (Tan, 1998) among women migrant workers in Guangdong, shows that many live in poor conditions, have little contact with the surrounding community, have poor access to services and are cut off from family and friends. Many do not relish the experience but endure it in order to send home money. She found that most women return home when it is time to marry.

9.6   Occupations and working environments of labour migrants

A wide range of findings exist on the conditions of migrant workers. Those who move to agricultural areas are most likely to engage in cash-crop production, or the raising of animals for sale in the market. The majority of urban labour migrants work in the secondary and tertiary sectors. In the industrial sector they generally take jobs that are more physically demanding, less skilled and potentially more hazardous. Construction and factory jobs are most common for men, while women work as 'outworkers' in small clothing enterprises or in factories. In the service sector, women work in restaurants and as cleaners, domestic workers, waitresses and prostitutes. Employers may be SOEs, TVEs, collectively owned enterprises, joint ventures or private companies. On the whole, however, the consensus is that 'compared with urban residents, China is no exception to the occupational concentration of temporary migrants to cities found in other Asian countries' (Yang and Guo, 1996, p. 785).

Both men and women also become self-employed as street vendors, selling vegetables, kebabs and numerous other products, or as peddlers, shoe and bicycle repairers, and hairdressers. They may emerge at night as part of the illegal 'ghost markets', or they may have official approval and pay taxes.

Access to jobs in urban areas is controlled in a number of ways. The absence of registration is one way of distinguishing between potential employees. Some cities openly list the jobs available to rural labourers without registration. In Beijing, for example, rural workers are only eligible for 271 types of job – the dirty, dangerous ones that the urban residents do not want. In Shanghai, all occupations are grouped into three categories: category A jobs can be filled by migrant workers after being advertised and not filled; category B jobs can be filled by migrants but are subject to quotas; and category C jobs can never be filled by migrant workers (Wu and Li, 1996).

Few migrant labourers appear to engage in 'blind migration'. Most surveys have found that kinship relationships and people from the same village/town play an important role in locating job opportunities, conveying job information and providing other help in job searching (Wu and Li, 1996). This results in people from the same area or village engaging in the same occupation in the city. For example, migrants from Leqing in Zheijiang mainly engage in garment making and marketing in Beijing. As a detailed study by Xiang (1998) shows, Zhejiang village in Beijing includes many people, especially women, who are involved in manufacturing and selling internationally. They have a complex network of suppliers and purchasers. Many businesspeople have moved out of their original job into other jobs or small businesses. Some have obtained local approval and support for setting up large commercial developments, and they have become an important part of the city's economy. Many other services, such as barbers, clinics, kindergarten, restaurants and repair shops, have emerged to service Zhejiang village.

Other examples are provided by migrants from Anhui who mainly engage in domestic service in Beijing, and migrants from Henan who have established rubbish collection and recycling industries in Nanjing and Beijing. In Beijing, about 1 000 trash collectors live in 'Henan village'. This is both a geographic area and a generic name for people who perform this activity (Xiang, 1998). 'Xinjiang village' in Beijing is another example where people of particular nationality groups – Uygurs and Kazaks – have established a community consisting largely of restauranteurs and street food sellers.

Government employment networks are beginning to be established, but migrants mostly do not rely on organizations for finding work. However, a small percentage do find jobs through their local communities. This type of arranged labour migration is similar to international labour migration with agents acting as go-betweens. Sometimes, local government officials recruit and send out young workers as a means of earning money for poor areas in China. Once people have reached their destination they may change jobs. Some people are directly recruited by urban enterprises, but this is usually once they already have another job in the city.

No analysis has been done on the relationship between the level of human capital investment and nature of employment. It appears, however, that there is considerable downgrading, as migrants are excluded from more skilled jobs. The exception, of course, is where skilled migrants gain permanent registration, either on the basis of marriage, or selection by the city or by an employer.

9.7   Understanding China's labour migration

Government restrictions on movement have led to a system where people without permanent household registration in the place they are living are disadvantaged. Many jobs are simply not open to them, as defined lists of jobs available for temporary workers have been compiled. The continued maintenance of the household registration system, *hukou*, to retain order over population distribution and to control the level of mobility, has encouraged labour market segmentation. In an effort to control inflows, Shanghai has also introduced a 'blue seal' system to enable the permanent settlement of desirable skilled and business migrants. The points system used to decide who can gain permanent registration in Shanghai is akin to the migration selection systems of Australia and Canada.

At the same time, temporary and permanent movement has been officially encouraged by local administrators, by the establishment of computer information networks of jobs and by loans. Mobile workers are seen as a tool for development by providing a cheap supply of labour, and as a means of alleviating poverty in rural areas. Other migration movement has been encouraged primarily by informal networks.

The creation of four Special Economic Zones, with special policies and economic opportunities, on the eastern seaboard in the early 1980s, along with the loosening of control over movement and policies promoting in-migration, led to the initiation of the pattern of easterly movement. In 1984 the open-door policies were expanded to 14 coastal cities and Hainan Island, coastal development strategies were boosted, and Shanghai's Pudong district was opened up. This all led to an increased flow of migrants.

Wei's correlation analysis (see Wei, 1997) reveals that net interregional migration is most closely correlated with regional differentials in foreign investment and state investment. He concludes that global forces and the state largely determine interregional migration in China, and conventional variables that most commonly explain internal migration, income and job opportunities, are not as important. Wei's earlier work (see Wei, 1996) shows that the location pattern of foreign investment is determined by the size of the domestic markets, access to international markets, transport facilities and state policy. The significance of the most recent finding is that 'state policies alone, though influential, are insufficient to understand migration behaviour in transitional socialist countries' (Wei, 1997, p. 213).

The Todaro model (Todaro, 1969), the best-known economic model of migration decisions, has been questioned as it gives no explicit consideration to the impact of remittances. By contrast, the New Economics of Labour Migration (NELM) approach argues that, firstly, migration decisions are part of family strategies to raise income, obtain funds to invest in new activities, and insure against income and production risks; and, secondly, that remittances set in motion a development dynamic by lessening production and investment constraints faced by households in poor developing-country environments (Castles, 1998). Bilsborrow (1998) notes that one of the implications of the NELM theory is that if migration is a tool used for risk minimization, it could occur even in the absence of income differentials. Income differentials were considered a necessary precondition in the neo-classical theory of migration based on human capital models. It is now realized that not only the poor move, and that migration is a strategy employed for a variety of reasons and not just for earning extra income or overcoming poverty.

A number of empirical studies support the NELM hypothesis that migration and remittances have positive indirect effects on the incomes of migrant-sending households, easing capital and risk constraints on local production. Market linkages, in turn, transmit the impacts of migration from migrant to non-migrant households in the sending economy. Taylor (1998) argues, however, that the economic environment that encourages out-migration may also limit the potential for remittances to stimulate development. Poor market infrastructure and lack of credit facilities made it hard to realize the development potential of remittances. This implies that source regions/countries could adopt a variety of economic policies to increase the potential positive contributions of remittances to broad-based income growth.

The NELM approach appears to apply within China where much of the mobility is related to more than seeking a higher income. Migration is a complex process where the decision to migrate is based on a range of historical, personal, family, economic and social factors. For example, Wenbao (1996, p. 125) found that people in a poor village were less likely to be attracted to going out to work to earn extra income than people in wealthier villages. The poor 'prefer to stay at home if the income in the destination areas is not high enough'. On the other hand, Wenbao found that contacts, both direct and indirect, are very important in influencing migration behaviour. The newly emerging *Baogongtou*, private contractor in rural areas, and government-organized labour export companies are also playing an increasing role.

9.8   Consequences for sending areas

Some of the income which is earned in the destination may be sent home to the countryside. As we have seen, *hukou* acts as a barrier to the permanent settlement of families in cities and thus it discourages migrant labourers from investing in cities. 'To secure their future they have to keep a close tie with their family land and village community' (Wu and Li, 1996, p. 27).

A survey in Shandong province found that 82 per cent of migrant workers sent home 30 per cent of their earnings per year, an average of 1 776 yuan or US$350. Cai (see Cai, 1998) extrapolated this figure and calculated that if all rural out-migrants sent home this amount it would equal 80 per cent of rural expenditure on fixed assets, and 3.7 times the state expenditure on agricultural production and administration. Households receiving remittances are more able to use modern inputs in farming as substitutes for labour and land. A study in Sichuan found that about one-third of remittances was spent on fertilizers, pesticides and plastic films for hothouses.

On the whole the effect of out-migration has been positive in rural areas and associated with steadily increasing grain production.

Nevertheless, some areas have experienced a negative impact. While the money sent home has helped alleviate poverty, the young people going out to work changed the composition of the village so that agricultural production often declined. Women were left to do both farming and caring for the children, and as a consequence the 'younger children left in school seem not interested in farming at all when they grow up. They are definitely potential migrants' (Huang et al., 1995, p. 49).

Many migrants return home after a period, though this does not spell failure as is often the case with return migration. Migration has often been for a certain period with a specific goal in mind. Most return migrants have worked in cities for five-to-seven years and return home looking for new but more stable opportunities that are more likely in the rural non-agricultural sector. In Guangfeng County, Jiangxi, most of the 60 recently opened rural enterprises were owned or managed by returned migrants, and, in Mengcheng County, Anhui, 57 per cent of the existing 21 000 rural enterprises were established by returned migrants (Wu and Li, 1996, p. 28). The rate of return migration is not known and the tendency to re-migrate certainly appears to be high, especially for those who have already been away for a considerable period. The opportunity cost of remaining at home has become greater.

9.9 Consequences for receiving areas

The urban labour employment system has moved from a planned one to a market one as a result of labour migration. According to Wu and Li (1996, p. 29), 'migrant labourers have formed the most competitive part of the urban labour market, in which labourers are free to choose jobs and enterprises while enterprises are free to select workers'. In fact it is not quite as open and non-discriminatory as this. As we have seen a dual labour market has developed in many cities, where people with permanent registration take the better jobs and floating or temporary migrants take the dirty and dangerous jobs. The continued maintenance of *hukou* seems to be having the effect of entrenching a segmented labour market structure, to some extent. Migrant labourers are consistently disadvantaged by being confined to the status of temporary or floating and are unable to access many services.

The wages paid to migrant workers are around half those paid to non-migrants, thereby providing an incentive to all enterprises to hire them. Employers are not required to provide on-the-job training, promotion and superannuation, or to provide services such as housing, health care and child education to temporary workers. Therefore, the level of service provision is poor and workers' rights are given little emphasis. This pattern depends on a continuous flow of migrant workers who are employed on contract for a specified period.

There is an increasing tendency for migrant workers to send for their families, once they are set up, and this is having the effect of making for more permanency. The worker may rent a house and the family will join them and establish contacts with teachers, doctors, security officials and other organizations to get benefits. Access to services may depend on bribes or they may get temporary residence permits that enable access to some services.

In the heavily industrialized Shenzhen region of southern China, a plan introduced in 1995 encourages fixed migration, rather than a floating flow, as this can be more easily managed and controlled (Shi Xian, 1998). But fixed migration requires the provision of better services and these changes are having the effect of raising the relative cost of hiring migrant workers. Nevertheless employers are finding this beneficial, and this pattern is likely to spread elsewhere. Shenzhen was one of the first regions in China to open to the outside and has often led the way in industrial reform.

Zhao (1998) states that since 1995 the outflow of rural labour has slowed down, but agrees that it has also become more organized and rural labourers are now more competitive with urban workers. Some cities' officials have responded by providing laid-off urban workers with alternative employment, through re-employment projects. Others have responded by placing further restrictions 'on the scope of industries and types of work in which rural labourers may be employed. In addition, some administrative measures have been taken to encourage migrants to leave cities' (Zhao, 1998, p. 1).

9.10 Conclusion

Labour migration is one of the major labour market dilemmas facing the Chinese authorities. The two major issues influencing labour migration are the maintenance of *hukou* and the continued protection of the SOEs.

There is consistent debate in China now as to whether *hukou* should be retained. Some argue that it is the best way to keep some form of discipline and control over mobility, and that it will be a long time before it can be eliminated. They pose the question whether China can afford to have hundreds of millions of surplus rural labourers flooding the cities? *Hukou* is seen as slowing down the rate of urbanization and the development of some of the social, economic and environmental problems attendant on the growth of large cities. Others argue that it should be retained from a welfare and income distribution effect. They maintain that the *hukou* system encourages saving by migrants so that they can send home remittances, thereby cutting down on wasteful consumption, and participation, in cities, and discourages investment in cities. Migrants also return home with money and new skills and ideas which benefit the rural economy. It is argued that these processes help to reduce the urban–rural differential. On the other hand, many Chinese social scientists are pressing for a freeing up of the system and the elimination of *hukou* as China moves further down the road to economic reform. They argue that the household registration system is outdated, discriminatory and runs counter to economic development.

The Chinese Government is becoming increasingly aware of the long-term social effects of temporary labour migration, as demonstrated in the March 1998 Central Government decision to enable the children of floating migrants to gain easier access to schools. The government announced that the children of temporary migrants should be enrolled in urban schools without incurring heavy enrolment costs. In the past, school principals had been at liberty to admit children from the floating population at a fee that they themselves nominated. In some areas, for example Beijing, this led to high fees for children of floating workers while in other areas, for example Urumqi, Xinjiang, local education officials provided almost free education to such children. The former position was leading to high rates of non-enrolment in some urban areas. The policy change is designed to militate against the development of future social problems, but the tendency to permanency is likely to increase due to this policy change.

The continued protection of the state workforce is also a matter of ongoing debate. The sacking of 15 million surplus urban labourers currently employed in SOEs would add considerably to the pool of unemployed, and could be very destabilizing. Two-thirds of all state enterprises are experiencing financial difficulties and central government deficits are rising (Karmel, 1996). The government continues to offer subsidies to state enterprises but it may soon have no choice but to close down most state enterprises. The government also has the problem of increasing corruption that has come about as a result of the decentralization of decision-making from the national to local level, and the opportunity for asset removal by managers and employees of state enterprises often 'aided and abetted by local government officials' (Hughes, 1998, p. 75).

Outside commentators, such as Karmel (1996) in 'The Neo-authoritarian Dilemma and the Labor Force: Control and Bankruptcy vs Freedom and Instability', conclude that unless change happens quickly it may need to be more radical than that which is presently required. Unrest and protest are highly likely. This position is supported by Hughes (1998, p. 77), who argues for rapid change and says that the 'iron rice bowl will be broken. The only question is whether China will be ready'.

Within China, however, many are arguing for gradual change as a better choice for the country. Recent developments have shown that the leaders are afraid of instability and are unwilling to promote dramatic labour market reforms, even though they regard them as necessary.

Of the two issues the flow of rural migrants has not created a major political problem for the government, as most left behind little and had everything to gain by seeking work elsewhere. By increasingly closing their eyes to labour migration, the government has allowed it to happen as one way of trying to overcome regional inequalities. However, unemployed state-enterprise workers are the privileged elite of China, along with civil servants, and if they lose their jobs they also stand to lose their welfare services. China must act to create a national welfare system the cost of which is shared by enterprises, workers and national and local governments for the benefit of all workers. Elimination of the dual social structure that currently exists in employment and social security, between the city and the countryside, is imperative and may help stem the outflow from rural areas. Retraining schemes and public works programs must also be put in place to reorient and absorb displaced state workers. Otherwise, urban discontent will prevail and this will be much more destabilizing than the high level of rural discontent that has already manifested itself in the process of labour migration.

Notes

1   See Chapter 4.
2   173 000 in 1993.
3   They employed 1 12 440 000 workers in 1996.

References

Bai, N. (1998), The Effect of Labor Migration on Agriculture: An Empirical Study, presentation at the *Labour Mobility and Migration in China and Asia Conference*, Institute of Asia-Pacific Studies (Chinese Academy of Social Sciences) and International Institute of Asian Studies (Leiden), Beijing, 17–18 April.

Bilsborrow, R. (1998), Discussant's Comments on a paper by E. Taylor, The New Economics of Labour Migration and the Role of Remittances in the Migration Process, *UN Technical Symposium on International Migration and Development*, The Hague, 29 June–3 July.

Bu. Z. (1998), The Research on the Status of Temporarily-staying Population Engaged in Industry, Business and Service Trades in China, presentation at the *Labour Mobility and Migration in China and Asia Conference*, Institute of Asia-Pacific Studies (Chinese Academy of Social Sciences) and International Institute of Asian Studies (Leiden), Beijing, 17–18 April.

Cai, F. (1998), Regional Characteristics of Labor Migration in China's Transitional Period, presentation at the *Labour Mobility and Migration in China and Asia Conference*, Institute of Asia-Pacific Studies (Chinese Academy of Social Sciences) and International Institute of Asian Studies (Leiden), Beijing, 17–18 April.

Castles, S. (1998), Report on the UN Technical Symposium on International Migration and Development, Conference, The Hague, 29 June –3 July.

Chan, K.W. (1994), 'Urbanization and Rural–urban Migration in China since 1982 – A New Baseline', *Modern China*, Vol. 20, No. 3, pp. 243–81.

China Daily (1998), '2.86 million transient workers in Beijing', 20 March, p. 3.

Day, L., and X. Ma (eds) (1994), *Migration and Urbanization in China*, M.E. Sharpe, Ardmonk, NY.

Fan, C. (1996), 'Economic Opportunities and Internal Migration: A Case Study of Guangdong Province, China', *The Professional Geographer*, Vol. 48, No. 1, pp. 28–45.

Goldstein, A. (1990), 'Urbanization in China, 1982-1987: Effects of Migration and Reclassification', *Population and Development Review*, Vol. 16, No. 4, pp. 673–702.

Hoy, C.S. (1996), 'The Fertility and Migration Experiences of Migrant Women in Beijing, China', PhD thesis, University of Leeds, United Kingdom.

Huang, P. (1997), *Personal Communication*, Institute of Sociology, Chinese Academy of Social Sciences, Beijing.

Huang, P. et al. (1995), *Rural Migration and Rural Development: A Report on the Field Investigation of Eight Villages from Four Provinces in China*, Institute of Sociology, Chinese Academy of Social Sciences, Beijing.

Hughes, N.C. (1998), 'Smashing the Iron Rice Bowl', *Foreign Affairs*, July/August, pp. 67–77.

Karmel, S. (1996), 'The Neo-authoritarian Dilemma and the Labor Force: Control and Bankruptcy vs Freedom and Instability', *Journal of Contemporary China*, Vol. 5, No. 12, pp. 111–33.

Kwan, F. (1997), 'The Use of Capital and Labour in Township-Village Industries in China: An Application of CMEC Analysis', in C.A. Tisdell and J. Chai (eds), *China's Economic Growth and Transition*, Nova Science Publishers, New York.

Kwong, C.L. (1997), 'Property Rights and Performance of China's Township-Village Enterprises', in C.A. Tisdell and J. Chai (eds), *China's Economic Growth and Transition*, Nova Science Publishers, New York.

Lee, W.O., and B. Hook (1996), 'Human Resources', in B. Hook (ed.), *Fujian Gateway to Taiwan*, Oxford University Press, Hong Kong.

Liu, X. (1995), 'On the Issues of Immigrant Labour Tide in Quangdong', *Shehuixue Yanjiu* (Sociology Research), No. 4, pp. 68–74.

MoA Migrant Labour Survey Project (Ministry of Agriculture) (1995), 'Rural Labour Mobility in Economic Development', *Zhongguo Nongcun Jingji* (Chinese Rural Economy), No. 1, pp. 43–50.

PRURS (Policy Research Unit, Rural Section, CCP Central Committee) (1994), 'A Preliminary Study on the Issues of Rural Labour Inter-Regional Mobility', *Zhongguo Nongcun Jingji* (Chinese Rural Economy), No. 3, pp. 3–13.

Shi Xian, M. (1998), Structural Cost and Institutional Origins: the Management of Out-coming Labor in Shenzhen, paper delivered at *China Research Network Workshop*, Beijing, 28–29 March.

State Statistical Bureau (1996, 1997), *China Statistical Yearbook*, China Statistical Publishing House, Beijing.

Tan, S. (1998), Approach to Female Out-going Labourers, paper delivered at *China Migration Research Network Workshop*, Beijing, 28–29 March.

Taylor, E. (1998), The New Economics of Labour Migration and the Role of Remittances in the Migration Process, *UN Technical Symposium on International Migration and Development*, The Hague, 29 June–3 July.

Todaro, H. (1969), 'A Model of Labor Migration and Urban Unemployment in Less Developed Countries', *American Economic Review*, Vol. 3, pp. 393–423.

Wei, Y. (1996), Regional patterns of Foreign Direct Investment in China, Manuscript, University of California, Los Angeles.

—— (1997), 'Interregional migration in socialist countries: the case of China', *GeoJournal*, Vol. 41, No. 3, pp. 205–14.

Wenbao, Q. (1996), *Rural–urban Migration and its Impact on Economic Development in China*, Avebury, Aldershot.

Wu, H.X. (1994), 'Rural to Urban Migration in the People's Republic of China', *China Quarterly*, No. 139, pp. 669–98.

Wu, H.X., and Z. Li (1996), *Research on Rural-to-Urban Labour Migration in the Post-reform China: A Survey*, Chinese Economy Research Unit, University of Adelaide.

Xiang Biao, M. (1998), Embedded Floating Population: the Relation of the Floating Population Community to Residence Community in Beijing, paper delivered at *China Migration Research Network Workshop*, Beijing, 28–29 March.

Yang, Q. and F. Guo (1996), 'Occupational Attainments of Rural to Urban Temporary Economic Migrants in China, 1985–1990', *International Migration Review*, Vol. 30, No. 3, pp. 771–87.

Zhang, Q. (1998), Research on the Status of Temporarily-staying Population Engaged in Industry, Business and Service Trades in China, paper delivered at *Labour Mobility and Migration in China and Asia Conference*, Institute of Asia-Pacific Studies (Chinese Academy of Social Sciences) and International Institute of Asian Studies (Leiden), Beijing, 17–18 April.

Zhao, S. (1998), China's Rural Labour Mobility and Migrant Unemployment in Cities, paper delivered at *Labour Mobility and Migration in China and Asia Conference*, Institute of Asia-Pacific Studies (Chinese Academy of Social Sciences) and International Institute of Asian Studies (Leiden), Beijing, 17–18 April.

Zhou, D.M. (1997), Internal Migration to the Quangdong Region of China, paper presented at *China Migration Research Network Workshop*, Zhongshan University, Guangzhou, October.

10

Regional Income Inequality in China

Khorshed Chowdhury
Charles Harvie
Amnon Levy

This chapter is concerned with analyzing developments in income inequality in China during the period of its economic reform. An overview of regional income disparity is conducted, focusing upon that between the coastal, central and western provinces, and the key factors behind this. A conceptual framework for measuring income disparity both between and within provinces is presented, and utilizing appropriate data the Theil index is calculated. It is found that income disparities within provinces have declined. However, income disparities between regions and provinces have increased significantly during the period of the 1990s. The government's policy response to such a widening disparity and its prospects of being successful is discussed.

10.1 Introduction

China's economic reforms have produced rapid economic growth, the benefits of which have spread to all of its regions. However, the coastal provinces in particular have been by far the major beneficiaries. This has primarily arisen from the fact that through deliberate policy measures by government the coastal provinces have attained greater integration into the international economy through trade and investment, which has contributed to a noticeable divergence of regional growth rates. This has accelerated in recent years with the further opening up of the economy and its greater market orientation. Per capita income in the wealthier coastal provinces has been approximately double that of the poorer hinterland provinces since the middle of the 1970s, and this gap has continued to widen. As a consequence, the Chinese government is having to face up to a major policy dilemma. While the coastal region has provided the engine of market-oriented economic reforms and growth, its rapid development has contributed to an increasing regional income divergence which threatens to create the conditions for serious social and political tensions.

During the 1980s the initial focus of economic reform was placed upon attracting foreign investment to Special Economic Zones, and then later to 'open' cities located in coastal provinces. These presented an attractive opportunity for foreign investors because of lower relative costs of production. However, during the 1990s, lower cost structures in production locations away from the main early growth areas on the coast, now represent a major potential source of opportunity for both local and foreign investors. A flow of local and foreign investment into the hinterland is already underway and has the potential to reduce the widening income disparities alluded to, but these provinces will require substantial infrastructure investments involving significant inter-regional fiscal transfers to sustain their income and growth momentum.

The remainder of this chapter proceeds as follows. A review of changing regional patterns of income, productivity and growth is identified in section 2. The major factors behind this diverging regional performance is discussed in section 3. A conceptual framework that can be utilized to analyze developments in income disparity for China is presented in section 4. Income disparity trends within and between China's provinces and regions are summarized in section 5. Recent government policy initiatives to address regional disparities, and the likelihood of future convergence, are discussed in section 6. The major conclusions are summarized in section 7.

10.2 Overview of regional disparities and its major causes

Regional income divergence in China has become most pronounced since the early 1990s, particularly since 1992, due to the acceleration of economic reforms and the increased market orientation of the economy. The latter enabled provinces to increasingly focus their production upon areas of comparative advantage. China has 23 provinces, five autonomous regions, and four centrally controlled municipalities.[1] A useful starting point for the analysis of disparities in the provinces' recent economic performance is to divide these into the coastal, central and western regions (see map on page xxiv). As indicated from Table 10.1 the distribution of income, population and land between these three regions is highly uneven.

Table 10.1   **Regional Income and Shares of Population and Land, 1995**

	GDP per capita US$	Share of national GDP %	Share of total population %	Share of national land %
Coastal	810	58	41	21
Central	441	28	36	19
Western	350	14	23	60

Source: State Statistical Bureau (1996)

The coastal region comprises the dynamic economic provinces of Guangdong, Jiangsu, Zhejiang, Fujian, Shandong,[2] the three rapidly growing municipalities of Shanghai, Tianjin and Beijing, the heavy industry province of Liaoning, and the poorer but rapidly growing provinces of Hebei, Hainan, and Guangxi which borders Vietnam. Traditionally, Shanghai in the east, Beijing and Tianjin in the north, and Liaoning in the north east coastal region were the most developed provinces in terms of industry. However during the period of economic reforms the poorer southern coastal provinces of Guangdong and Fujian achieved rapid economic growth,[3] and have now attained higher income levels than those in the north-eastern provinces. For example Liaoning, with a high proportion of assets in inefficient and financially distressed SOEs and with many redundant workers, is now poor by the standards of the southern provinces.

The first four Special Economic Zones opened in the early 1980s were in the southern coastal provinces of Guangdong (Shenzhen, Zhuhai and Shantou) and Fujian (Xiamen). Similarly, the 14 cities designated as open cities in 1984 are all in the coastal region (from north to south): Dalian, Tianjin, Yantai, Qindao, Qinhuangdao, Lianyungang, Nantong, Shanghai, Ningbo, Wenzhou, Fuzhou, Guangzhou, Zhanjiang and Beihai. All cities were commercial shipping ports,[4] and had a tradition of international as well as domestic commercial interaction. They were either Western-dominated 'treaty ports' before 1949 or had experienced substantial informal Western influence. After 1984 all of these 14 open cities became the focus of foreign investment, and consequently major centres of economic growth and development.

The central region comprises the middle and lower middle income-level provinces of Heilongjiang and Jilin in the north east, Inner Mongolia and Shanxi in the north, and the generally poorer central and southern provinces of Henan, Anhui, Hubei, Hunan and Jiangxi. Unlike the coastal region it is not heavily industrialized, and in terms of land area is the smallest of the three major regions. Hubei and Henan are the two most economically significant provinces in this region, while Inner Mongolia and Jilin are the least economically significant provinces.

The western region comprises the country's poorest and least developed provinces. It includes Sichuan, Guizhou and Yunnan in the south west; and the resource rich provinces of Shaanxi, Gansu, Qinghai, Ningxia, Xizang (Tibet) and Xinjiang in the north west. In comparison to China's two other regions it is very poor, even though it is well endowed with land and resources and has a relatively low population density. Its economic development has been severely hindered by its poor infrastructure links to the markets in the coastal provinces and other major markets, and its limited integration into the global economy. The most economically significant province in this region is Sichuan, China's largest province, with a population of over 100 million, and containing the two large cities of Chongqing and Chengdu. This province has the potential to become more important economically, but needs to overcome the disadvantages of being overpopulated, economically poor, and physically distant from the dynamic markets in the coastal areas. The provinces bordering Burma and Vietnam, especially Yunnan, have developed lucrative trade and investment links with their neighbours, which have contributed to a strengthening of their economies.

Indicators of regional divergence of economic growth and development

Three indicators are particularly useful in identifying the extent of divergence between the three regions, in terms of economic growth and development. Firstly, there is GDP growth and GDP per capita, the conventional indicators of economic activity, and the focus of the empirical analysis conducted in section four. Secondly, industrial output which can be used as a proxy for the rate of modernization and development. Finally, there is the gross value of retail sales, which reflects the level of effective demand and marketization of the economy.

Figure 10.1 indicates that the coastal region's growth rates are consistently higher than those of the western and central regions, even though by international standards the latter are high. Hence the divergence of regional economic growth is not a consequence of poor performance by the central and western regions, but rather due to the outstanding performance of the coastal region. While the coastal region's growth as a whole continues to outstrip the growth rates of the other two regions, there are five provinces within the coastal region, Jiangsu,

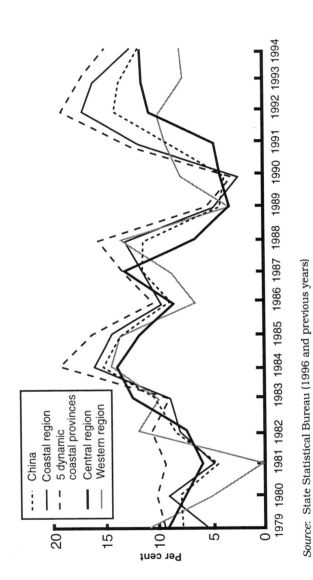

Source: State Statistical Bureau (1996 and previous years)

Figure 10.1   **Annual Growth Rates of Real GDP by Region**

Zhejiang, Fujian, Shandong and Guangdong, whose growth is outstanding. The contribution of these five fastest-growing provinces to national GDP increased dramatically from 25 per cent to over 36 per cent between 1978 and 1995. By contrast the economic performance of the traditional industrial provinces and municipalities of Liaoning, Hebei, Beijing, Tianjin, and until recently Shanghai, where most of the large SOEs are located, is only average.

Industrial production in China is dominated by the coastal region. Its contribution to the national total increased steadily in the second half of the 1980s and during the first half of the 1990s. By 1995 the region contributed approximately two thirds of total industrial production. However, the star performers in this region have been the five dynamic provinces, whose share of national industrial production increased from 24 per cent in 1978 to 44 per cent by the mid-1990s, overtaking the traditional coastal industrial provinces. The western and central regions have also achieved high rates of growth in industrial output, averaging about 20 per cent per year in current prices, compared with 25 per cent in the coastal region. However, as clearly indicated from Figure 10.2, industrial output is heavily concentrated in the coastal provinces, and particularly in the five dynamic coastal provinces. In 1978 the coastal region had an industrial production per capita greater than that of the national average, while that of the dynamic coastal provinces was about the national average. By 1995 the coastal region, and dynamic provinces in particular, had an industrial production per capita considerably above that of the national average. The central and western regions lag well behind the coastal region and the national average.

Finally, the value of retail sales has also grown consistently faster in the coastal region, as well as in the five dynamic provinces, than in the central and western regions (see Figure 10.3). This is not only due to higher incomes on the coast but also because markets have developed more rapidly there than in the hinterland, where semi-subsistence agriculture is still prevalent.

10.3 Factors behind the regional income and development divergence

The divergence of GDP, industrial output, and retail sales in the three regions has increased markedly since 1989. In the case of GDP per capita there is empirical evidence to suggest increasing divergence, although, as identified in section 5, this remains relatively small. Some of the major factors behind such regional disparities are now briefly identified.

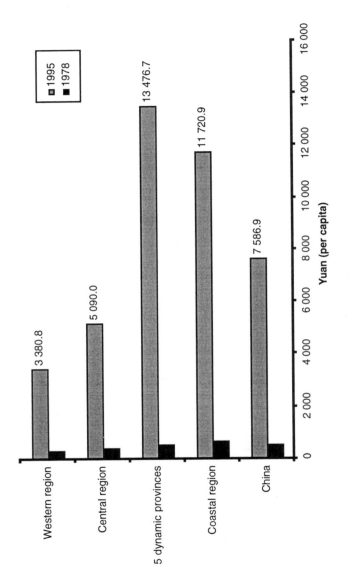

Source: State Statistical Bureau (1996 and Previous Years)

***Figure 10.2* Regional Industrial Output, 1978 and 1995 (in current prices)**

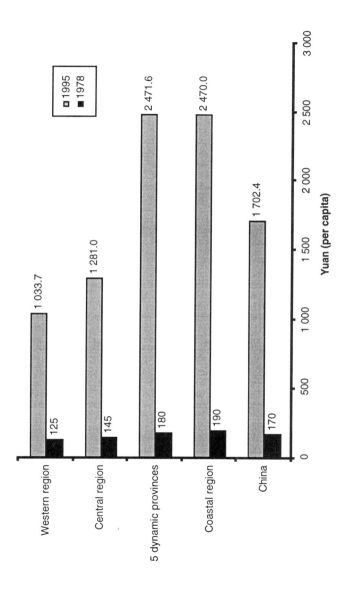

Source: State Statistical Bureau (1996 and Previous Years)

Figure 10.3 **Per Capita Value of Regional Retail Sales (in Current Prices)**

Disparities in new investment

During most of the pre-reform period the allocation of state-controlled investment was heavily biased towards the western region, primarily for strategic reasons. However with significant decentralization of economic power and fiscal resources from the central government to local governments and individual firms, state and non-state, during the period of economic reform, the coastal region received a larger proportion of total investment. This occurred due to the declining role of the state budget, and the increasing importance of enterprises' retained earnings as investment sources. By the mid-1990s retained earnings financed almost 50 per cent of total fixed investment while only 6 per cent was provided by the state budget, with most of the remainder coming from bank loans. The coastal region accounted for two-thirds of all retained earnings, with the remainder shared between the central and western regions. This arose from the greater propensity of non-state firms, dominant on the coast, to retain and reinvest their earnings. State firms, in contrast, depended on bank loans for investment. In addition, the open economic zones, based in the coastal provinces, also received most FDI.

Divergence in growth of TVEs

As discussed in Chapter 4, the most dynamic component of China's industrial sector during the period of economic reform has been the non-state sector and specifically that of the TVEs. These are concentrated in the coastal region, and more particularly in the five dynamic provinces (see Figures 10.4 and 10.5). After the demise of the commune system in agriculture in the early 1980s, TVEs emerged as a major source of growth in the industrial sector. They were particularly strong, initially, in provinces such as Jiangsu, developing links with SOEs in large cities such as Shanghai. A second wave developed in Guangdong and Fujian, initiated by individuals with relatives in Hong Kong and Taiwan, and later in Shandong, Liaoning and Hebei provinces. Although TVEs emerged in the central and western regions, and have also been growing rapidly, their role is still significantly smaller than in the coastal region. The differences in TVE industrial output account for more than half of the overall regional disparity in industrial output.

Decentralization of the trade regime and export growth

In Chapter 7 it was shown how significant the export sector has been to the growth of the economy. The coastal provinces, but again more particularly the five dynamic provinces, have been extensively involved in this process. For example, the share of China's total exports accounted

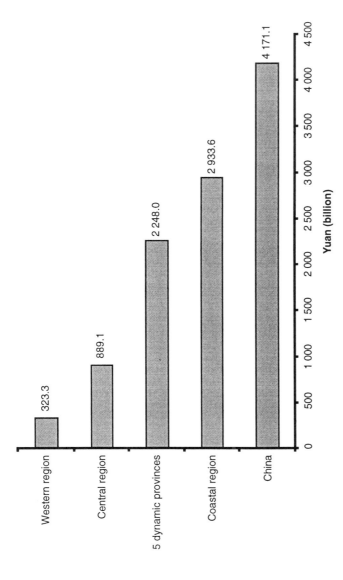

Source: State Statistical Bureau (1996)

Figure 10.4   **TVE Industrial Output by Region, 1995**

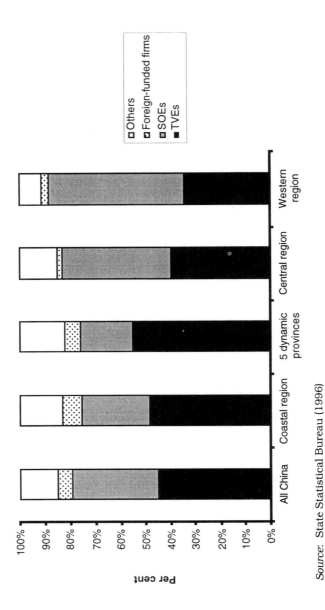

Source: State Statistical Bureau (1996)

Figure 10.5   Ownership Share in Regional Industrial Output, 1995

for by the five dynamic provinces rose dramatically from 30 per cent in 1978 to 64 per cent by the mid 1990s. These provinces have become China's export base (see Figure 10.6). Throughout the 1990s Guangdong dominated China's international trade accounting for about one-third of total exports and imports, and its foreign trade, including contract trade with Hong Kong, is more than double the combined trade of Shanghai, Jiangsu and Zhejiang. During this process of spectacular export growth by the coastal provinces, by contrast the export competitiveness of the central and the western regions deteriorated and export growth lagged behind in the 1990s

Concentration of FDI in the coastal region

The 'coastal development strategy' adopted during the early part of the 1980s favoured direct investment to the coastal areas. Only later were the central and western regions given permission to open their own development zones, although they still have far fewer than in the coastal region. However, the central and western regions have attracted relatively little foreign investment due primarily to a lack of basic economic infrastructure and lower incomes, and consequently smaller markets, rather than the absence of preferential policies. As a result of this, by the mid-1990s, the coastal region received 87 per cent of China's FDI, with the five fastest-growing provinces alone taking almost 66 per cent of the total (see Figure 10.7). In addition to capital, foreign investors have brought the region major benefits including: management skills, new technology, and knowledge of, and access to, international markets. By the end of 1995 more than 200 000 foreign firms were registered in China, mostly in the coastal region, generating almost one-third of China's exports. Their concentration in the coastal region has undoubtedly been a major factor in promoting the region's rapid export growth as identified previously.

Regional productivity and cost efficiency divergence

The divergence of regional economic growth can also be explained by not only increasing regional differences in capital accumulation, but also in terms of productive efficiency. The coastal region in general, and the five fastest-growing provinces in particular, has not only accumulated capital resources much faster than the central and western regions, for the reasons previously discussed, but has used these much more efficiently. This divergence can be explained to a large extent by the prevalence of state enterprises in the hinterland provinces. For example, industrial enterprises in the central and western regions have lower labour productivity, output per worker, and lower capital productivity, output per unit of capital, than enterprises in the coastal

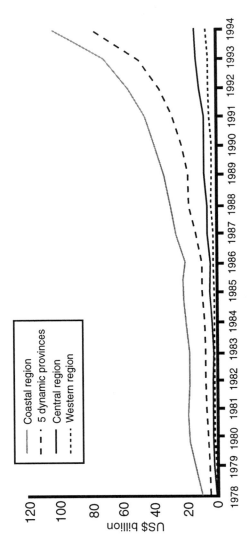

Source: State Statistical Bureau (1996 and previous years)

***Figure 10.6*   Regional Divergence in Exports[a]**

Note: a   The exports included are controlled by provincial trade corporations, agents and companies; those managed by the central foreign trade corporations are not. Exports are attributed to province of origin, not final export.

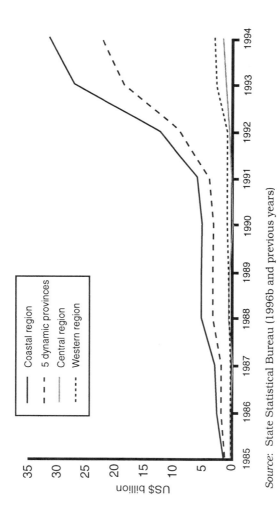

Source: State Statistical Bureau (1996b and previous years)

Figure 10.7   Regional Divergence in Used Foreign Investment

region. That is, they are technically inferior. Figure 10.8 indicates that in comparison to all other regions the five dynamic provinces are technically superior, using less of both labour and capital to produce a given amount of output.

Fiscal burdens of the regions

Within China it has been suggested that the relatively light tax burden on the coastal provinces, due to tax concessions given to foreign firms and special economic zones, and the high tax burden on SOEs,[5] which dominate interior provinces, have contributed to regional income disparities, as well as to a lack of capital accumulation among SOEs. However in 1993 the proportion of GDP paid as production taxes was 6 to 9 percentage points higher in the coastal region and five dynamic provinces than in the central and western regions. Although higher tax rates were applied to SOEs prior to 1995, because they were supposed to include a capital charge for state investment, the actual tax contribution of SOEs was limited because many were unprofitable and therefore could not be taxed. The inland regions also paid a higher share of their output to labour, and had lower profit to GDP ratios. Again this was probably due to the prevalence of SOEs in these regions.

World Bank data on fiscal transfers indicate that from 1978 to 1991 the coastal provinces ran budget surpluses, averaging 16 per cent of expenditure, that were transferred to the central government. At the same time the western and central regions had budget deficits, averaging 24 per cent of expenditure, which were financed by the central government. State-subsidized bank loans have also heavily favoured the interior regions.

Differences in regional economic policies

Since the mid-1980s every province has had the same autonomy to: encourage their non-state sectors; trade; reform agriculture; reform their SOEs; and generally develop a market economy. However the coastal provinces in general, and the five dynamic provinces in particular, have been more enthusiastic in reforming and opening their economies. In the central and western provinces a more cautious and conservative approach has generally been adopted. The personalities and capacities of regional and municipal leaders and administrators have also contributed to a greater determination and willingness to innovate in the coastal region.

In summary, it can be said that every province has adopted reforms and achieved high real economic and trade growth rates by international standards. However, the performance of the coastal provinces, centred on the five dynamic provinces, has been particularly impressive, and

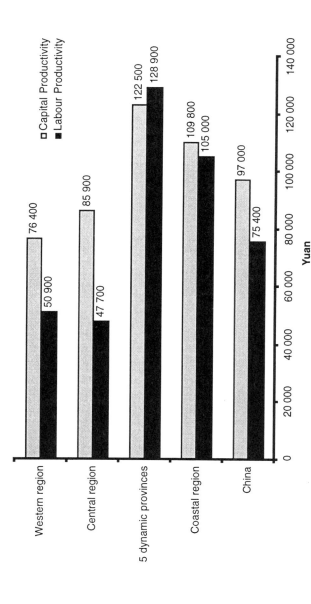

Source: State Statistical Bureau (1996)

Figure 10.8   Labour and Capital Productivity of Industrial Enterprises by Region, 1995

Note: Capital productivity is measured in terms of yuan of output per 100 000 yuan of capital employed. Labour productivity is yuan produced per worker.

this has contributed to increasing regional income disparity. Their proximity to sea links, more developed transport and other infrastructure, as well as the previously identified factors, have all contributed to increasing regional income disparities between them and the central and western provinces.

10.4 Measuring income inequality

Conceptual framework

In this section, Theil's (Theil, 1967) entropy index of income inequality, and its decomposition formula, is used to analyze China's regional income disparity. Theil's entropy index can be written as follows:

$$T(y:x) = \sum_{i=1}^{n} y_i \log \frac{y_i}{x_i}$$

where:

T = Theil index;

y_i = income share of province i;

x_i = population share of province i.

The Theil index indicates that the aggregate level of income inequality is equal to the weighted sum of the logarithms of the provinces' ratios of income share to population share, where the weights are the provinces' income shares. It can also be interpreted as the expected information of the indirect message that transforms the prior probabilities as represented by population shares of groups into the posterior probabilities as represented by the group's income shares.

The range of T is between 0 and log N. When income is equally distributed between the N possible provinces, the value of this index is equal to zero. On the other hand when all income is attained by one province then the index reaches its upper bound of log N.

Choice of Theil's Index

The choice of the Theil Index as a measure of income disparity is based upon its attractive properties. Firstly, it is very simple to calculate and is less demanding on data requirements. Secondly, it is a 'positive' measure of income inequality, that is the Theil Index does not make use of any explicit social welfare function in its calculation. Hence, it is free from bias and value-judgement. In addition, the Theil Index fulfills the desired axioms of an ideal income inequality measure:

1   it is independent of the mean income and population size;

2   it satisfies the Pigou-Dalton condition of income reversibility;

3   it is decomposable.

It has been shown (see Bourguinon, 1979) that the Theil Index is the only income-weighted decomposable inequality measure which is differentiable, symmetric and homogeneous of degree zero in all incomes. Hence, it can be considered as a good index for measuring income inequality between and within the provinces of China. Decomposability is a desirable property since the objective here is to measure income disparities between and within regions in China.

Decomposition of Theil's Index

The computation of China's income inequality index between and within its provinces is conducted in accordance with a decomposition formula offered by Fishlow (Fishlow, 1972), that measures the contribution of the constituents of the classification of provinces into three regions, namely coastal, central and western as identified previously.

$$T_{ij} = \sum_{i=1}^{3} y_i \log \frac{y_i}{x_i} + \sum_{i=1}^{3} y_i \sum_{j=1}^{30} \frac{y_{ij}}{x_i} \log \frac{y_{ij} / y_i}{x_{ij} / x_i}$$

where,

i = regional index;

j = provincial index;

y_i = income share of region i in China's total income;

x_i = population share of region i in China's total population;

y_{ij} = income share of province j affiliated to region i;

x_{ij} = population share of province j affiliated to region i.

The first term on the right-hand side indicates the level of income inequality between the three regions of China, and the second term indicates the weighted sum of income inequality within the provinces of China.

10.5   Data and substantive results

Data was extracted from the *Statistical Yearbook of China* for various years. The Theil Index was calculated for 1981, 1987, 1990, 1994 and 1997. Non-availability of data on a consistent basis precluded calculating the Theil Index for other years. However, the sample period is broad enough to enable us to compare and contrast the movement of income inequality in China before and after the reform process.

Table 10.2 presents a summary of the income inequality and its

Table 10.2   **Constituents of Income Inequality of China**

Year	Total	Between	Within
1981	0.0539	0.0119	0.0420
1987	0.0410	0.0140	0.0270
1990	0.0354	0.0146	0.0208
1991	0.0371	0.0159	0.0211
1994	0.0461	0.0266	0.0195
1997	0.0445	0.0256	0.0189

Source: Calculated from *China Statistical Yearbook*, various years

constituents in China between 1981 and 1997. These are also shown in diagrammatic form in Figures 10.9, 10.10, and 10.11. It is worth noting that the overall income inequality is found to be very small and miniscule over the sample period. It ranges between 2.4 per cent to about 3.7 per cent of the maximum value, log 30 = 1.48, of the Theil Index. Secondly, total income equality is found to be U-shaped. It starts to decline over the decade of the 1980s and then starts to rise by the mid-1990s (see Figure 10.9). This trend contradicts the view of Kuznets' inverted-U hypothesis, which suggests that in the early stages of economic growth the distribution of income will tend to worsen while at later stages it will improve. Thirdly, it has been found that income inequality between the regions of China has increased gradually from 1981 to about 1991 (see Figure 10.10). But the gap in income inequality noticeably widened after 1991. Fourthly, income inequality within provinces of China decreased substantially between 1981 and 1987. The decreasing trend continued after 1987 (see Figure 10.11), at a slower pace, and has now stabilized around a low figure.

10.6   The government's regional policies

In 1996 the government's policies on regional development were outlined in the Ninth Five Year Plan. It was anticipated that each region would develop in line with its comparative advantage, with the coastal provinces focusing upon developing manufacturing, information and service industries, while the central and western regions would focus on developing agricultural and resource based industries. The Chinese authorities would therefore not attempt to slow the rapid growth of

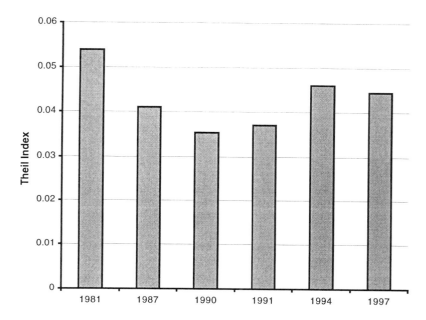

Figure 10.9 **Total Income Inequality in China**

manufacturing industry in the coastal region, implying that regional divergence is likely to continue. However, the government included several policy guidelines in the Ninth Five Year Plan to address widening regional disparities. These included high central government priority to resource development and infrastructure projects in the central and western regions. Resource processing and labour-intensive industries were to be encouraged to move to the central and western regions. Prices of resource products were to be further liberalized to increase the profitability of resource-based enterprises in the central and western regions. The central government's fiscal transfer system is to be enhanced, and the proportion of revenue transferred to the central and western regions will be gradually increased. FDI will be encouraged to go to the central and western regions. The proportion of policy loans from the new policy banks will be increased and more than 60 per cent of international soft loans will be allocated to the central and western regions. Coastal localities' assistance to the remote, poor and minority areas will be encouraged, as will economic and technological cooperation between coastal and interior enterprises. Coastal and interior enterprises will be allowed to cooperate in exploring for and using natural resources.

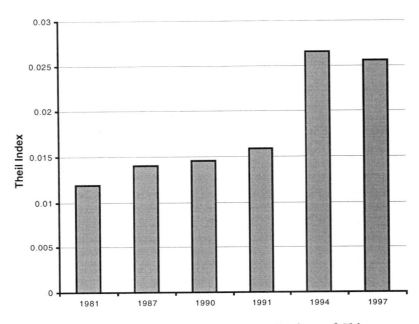

Figure 10.10   **Income Inequality Between Regions of China**

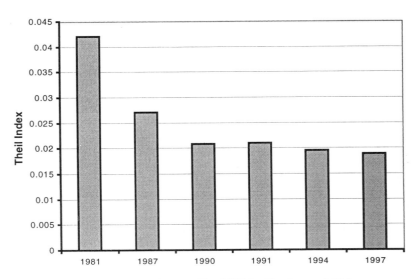

Figure 10.11   **Income Inequality Within Regions of China**

Coastal provinces will be encouraged to invest in the interior, and the interior will be encouraged to export labour to the coast.

However, without radical taxation reform the central government will have limited financial resources to implement these regional policies. Also missing are agricultural reform policies that would enable farmers in the predominantly agricultural hinterland to move out of lower value-added crops, such as grain and cotton, and the removal of price controls on these crops.

While a policy to encourage cooperation between coastal and interior enterprises may be important in reducing regional disparities, such cooperation cannot occur on a significant scale until better transport links enable coastal firms to cut production costs by subcontracting work to hinterland firms. Foreign investment will also be limited until such infrastructure is in place.

10.7   Summary and conclusions

This chapter has focused upon regional disparities in terms of income growth and economic development. In particular, China's provinces were divided into three regions – coastal, central and western. The success of the coastal region can be attributed mainly to the shift in national economic policy away from emphasis on a closed, centrally planned, and heavy industry-orientated economy, to a more open, market-oriented economy that used the coastal region's natural competitive advantage. In particular, the coastal region performed strongly in developing TVEs and export-oriented enterprises, increasing productivity, increasing the rate of reinvestment of retained earnings, and successfully attracting FDI. The rapid growth of household income and consumption has also supported local market and industrial development. In the early 1990s the coastal region entered a take-off stage, precipitated in part by the growing integration of key provinces and growth centres.

Empirical evidence supported the view that income disparities have widened between provinces but not within provinces. In addition the Theil indices calculated for China suggest a U-shape in terms of total income inequality instead of an inverted U-shape. The likelihood is that with disparities in natural endowments divergence of regional economic growth and incomes is likely to increase in the short to medium term, with the coastal areas continuing to grow rapidly and inland regions continuing to lag. However, this may not cause major concern, as such divergence will occur simultaneously with rapid economic growth in every province. Nevertheless, the central government will need to be prepared to deal with possible tension resulting from such divergence for a prolonged period, and therefore will be required to vigorously pursue policies to reduce such disparities.

The government will need to give high priority to policies that accelerate public and private provision of transport, energy and social infrastructure in the poorer regions to reduce their isolation, and that develop their human resources. Completion of price reform for agricultural and other raw materials will also help the hinterland provinces.

Foreign investors, however, are likely to continue to locate most of their investments in the more dynamic coastal provinces, and in a few of the stronger interior provinces such as Sichuan and Hubei. Government incentives to move FDI inflows inland to poorer provinces may not have a major impact in the short and medium term, due to their basic lack of attractiveness, poor infrastructure, lower incomes and less market-oriented economies. In the longer term, policies to reform inefficient SOEs in these provinces, encourage the growth of smaller, more dynamic, non-state firms, infrastructure investment by the government, aid donors, and domestic and multinational firms, should contribute to sustaining reasonably high growth rates and enable these provinces to reduce the disparities between them and the coastal provinces.

Notes

1   Chongqing, the newest of the municipalities, formally acquired this status in early 1997.
2   Referred to here as the five dynamic coastal provinces.
3   Links with Hong Kong and Taiwan respectively were particularly important.
4   Before or since 1949.
5   Before 1994, the Chinese government levied a 55 per cent tax rate on large and medium sized SOEs.

References

Bourguinon, F. (1979), 'Decomposable Income Inequality Measures', Econometrica, Vol. 47, pp. 901–20.

Department of Foreign Affairs and Trade. (1997), China Embraces the Market: Achievements, Constraints, and Opportunities, East Asia Analytical Unit, Canberra.

Fishlow, A. (1972), 'Brazilian Size Distribution of Income', American Economic Review, Papers and Proceedings, Vol. 62, pp. 391–402.

State Statistical Bureau. (1996), *China Statistical Yearbook*, China Statistical Publishing House, Beijing.

Theil, H. (1967), *Economics and Information Theory*, Amsterdam, North Holland.

11

Land Reform and the Competitiveness of China's Cities

Darren McKay

This chapter examines urban development issues and land market efficiency in Chinese cities, pre- and post-economic reforms in the 1980s. It notes that urban competitiveness is fundamental to continued economic development in China. For much of the post-war era Chinese cities were hindered by poor planning, lack of infrastructure and housing investment, and the absence of a real-estate market. The chapter outlines how reforms in these areas in the 1980s for selected cities has improved their competitiveness and changed their physical structure. However, it is also noted that problems still persist that threaten sustainable urban economic development. This includes poor infrastructure coordination between cities, congestion and pollution, land hoarding and housing shortages. Such problems need to be addressed if Chinese cities are to successfully absorb surplus rural immigrants and those displaced through the rationing of state owned enterprises. Consequently, various urban policy options from the literature are reviewed.

11.1 Introduction

For reasons of simplicity, this chapter often generalizes the major urban issues present in China. However it should be noted that in such a populous and complex country, the urban problems and reforms often vary between Chinese cities. Mostly reforms are trialed in selected cities before being replicated elsewhere, thereby creating diversity in urban competitiveness and living standards. However, given this note of caution, three major factors can be identified as impacting on Chinese cities in the post-reform era. Accelerating economic growth has been associated with rapid urbanization, which has put increasing demands on the infrastructure, housing, and employment of cities. The latter is exacerbated by retrenchments from urban state owned enterprises (SOE's). Secondly, post-1988 urban land reforms have induced changes to the physical structure of many cities, in particular promoting inner city re-development and suburbanization, as well as invoking problems of property speculation. Finally, government decision making has been increasingly decentralized to the regional level, which has provided cities with greater autonomy as well as being a catalyst for regional protectionism and widening spatial inequality as outlined in chapter 10. To the extent that these factors impact on the economic performance of China's cities, they must be seen as important considerations in its future economic development. Consequently, these factors are recurring themes in this chapter.

The chapter proceeds as follows. Section 2 provides a justification of why an analysis of urban issues is important to the economic development debate in China. Section 3 discusses the processes and problems of urban land management prior to 1980. Section 4 focuses on the significant impact that urbanization, decentralized political decision making and land reforms have had on Chinese cities. A case study of two Chinese cities that have introduced land reforms at different rates is provided in section 5. Unresolved urban problems post-land reforms are discussed in section 6, while section 7 reviews urban land-policy options for China. The major conclusions are provided in section 8.

11.2 The importance of cities in the development debate

Many authors, such as Jacobs (1986), believe cities are the engine rooms for economic growth. Large cities, in particular, are able to take advantage of agglomeration economies, maximizing interaction between agents while providing the advantage of scale economies. These factors not only allow cities to become the centres of culture, but also of invention, innovation and development. In contrast, for most of the socialist period, the Chinese government perceived cities as net consumers of society's wealth rather than producers (Zhao and Zhang, 1995). Urban residents were provided with subsidized food, housing, and health, with superior education facilities and government employment opportunities. In particular cities were seen as a drain on the national budget and the rural surplus, and consequently the home registration scheme was established to discourage urbanization.

In the 1980s government reform policies allowed selected cities to improve their economic competitiveness and move toward being net wealth creators. In particular, the national government allowed certain cities to experiment with international openness and market reforms. From 1978 the cities of Shenzhen, Zhuhai, Shantou and Xiamen were chosen to trial market reform. Following success in these centres, a further fourteen coastal cities were selected for reform experiments in 1984. The 1990s extended the privileges of market reforms possessed by the coastal cities to all inland provincial capitals. Consequently, China's cities have been an integral component of its reform process since 1978. In fact, Zhang and Yi (1997) argue that market initiatives adopted by autonomous cities influenced national reforms in the late 1980s.

The experiment with market reform in many of China's cities has significantly accelerated their economic growth, and subsequently encouraged rural-to-urban migration. Over the last twenty years, for instance, Shenzhen, situated in a special economic zone, has grown from around 10 000 to 3.8 million people. No doubt the growth of many of these cities has promoted the benefits of agglomeration economies, though such growth has also exacerbated the negatives of congestion, pollution and high property rents. These problems can be somewhat offset by facilitating an efficient land market, effective provision and pricing of infrastructure, and comprehensive urban planning. Progress has been made on these factors to varying degrees between cities, with land leasing and the adoption of comprehensive urban planning, though much remains to be done.

Increasingly city governments have been provided with the economic and land-use tools to influence their own development (Wu, 1997). Combinations of good management, incentive schemes and comparative advantage have allowed some of these cities to achieve standards of living notably in excess of other regions. It is important that the central government continues to analyze how the success of some of these cities can be transferred to other lagging regions for two reasons. Firstly, failure to do so will perpetuate regional inequity, thereby adversely affecting social cohesion and political stability. Recently there has been greater recognition of this point by the Chinese government, with moves to divert capital funds to inland regions (Fan, 1997). Secondly, because the more numerous are cities with successful urban development policies, the greater will be national economic growth (Zhao and Zhang, 1995).

11.3 Urban efficiency pre-reforms

In the 1950s the Chinese government set about nationalizing urban land, and though it distributed rural lands to farmers, such land could not be sold. In effect a market for land ceased to exist, and property lost its exchange value (Tang, 1994). This would prove to have profound effects on the way land would be used and the physical form of Chinese cities. Private rental properties and factories were appropriated by the state and mostly allocated to work units. Land for new housing and industry was administratively allocated to work units according to set criteria, and at no price.

The period of land nationalization led to allocation inefficiencies, which arguably retarded urban economic growth. To appreciate this point the Chinese land system at this time can be compared to the neoclassical model of land allocation under market forces. This model illustrates that proximity and fertility of land impacts on its exchange value and its use intensity. In relation to urban centres, the premise is that land closest to the city centre offers greatest utility and profit. This results from it being central to a market catchment area and offering such benefits as infrastructure facilities for business, and employment for workers. These benefits diminish with distance from the city or catchment centre, and agents incur increasingly higher transport costs. Consequently, a downward-sloping bid rent curve can be derived for urban land use which illustrates that agents' property bids fall with distance from the city centre. Under this situation the most efficient producers are able to outbid those less efficient, thereby encouraging re-development and ensuring valuable sites are used most productively and intensively. Householders, or less-efficient businesses, will be pushed further into the suburbs, establishing a city structure of high-rise inner-city development falling to more dispersed low-rise suburban development. This model can be applied to a multi-nuclear as well as a mono-nuclear city. In the former a downward-sloping bid rent curve radiates from each metropolitan sub-centre.

Chinese cities in the pre-reform era varied from the above market model in three major ways: no exchange value for land; low land use intensity in the inner city; and little re-development of urban land. As land could not be traded, land-price differentials did not arise that would otherwise promote changes to existing land uses. Government regulations regarding compensation further inhibited urban re-development. Although households and businesses occupying inner-city sites were not permitted to own land, they did have strong land-use rights. If a state enterprise wished to acquire an inner-city site for re-development, existing occupiers were to be fully compensated.

Preferably with displaced households receiving a new apartment on the existing site. Unfortunately, this compensation requirement, combined with low density, low plot ratio, planning regulations and fixed rents, meant that the re-development of a site was often non-viable. A further factor inhibiting re-development was the scarcity of urban services toward the fringe, including public transport, which made relocation for residents and small business unattractive. Similarly, because occupiers could not sell their inner-city properties they could not derive adequate revenue for relocation even if they desired to do so. Residents would only be inclined to relocate if they were assured of employment in a suburban work unit, which could provide them with housing. Finally, the small size of the tertiary sector in Chinese cities also provided little impetus for inner-city re-development (Wu and Yeh, 1997).

During this period the major property developers were state-enterprise work units administered by sectoral departments financed by the central government. This was the main influence of the central government on the physical structure of cities. Work units produced output as designated by state planning strategies, which were then collected and distributed by the state. Finance for production projects would often include funding for constructing employee housing, and often required the requisition of additional land. However it was common that they would apply for more land than they would actually use in their production and housing of workers (Wu, 1997). Two reasons can be given for this. Firstly, land had no value placed on it to reflect the opportunity cost of its usage, thereby inducing excess demand. Secondly, the economic aim of state enterprises was to maximize output rather than profit, and as such they acquired a hunger for all resource inputs including land. Work units often overstated their input needs to state departments so that future targets could be more easily met. Once new land was acquired it was promptly occupied, even if it was put to an unproductive use. This ensured it was unavailable for distribution to rival work units. This land allocation system frequently resulted in some work units possessing idle land, while others experienced a shortage, which inhibited their growth. Similarly, there was little certainty that the more efficient work units would receive greater land, or more valuable locations, than the less-efficient units. According to Tang (1994) land was often simply distributed according to who shouted the loudest.

The above factors combined to form inner cities that are congested, yet characterized by low-rise and stagnant development. New building development has mostly occurred on the agricultural fringes of cities through the work-unit system. The latter involves construction of self-contained communities for the purpose of state production. Construction occurred on the fringe to avoid the costs of compensating inner-city land occupiers, while still maintaining access to city infrastructure. Work-unit communities combined living with work place, the work unit being the property developer and housing allocator. The lack of re-development of inner-city areas and the self-contained industrial development on city fringes meant there was little commuting in Chinese cities compared to western cities. These factors led to a very immobile labour force, with workers fearing if they left a work unit it would mean a loss of housing and other benefits. Overall, Chinese cities displayed little variety in land-use intensity because of the lack of a land-price differential.

Though accommodation expenses for many workers were extremely low by world standards, with many families paying around 3 per cent of their income in rent to the government, this was also associated with perpetual housing shortages. Those outside the work-unit system were particularly disadvantaged by housing shortages. Shortages arose from the state biasing investment away from housing toward industry because the former was seen as an unproductive form of investment. Highly subsidized rents also prohibited adequate revenue from being raised through this sector for dwelling re-investment to alleviate shortages (Lee, 1988).

This period was also one of poor urban planning, with little coordination between the various government departments involved in land use (Tang, 1994). City governments during this period had minimal influence over land use, being merely expected to respond to work-unit demands for additional infrastructure when the former acquired more land. Such demands were often impossible to fulfil given the financial constraints of city governments. Consequently poor urban planning and lack of market signals resulted in less-competitive Chinese cities, which dispersed more than necessary. Arguably this resulted in higher transport and infrastructure costs, reduced economic interaction between agents, and absorbed unnecessary scarce farmland.

On a broader scale the central government attempted to constrain the growth of large cities prior to the mid-1970s, particularly in coastal areas. As previously noted, cities were seen as a drain on the national budget due to their residents' privileged health, food, education and housing conditions (Zhao and Zhang, 1995). Consequently, the rural population was discouraged from migrating to cities through the home registration scheme (Quan, 1991). The state also wished to avoid problems of congestion, slum creation and pollution that were present in other developing countries' large cities. Consequently throughout the 1960s and 1970s urbanization rates were kept to modest levels, which was true of towns as well as cities. With regard to towns, collectivization and central distribution of agricultural output by the state had denied them of their traditional role as rural commercial centres and so their growth stagnated (Ma and Fan, 1994).

11.4   Urban performance post-reforms

From 1978 China entered a period of greater economic openness with the rest of the world, aiming to accelerate economic development. To this end fourteen coastal cities were selected as centres to promote foreign direct investment (FDI) and exports. The philosophy being that growth in these cities, particularly from manufacturing exports, would generate wealth that would filter down to undeveloped cities and regions (Fan, 1997). Essentially this was a growth pole approach to economic development. To maximize the chances for success, this growth centre approach was targeted at areas of perceived existing comparative advantage. Many of these selected cities had the advantage of port access for exporting, and relatively close proximity to the developed economies of Hong Kong, Taiwan and Macao. It was felt that concentration of government efforts needed to occur in set locations, as to disperse the state's efforts would only dilute the desired effect (Chen, 1991).

The state supported these cities by loosening their foreign investment controls, providing them with tax incentives and favourable infrastructure provision relative to other cities (Zhou, 1993). These factors, combined with China's low labour costs, encouraged significant FDI into these cities, which lifted their per capita incomes above other inland centres. For much of the 1980s the FDI was predominantly in industrial investment, often through joint ventures. This success encouraged significant immigration into these centres, particularly from inland rural areas. However this increased stress on these cities' infrastructure, housing and employment demands.

In terms of the impact on urban structure, investments in factories and the like for much of the 1980s was predominantly constructed on the fringes of these cities. This was due to the prohibitive costs of compensating inner-city residents for re-development of their sites (Wu, 1998). Often special industrial areas or zones with serviced land were made available by the state for FDI and joint ventures on the urban fringes. Consequently, these cities continued to expand outwards rather than through infill re-development. Concerned with the issue of urban land inefficiency and the disappearance of valuable agricultural land, the Chinese government in 1988 approved the commercial transfer of land-use rights in cities. This, in practice, created urban real estate markets (Liu and Yang, 1990). City governments were now custodians of state land, which they could acquire and then distribute on a leasehold basis if they wished. Market distribution could now occur via negotiation with developers, tender, or by auction. The adoption of this market mechanism now supplemented traditional bureaucratic land allocation, which occurred to varying degrees among different cities. Some cities continued to rely predominantly on bureaucratic land allocation, while others, such as Guangzhou, took advantage of the new law, preferring to increase their reliance on the market for land allocation.

Land now had an exchange value that would result in adjusting the structure and form of many cities towards that predicted by neoclassical land-use models (Wu, 1997). They began to move away from a structure of low-rise inner-city residential development and industrial fringe development, towards more intensive commercial inner-city re-development and residential suburbanization, as is more common in western cities. In effect land reform unleashed a rent gap in Chinese cities, where the value of inner-city land in its highest and best use was now in many cases significantly higher than its current use. Consequently, developers could be assured of healthy rent returns from inner-city office or residential developments, which would make projects viable after compensating existing residents. Potential rent returns would influence developer bids for land during the negotiation or auctioning process with city governments. Development was even more likely where agents were permitted to compensate existing occupiers with new housing, utilizing cheaper land in the suburbs. Subsequently, since 1988, there has been substantial re-development of many inner city areas, particularly in those favouring FDI and which have implemented more extensive land market reforms. Investment in property development is now the second largest area of FDI in China. Not surprisingly this process has also been associated with the expansion of the tertiary sector, which favours inner-city locations (Wu and Yeh, 1997).

The above changes in urban structure need to be seen in the light of movements in the political economy of China. In essence, the period since 1978 has seen a significant devolution of decision-making power and investment from the central government through its sectoral departments to city governments and local work units. In the late 1970s the central government was facing fiscal difficulties due to agricultural subsidies, industrial imports and growing youth unemployment, and consequently transferred many expenditure responsibilities to individual work units and city governments (Bian and Logan, 1996, and Wu, 1998). However this led to cities and work units gaining greater revenue-raising power with which to conduct their operations. City governments were given power to charge enterprises for infrastructure usage as well as imposing fees and taxes for property development. Post-1988 they were also provided with the ability to raise revenue by acquiring and leasing land to developers, occurring through a process of auction, tender or negotiation. Proceeds were intended to be shared with the central government. However, city governments would often keep a larger share by negotiating with the developer to provide 'in kind' community infrastructure in return for discounted land. This has helped City governments to expand urban infrastructure without budgetary burdens, which in turn attracts FDI.

The central government has also imposed greater burdens on work units in providing their own funding for employee housing provision (Bian and Logan, 1996). In turn they have been provided with greater autonomy in their production management and were increasingly permitted throughout the 1980s to sell output in the private market. However, they have retreated from their past role as property developers to one of utilizing part of their surplus to purchase housing from private developers, which are then provided at subsidized rates to their workers. Consequently, employees are increasingly being provided with housing in residential locations separate from work-unit operations, breaking the work and home connection, thereby promoting greater commuting. Furthermore, greater amounts of labour surplus are being diverted into housing, which was in the past seen as an unproductive investment and negative to economic growth.

In terms of urban land allocation, it is firstly acquired by city governments who either allocate it directly to work units or lease it to property developers. Developers may then construct apartments or offices for rent or sale to private agents or work units. In 1984 the national government required all cities (666 according to Tao, 1997) to produce a master plan for their physical development. Until this stage urban planning was a very uncoordinated process. In 1989 the central government produced the city planning Act, which provides guidelines for the production of city master plans that would identify areas for re-development and residential expansion. Mostly they aimed to free more central city land for more intense commercial development, while decentralizing residents and factories to the suburbs. City governments would acquire land for re-development, as consistent with their master plans, and then in many cases auction it to developers. Note that work units may wish to re-develop their inner-city site themselves, or enter into joint venture projects to do so. Legally they can only sell property to other work units, though in practice stronger work units may be able to bend the rules and sell to private agents. Influential work units may also be able to sell leases outside of the designated re-development areas, thereby compromising city master plans.

Consequently city governments now more strongly influence the location and supply of land allocation and property development. This allows them to better manage the physical form of their cities and to achieve scale economies in infrastructure provision. Large residential developments are now approved by them in suburbs that serve multiple work-unit locations. The post-reform era has allowed many cities, through their governments and work units, to have a much greater role in determining their own regional growth and wealth distribution. In particular, land-leasing arrangements and tax incentives have enabled them to raise revenue and expand investment.

In summary the 1980s and 1990s have seen selected Chinese cities develop industrial zones for foreign investment and joint ventures on their fringes, that have now become suburban sub-centres. Cities have also experienced increased high-density commercial and residential re-development in their centres, with large residential areas being developed in their suburbs from which residents commute to work. This period also saw a resurgence of township development, with expansion within them of many small manufacturing establishments. Increased market involvement in the agricultural sector has also returned the traditional commercial role to townships (Ma and Fan, 1994).

11.5   The cases of Tianjin and Guangzhou

As previously noted, economic and land reforms have been instigated at different rates depending on the city. Thus, not surprisingly, the pace of economic development and physical structural change of Chinese cities varies. A comparison of land policy in the cities of Tianjin and Guangzhou until 1994 by Dowall (1994) illustrates this point. Both cities had land bureaus, which developed master plans for future industrial, commercial and residential location, and other development. However, within this, Tianjin maintained traditional bureaucratic methods of land allocation while Guangzhou moved towards adopting more radical market mechanisms.

In Tianjin the Urban and Rural construction committee was responsible for physical planning and development. It developed a master plan for the city, which the land bureau was required to uphold when allocating land. The master plan would determine what new land would be made available for expansion of industry and residential development. Under this system enterprises wishing to expand their operations would need to request land from the land bureau, which conformed to the master plan's new release areas, planning and zoning regulations. The land bureau would determine whether the enterprise conformed to these regulations, as well as ensuring the demand for new land was consistent with the enterprise's future production projections. If the bureau was satisfied on these points it would ask the enterprise to compensate existing residents on the site being re-developed. A similar process applied to corporations developing new housing, to which a quota for expanded dwelling output was set each year. New housing would be encouraged in suburban areas in line with a policy to decentralize workers toward industrial areas. On most occasions the decision on land allocation was a bureaucratic one, particularly in the established city area.

In Guangzhou, the city government, through its planning bureau, has been negotiating the allocation of land leases with real estate corporations since 1984. New release areas were determined by a master plan, though the allocation process incorporated a bidding component. Enterprises would need to establish that their developments were in accordance with the master plan, which identified inner-city locations for re-development and suburban areas for residential and industrial use. Developers would also be asked to submit an offer on the provision of off-site infrastructure, which allowed the city government to finance urban development. Efficient producers who could earn the highest income from a site would theoretically submit the largest bid or infrastructure offer. Consequently the bid was determined with reference to expectations of potential site income. Another allocation method was for the purchaser to develop the land and transfer parcels of it fully serviced back to the municipal government for public use. However, by 1994 Guangzhou was moving towards a system of selling leases for cash, as is the case in nearby Hong Kong.

The net outcome of Tianjin's land allocation methods was that it had badly located residential areas relative to industry, which increased work travel times. Alternatively, Guangzhou's policies had encouraged more inner-city re-development, thereby reducing its travel times. Also, because land in Tianjin is bureaucratically allocated there was less incentive to vary the intensity of its land use. Consequently, land in the inner areas of Tianjin was utilized less intensively than that of Guangzhou, where the later developers were forced to utilize the valuable central city sites more intensively due to higher land acquisition costs.

According to Dowall (1994), the lack of land pricing as well as Tianjin's regulations on open-space allocation and density use flattened its bid rent curve. This in turn adversely affected its transport costs and infrastructure provision requirements. The latter reflected the point that if a population is dispersed, then average infrastructure and transport costs would increase. Finally, Guangzhou captured some of the land value its development created in order to finance infrastructure for future urban development, while this was forgone in Tianjin. Consequently, the more extensive market land reforms occurring in Guangzhou arguably aided its faster development relative to Tianjin. Since Dowall's (1994) case study Tianjin has moved towards a greater reliance on the market, with land on the city's fringes incorporating a more competitive allocation process.

11.6   New and unresolved urban problems

The reforms discussed in the previous section have moved many Chinese cities towards more competitive physical structures and efficient land use allocation, while increased managerial power to city governments has allowed them to promote their own growth. However, though cities that have adopted land reform have improved their competitiveness, certain land-use problems still persist. These include continued housing shortages within a climate of property vacancies, land hoarding and leapfrog development, congestion and pollution. Two reasons can be given for this. Many of the cities adopting land reform have maintained levels of government regulation that distort land market efficiency, in particular a dual land-allocation market, occupier compensation policy and rent subsidies. Secondly, cities adopting a real estate market may suffer from problems of land speculation, which is a form of market failure. Other problems relate to concerns that urban economic growth in China is inequitable, and that some cities have grown too large, causing diseconomies.

At present many Chinese cities are operating a dual land market system, where a commercialized market now coexists with authorities' continued free allocation or subsidized distribution of property, particularly to work units for industrial use (Chen, 1996, and Zhu, 1994). That is, market land reforms have been introduced to some but not all land uses. In particular the issue of property rights is confusing. Leases sold by city governments entitle the owner to sell, mortgage and bequest that property, though allocated or subsidized properties carry only use rights and supposedly can not be sold. This issue is often ambiguous, with strong work units being able to bend the rules and work-unit properties purchased by workers being allowed to be sold after a five-year period. This situation distorts the market, restricts potential property supply, and encourages black-market activity.

Work units purchase the majority of new residential development for the subsidized market. Limitations on selling these properties restrict supply in the commercial market, thereby maintaining high prices in that market for those who demand housing but are not in work units. Similarly, some work units which have been allocated land may be hoarding it or trading it on the black market. Furthermore, some foreign firms and joint ventures that negotiate discounted land from city governments on the basis of its use for production may default on these initial plans, under utilizing or hoarding the land for speculative purposes. Therefore the dual land market encourages land banking and black-market activity which restricts market supply, imposing higher prices on genuine producers (Wu, 1998, and Zhu 1994).

Another market distortion involves restrictive policies on compensating land occupiers, which Dowall (1994) argues deters the level of re-development and is passed on to consumers in higher rents or apartment prices. Various development fees and contributions may add to this problem. Residents compensated with valuable new apartments are also known to sublet on the black market, receiving high returns. Another factor reducing potential supply involves the significant subsidies provided to government housing tenants, particularly to work-unit employees. This subsidy to the fortunate occupiers comes at the expense of little funds being recouped by government for re-investment in expanding the public housing stock. This leaves those unable to acquire government housing to bid up the private-sector property market, thereby reducing affordability in that sector.

In general, speculation in real estate is not only encouraged by market distortions but is also a failure in the market system (George, 1879). It was noted by George that as urban economic growth escalated, investment would be increasingly diverted away from productive areas toward speculative property. Escalating rents and property prices would, in turn, drain profits and incomes. He concluded that productive investment would be adversely affected, while a greater bias toward property investment would undermine the financial system. These ideas have been noted by Marxist urban economists who argue that wealthier classes may appropriate and hoard land, thereby restricting supply to increase their rental returns. This would result in the bid rent curve in the neoclassical land use model being pushed upwards, thereby increasing rents for all distances from the city centre.

These arguments appear to have some relevance to those Chinese cities that had freed their land markets from the period of the early 1990s. By this time property investment in China became the second largest area of FDI. Growth in building construction increased significantly from the pre reform era. Since 1978 approximately 3 billion square metres (sq.m) of housing has been constructed with average city and town dwelling space increasing from 3.6 sq.m in 1979 to 8.47 sq.m in 1996 (Tao, 1998). However, given this, the level of commercial and up-market residential vacancies have also notably increased in the 1990s, at a time when there has been excess demand for down-market housing. According to Tao (1998) there were 70.38 million sq.m of commercial houses unsold in 1997. Such excess supply at the same time as there are housing shortages, points to failures in the property allocation system. Arguably too many resources were going into up market offices and apartments in the 1990s for speculative reasons, where owners were more likely concerned with capital gains rather than their properties' use value. As the theory suggests this created vulnerability in the Chinese financial system, and made it difficult for genuine producers to establish, or expand, operations in those cities experiencing severe property speculation.

To the extent that continued market distortions and property speculation have resulted in land hoarding and higher property prices, this may well have retarded potential re-development and induced leapfrog development. Theoretically, this adds to transport and infrastructure costs. Therefore, although the land-allocation process has improved relative to the planned system, there are still problems and therefore room for improvement. This is particularly important if China is to expand the producer services side of its economy, which requires central city locations. It is noted by Dowall (1994) that Shanghai, for example, would need to clear out 25 per cent of the factories in its inner city if it is to make way for expansion of service-sector office blocks comparable to that of Hong Kong. The development of this sector is particularly important to the absorption of surplus rural labour migrating to the cities, which Tao (1998) notes will reach 200 million people by the year 2000. Beijing alone already has 3.3 million transient rural residents. Added to this are those urban residents who will become unemployed due to rationalization reforms in state-run enterprises.

The reforms since 1978 have also facilitated greater growth in some cities relative to others, thereby creating greater regional inequality. This situation raises several issues. Firstly, how compatible is this situation with socialist ideology of fairness of wealth distribution. Deng Xiaoping promoted this policy of uneven development, believing in the trickle-down theory of economic growth (Chen, 1991, and Zhou, 1993). However, unrest from inland cities and regions, who feel that they are being left out of China's new economic prosperity, has recently forced a change in policy, with more investment now to be diverted to interior regions (Fan, 1997). However, China must be careful not to re-balance regional growth at the expense of slowing economic development in the coastal cities. A related issue is the poor coordination of infrastructure between cities, with items such as airports and freeways being duplicated between adjoining regions. This increases the average costs of infrastructure, retarding regional and national development.

China also needs to be vidual regarding changes in its urban hierarchy. There are concerns that some of its large cities are experiencing too much population growth, which promotes urban diseconomies thereby accelerating problems such as that of pollution, poor sanitation and congestion. Between the reform years from 1982 to 1992 sulphur dioxide emissions increased by one-third in China's cities (Tisdell, 1997). Consequently, most Chinese cities' air quality is lower than World Health Organization standards, causing respiratory illnesses and other health problems. Both congestion and pollution derive from the successful economic development of cities, which unfortunately in turn retard their competitiveness. Conversely, in terms of the significant growth of small towns, local manufacturers in them may be less efficient due to the lack of agglomeration economies in towns relative to the cities (Quan, 1991). For these reasons Chinese officials have adopted policies to promote the development of medium-sized cities (Zhao and Zhang, 1995).

11.7   Future policy approaches

It was noted in the previous section that problems still persist in China's cities even though land and economic reforms have notably improved their competitiveness. However the challenges for China's cities are immense, in particular in employing and housing surplus labour displaced through increased rural sector productivity. Related issues include maintaining property affordability, lowering transport costs and pollution, promoting infrastructure efficiency and provision. No doubt authorities are well aware of these issues and have investigated various policies that would continue to improve the competitiveness of their cities. They would also be aware that urban efficiency impacts on national economic growth (Zhou, 1993).

In the following a short review of ideas presented in the literature to address some of these urban problems is presented. Possible policy alternatives fall into categories of: a) reducing urban land market distortions; b) improved urban planning; and c) addressing market failure.

Removing market distortions in the urban land market would include dismantling government impediments to property development and trading, such as compensation payments and restrictive plot ratios, removing the dual property market (Zhu, 1994), and reducing rent subsidies and the like. According to Dowall (1994) it would be more efficient for developers to compensate existing property occupiers monetarily, rather than forcing them to provide on-site replacement accommodation which is mostly more valuable than their initial dwelling. This would decrease the costs of re-development and encourage individuals and companies who do not need inner-city sites to relocate to a suburban site, therefore transferring the inner-city site to a higher economic use. The loosening of height or density restrictions for new building development would similarly promote greater re-development. This would allow the developer greater profit or rental opportunity for a given site. Inner-city re-development is particularly important for the development of producer services in China.

Dismantling the dual property market would require government enterprises to bid for land, as do private firms. Presently government work units are still allocated land bureaucratically. This applies to such units as industrial enterprises and universities, but not to those seeking commercial development. Dismantling the dual land system, as advocated by Zhu (1994), would reduce future black-market opportunities in property trading. Furthermore, existing land allocations and subsidized housing if allowed to be sold would expand supply in the property sector, thereby dampening private housing prices and rentals. Lee (1988) also advocates increasing rents on subsidized public housing, so those additional funds may be raised by government for re-investment in expanding the housing stock. Recently progress has been made in this area, with rents increasing and government adopting a policy to withdraw from any new provision of work-unit subsidized housing in 1999.

As noted previously, Chinese cities have improved their urban planning since the 1980s. However, many cities still have room for improvement. The process of comprehensive planning occurring in cities such as Guangzhou and Shanghai, which have promoted inner-city development and improved transport infrastructure, should be more universally adopted. It is argued by Pugh (1996) that Chinese urban planners should utilize an example such as Singapore in their urban development plans, which is a good model of how urban policy may foster economic development. Planners in that city have been very successful in influencing development in such a manner as to maximize infrastructure efficiency, while reducing congestion and pollution through coordinating residential, commercial and public transport development.

Finally, urban problems may also result from market failure. It cannot be assumed that urban inefficiencies in China will completely be resolved by the introduction of the market. Problems of congestion and pollution, referred to as negative externalities, have long been seen as a failure of the market economy, which retards urban competitiveness. The traditional solution is to charge cars, factories and so on the external costs of their activities, thereby rationing their production. In Singapore this occurs through a driving-permit quota system, where the permits are traded on a market. Not only does this ration car usage to control pollution and congestion, but it also raises substantial revenue for the government. If successfully applied to Chinese cities, such a system would help control the negative externalities that retard urban competitiveness, as well as generating funds for infrastructure provision. Progress has been made in Shanghai, which has introduced a car quota system. However, little is being done elsewhere due to the national government's eagerness to continue car consumption, and hence production, as a means of driving economic growth. In terms of factory pollution the government has introduced a polluter permit system, though Tisdell (1997) notes it is currently insufficient.

Another aspect of market failure derives from the speculation and hoarding of land. China cannot afford to have land lie idle or under utilized, particularly because its land resources per capita are notably below the world average (Tisdell, 1997). Land and property hoarded in Chinese cities disperses them more than is needed, thereby increasing their transport costs. Similarly, hoarding increases rents as it restricts land and building supply entering the market. Hoarding also under-mines the urban planning process and retards the efficient use of urban infrastructure. To address this, Zhu (1994) advocates the introduction of a vacant land tax to force land to be utilized for production. He notes that land is sometimes being acquired by private and work-unit entities for speculation, while genuine companies are discouraged by resultant high property values. Another method to discourage land speculation is to impose a capital gains tax on property, which should encourage users to derive income from production on the site rather than through its mere exchange. According to Li (1997) the authorities have already discussed this, though there have been no clear initiatives to implement such a policy. To date the authorities have attempted to address the problem by monitoring land and demanding that a site purchased be developed within a set time, in many cases twelve months, otherwise that land may be confiscated by the state. Similarly, the authorities in Shanghai require 25 per cent of a site to be developed before it may be resold. Though this ensures that land leases purchased are used, it does not necessarily ensure the land is used in the most productive manner. Furthermore, such regulations do not apply to the larger proportion of land occupied by state enterprises. In theory, the most effective policy to discourage the hoarding and under utilization of land is to apply an annual tax on its value. Such a land tax is advocated for China by Trescott (1994).

11.8 Conclusions

In the past, Chinese cities were perceived as being a drain on national development and consequently government attempted to control their growth. In the 1980s perceptions changed as coastal cities experiencing market reforms were now relied on to boost the national economy. This has generated some success, but in its wake has arisen new problems. The significant migration of people towards these successful urban centres has created new problems and challenges. If China's large cities are well managed then this urbanization will accelerate national growth. However, if they are poorly managed then problems of congestion, poor housing affordability, and urban pollution will retard the national economy. Good management policy must ensure that scarce urban land is not only used, but is used by the most efficient occupier so that a city's output may be maximized. There are no shortages of ideas on how cities may be better managed to improve their competitiveness, though one should never underestimate the immense political problems facing China in attempting to implement such schemes, in particular, in coordinating the many cities and regions which have been recipients of increased political autonomy.

References

Bian, Y. and J. Logan (1996), 'Market Transition and the Persistence of Power: the Changing Stratification System in Urban China', *American Sociological Review*, Vol. 61, pp. 739–58.

Chen, A. (1996), 'China's Urban Housing Reform: Price-Rent Ratio and Market Equilibrium', *Urban Studies*, Vol. 33, No. 7, pp. 1077–92.

Chen, X. (1991), 'China's City Hierarchy, Urban Policy and Spatial Development in the 1980s', *Urban Studies*, Vol. 28, No. 3, pp. 341–67.

Dowall, D. (1994), 'Urban Residential Redevelopment in the Peoples' Republic of China', *Urban Studies*, Vol. 31, No. 9, pp. 1497–516.

Fan, C. (1997), *Uneven Development and Beyond: Regional Development Theory in Post-Mao China*, Blackwell USA, pp. 620–39.

George, H. (1879), *Progress and Poverty*, Century Edition, 1979, Robert Shabkenbach Foundation, New York.

Jacobs, J. (1986), *Cities and the Wealth of Nations*, Penguin Books, Middlesex, UK.

Lee, Y. (1988), 'The Urban Housing Problem in China', *China Quarterly*, No. 115, pp. 387–407.

Li, L. (1997), 'The Political Economy of the Privatization of the Land Market in Shanghai', *Urban Studies*, Vol. 34, No. 2, pp. 321–35.

Liu, W. and D. Yang (1990), 'China's Land Use Policy Under Change', *Land Use Policy*, July, pp. 198–201.

Ma, L. and M. Fan (1994), 'Urbanization from Below: The Growth of Towns in Jiangsu, China', *Urban Studies*, Vol. 31, No. 10, pp. 1625–45.

Pugh, C. (1996), 'Urban Bias, the Political Economy of Development and Urban Policies for Developing Countries', *Urban Studies*, Vol. 33, No. 7, pp. 1045–60.

Quan, Z. (1991), 'Urbanization in China', *Urban Studies*, Vol. 28, No. 1, pp. 41–51.

Tang, W. (1994), 'Urban Land Development Under Socialism: China Between 1949 and 1977', *International Journal of Urban and Regional Research*, Vol. 18, No. 3, pp. 392–415.

Tao, M. (1998), Monetization of Housing Allocation to Start the Residential Housing Market and Promote Circulation of Capital, Presented at the *Third International Conference on Management*, Shanghai, July 25–28.

Tisdell, C. (1997), 'China's Environmental Problems and its Economic Growth', in C. Tisdell and J.C. Chai (eds), *China's Economic Growth and Transition*, Nova Science Publishers, New York, pp. 295–316.

Trescott, P. (1994), 'Henry George, Sun Yat-sen and China: More Than Land Policy Was Involved', *American Journal of Economics and Sociology*, Vol. 53, No. 3, pp. 363–75.

Wu, F. (1996), 'Changes in the Structure of Public Housing Provision in Urban China', *Urban Studies*, Vol. 33, No. 9, pp. 1601–27.

—— (1997), *Urban Restructuring in China's Emerging Market Economy: Towards a Framework for Analysis*, Blackwell, USA, pp. 640–63.

—— (1998), 'The New Structure of Building Provision and the Transformation of Urban Landscape in Metropolitan Guangzhou, China', *Urban Studies*, Vol. 35, No. 2, pp. 259–83.

Wu, F. and A. Gar-On Yeh (1997), 'Changing Spatial Distribution and Determinants of Land Development in Chinese Cities In The Transition From A Centrally Planned Economy To A Socialist Market Economy: A Case Study of Guangzhou', *Urban Studies*, Vol. 34, No. 11, pp. 1851–79.

Zhang, W. and G. Yi (1997), 'China's Gradual Reform: A historic Perspective', in C. Tisdell and J.C. Chai (eds), *China's Economic Growth and Transition*, Nova Science Publishers, New York, pp. 19–56.

Zhao, X. and L. Zhang (1995), 'Urban Performance and the Control of Urban Size in China', *Urban Studies*, Vol. 32, No. 4–5, pp. 813–45.

Zhou, Q. (1993), 'Capital Construction Investment and Its Regional Distribution in China', *International Journal of Urban and Regional Research*, Vol. 17, No. 2, pp. 159–77.

Zhu, J. (1994), 'Changing Land Policy and its Impact on Local Growth: the Experience of the Shenzhen Special Economic Zone, China, in the 1980s', *Urban Studies*, Vol. 31, No. 10, pp. 1611–23.

Index